Cognitive
Foundations
of Grammar

Cognitive Foundations of Grammar

BERND HEINE

New York   Oxford
OXFORD UNIVERSITY PRESS
1997

Oxford University Press

Oxford   New York

Athens   Auckland   Bangkok   Bogota   Bombay   Buenos Aires
Calcutta   Cape Town   Dar es Salaam   Delhi   Florence   Hong Kong
Istanbul   Karachi   Kuala Lumpur   Madras   Madrid   Melbourne
Mexico City   Nairobi   Paris   Singapore   Taipei   Tokyo   Toronto   Warsaw

and associated companies in
Berlin   Ibadan

Copyright © 1997 by Bernd Heine

Published by Oxford University Press, Inc.
198 Madison Avenue, New York, New York 10016

Oxford is a registered trademark of Oxford University Press

Library of Congress Cataloging-in-Publication Data
Heine, Bernd, 1939–
Cognitive foundations of grammar / Bernd Heine.
    p.   cm.
Includes bibliographical references and index.
ISBN 0-19-510251-7; ISBN 0-19-510252-5 (pbk)
1. Cognitive grammar.   I. Title.
P165.H45   1997
415—dc20   96-34670

1 3 5 7 9 8 6 4 2

Printed in the United States of America
on acid-free paper

PREFACE

During the Australian Linguistic Institute 1994, which took place in July 1994 at LaTrobe University, Melbourne, I gave a course on the cognitive foundations of grammar. I was then asked by students of the course whether what I was saying was available in print. I decided to work on an introductory account that could be of use to students of linguistics, cognitive science, psychology, anthropology, and related disciplines. One year later I had the opportunity to discuss the same subject matter when giving a course at the Institute of the Linguistic Society of America at the University of New Mexico, Albuquerque. This book owes much to discussion with my students in Melbourne and Albuquerque, and it is dedicated to them.

A number of other people have contributed to this book in some way or other. My thanks are due in particular to Jürgen Broschart, Joan Bybee, Ulrike Claudi, Bernard Comrie, Karen Ebert, Suzanne Fleischman, Orin Gensler, Tom Givón, Ingo Heine, Paul Hopper, Christa Kilian-Hatz, Chirsta König, Tania Kuteva, George Lakoff, Dirk Otten, Mechthild Reh, Heinz Roberg, Franz Rottland, Hans-Jürgen Sasse, Mathias Schladt, Fritz Serzisko, Eve Sweetser, and Elizabeth Traugott for critical comments and advice. I also thank Hassan Adam (Swahili), Kossi Tossou (Ewe), and Mohamed Touré (Bambara) for their patience when providing me with information on their mother tongues, and two anonymous reviewers of Oxford University Press for comments on an earlier version of the manuscript. Finally, I thank the Australian Research Council, the Deutsche Forschungsgemeinschaft (German Research Society), the Alexander von Humboldt-Stiftung (Humboldt Foundation), and the Volkswagen-Stiftung (Volkswagen Foundation) for having sponsored the research on which this book is based in some way or other.

Cologne, Germany
March 1997

B. H.

CONTENTS

Abbreviations   ix

1   The Framework   3
    1.1   Assumptions   3
    1.2   Methodological issues   7
    1.3   This volume   15

2   Numerals   18
    2.1   The body-part model   19
    2.2   Variation   24
    2.3   Morphosyntax   29
    2.4   On transparency   31
    2.5   Summary   32

3   Spatial Orientation   35
    3.1   Deictic orientation   37
    3.2   Cardinal orientation   49
    3.3   Some principles of spatial orientation   57
    3.4   Notes on grammar   58
    3.5   Summary   62

4   Indefinite Articles   66
    4.1   Generalizations   67
    4.2   Evolution   71
    4.3   Answers   76
    4.4   Discussion   78
    4.5   Summary   81

ABBREVIATIONS

A	subject of a transitive or ditransitive verb
ABS	absolute
ABSO	Absolutive
ABSTR	abstract possession
ACC	accusative
AL	alienable
ALL	allative
ART	article
ASP	aspect
ASSOC	associative
AUX	auxiliary
CL	noun class
CLASS, CLFR	classifier
CLIT	clitic
COM	comitative
COMPL	completive
CONJ	conjunction
CONN	connector
COP	copula
DAT	dative
DEF	marker of definiteness
DEM	demonstrative
DUAL	dual
EMPH	emphatic marker
ERG	ergative
EXIST	existential marker
F	feminine gender
FOC	focus
GEN	genitive
IMP	imperative
IMPERF	imperfective
INAL	inalienable possession
INDEF	marker of indefiniteness
IN/A	inanimate alienable possession
IN/I	inanimate inalienable possession
INSTR	instrument
IPFV	imperfective
LOC	locative
M	masculine gender
NEU	neuter gender
NF	nonfeminine gender
NOM	nominative
NSP	nonspecific
O	object of a transitive verb
PART	participle
PARTIT	partitive
PAST	past tense
PERF	perfect
PERM	permanent possession
PFV	perfective
PHYS	physical possession

Cognitive
Foundations
of Grammar

1

THE FRAMEWORK

1.1 Assumptions

Language structure is the product of our interaction with the world around us. The way we build discourses and develop linguistic categories can immediately be derived from the way we experience our environment and use that experience in species-specific communication.

A common human strategy of communication consists in relating different concepts by describing one in terms of the other. This strategy, it is argued here, can be held responsible for much of why grammar looks the way it does, and perhaps also why grammar exists in the first place. And it also constitutes the foundation of the framework used in this book. This framework is based primarily on the following assumptions:

A. The main function of language is to convey meaning. The question of why language is used and structured the way it is must therefore be answered first and foremost with reference to this function.
B. The forms used for expressing meaning are motivated rather than arbitrary (where "motivated" means that linguistic forms are not invented arbitrarily but are, rather, already meaningful when they are introduced for some specific function).
C. Since the motivations for using and developing language are external to language structure, external explanations of language are more powerful than internal ones.

3

D. Language is a historical product and must be explained first of all with reference to the forces that have shaped it.

E. The synchrony/diachrony distinction derives from the perspective adopted, rather than from the facts considered.

F. Grammatical change is unidirectional, leading from lexical to grammatical, and from grammatical to even more grammatical, forms and structures.

Some of these assumptions are perhaps trivial, others may seem unusual, and still others are hard to reconcile with widely held views of mainstream linguistics. A few elucidating remarks are therefore in order.

Assumption A is based on the observation that when using language, people are less worried about what kind of syntax or phonology to use than they are about how to encode the meanings they want to communicate in the best way possible. This suggests that, first, language use is goal-oriented: People use language to accomplish purposes and goals. Second, linguistic form will tend to adapt to the meaning expressed by it, and not normally the other way round. Third, linguistic explanations in terms of such exponents of language structure as syntax or phonology are likely to highlight peripheral or epiphenomenal rather than central characteristics of language use and language structure (note that we are using the term "meaning" in a wider sense, to include, for example, discourse-pragmatic functions). Furthermore, as we will see, language is not a simple reflection of meaning; content alone is not sufficient to explain why languages look the way they do (cf. Bates & MacWhinney 1989:7).

Assumption B might seem to contradict one of the basic axioms of post-Saussurean linguistics. Following Ferdinand de Saussure (1922:101c, 102b, 180–4), it has become habitual in linguistic works to assume that linguistic signs are "arbitrary" or "unmotivated," where the two terms tend to be used synonymously: There is no natural, inherent connection between a form (*signifiant*) and its meaning (*signifié*)—any *signifié* could be expressed by any *signifiant*. This is proved a posteriori, Saussure argues, by the existence of different languages and by the fact that languages change (cf. Wells 1947).

As a matter of fact, however, B does not contradict Saussure's arbitrariness axiom. There are a number of contrasting senses in which the notions of arbitrariness and motivation can be used; the following example may help illustrate the most common senses:

(1) a. They keep the money.
      b. They keep complaining.

It would seem that there are at least three different ways in which the distinction motivated/arbitrary can be used with reference to examples like (1). One approach concerns language structure. The item *keep* in (1) is associated with two different morphosyntactic structures and two different meanings: It functions as the main verb and has the lexical semantics of an action verb in (1a), while it is commonly described as an auxiliary (or catenative) verb that expresses an aspectual notion in (1b). On the basis of such structural linguistic criteria, one may decide that the phonological identity of *keep* in (1a) and (1b) is coincidental or arbitrary—hence, unmotivated. But it is equally possible to highlight other structural properties (such as shared semantic features or syntactic rules) that suggest the existence of a linguistically definable, motivated relationship.

The second approach has to do with native speakers' intuitions. For example, instead of using structural, linguistic criteria, one could choose a sample of one thousand speakers of English and ask them whether the items *keep* in (1a) and (1b) are related. If a statistically significant majority says yes, then one may conclude that the relationship is motivated.

The third approach relates to diachrony: *keep* in (1a) and (1b) is etymologically the same—that is, both can be assumed to be historically derived from one and the same root—hence, their relationship is motivated rather than arbitrary.

For want of more appropriate terms, the three kinds of motivation just sketched may be called *structural, psychological,* and *genetic* motivation. This distinction is not entirely satisfactory, nor is it exhaustive: There are other kinds of motivation that one could think of, such as sociological or areally induced motivation. Like most other linguists, however, I will confine myself to these three notions. Saussure (1922), for example, appears to have been preoccupied with structural and/or psychological motivation (1922:180ff.; see chapter 2).

My interest here is exclusively with genetic motivation since, of the three kinds of motivation discussed, only genetic motivation lies unequivocally within the scope of the linguist. The linguist can make a useful contribution to the study of psychological motivation, but this domain falls essentially within the scope of the psychologist. And, although structural motivation has been a dominant concern of linguistics since Saussure, it is not entirely clear what reason there should be for structural motivation. Finally, genetic motivation has the advantage of being less theory-dependent than the other two kinds of motivation since its reconstruction allows for a straightforward evaluation procedure: It can easily be falsified by means of diachronic evidence. For example, the question of whether the relationship between (1a) and (1b) is genetically motivated is a matter not of the theory or the model adopted but of whether a certain event has or has not taken place (see section 1.2.2). Note, however, that genetic motivation is not an explanatory notion; rather, it has to be explained with reference to other factors, most of all with reference to Assumption A.

Assumption C is based on Assumption A, that the main function of language is to convey meaning and to communicate successfully. Hence, explaining language structure with reference to the goals of communication is likely to yield more insights than explaining it with reference to language-internal mechanisms. For example, an account of lexical borrowing in terms of lexical, syntactic, or morphological structure is probably less "explanatory" than an account in terms of the motivations speakers have for conveying meaning.

Assumption D rests on the observation that language has not been created by the people who are presently using it but, rather, has evolved over the course of centuries and millennia. Grammar, as we now use it, can be described as the conventionalized (and to some extent fossilized) product of earlier patterns of less constrained language use. Explanations of language in terms of its synchronic structure are there-fore likely to account for only a small part of why language is structured the way it is. Many characteristics of language and its uses can therefore be explained satisfac-torily only with reference to its diachronic evolution. The following example may illustrate this point. In English, as in a number of other languages, there is an asym-metry in use between definite and indefinite articles: One can utter (2a), (2b), and (3a) but not (3b)—that is, the indefinite article may determine singular nouns but not plural nouns.

(2) a. I see the child.
     b. I see the children.
(3) a. I see a child.
     b. *I see a children.

Any attempt to explain this asymmetry must take account of the historical develop-ment of the articles in question. The English indefinite article *a(n)* can be traced back to the numeral *one*. Obviously, numerals for 'one' are inappropriate as modifiers of plural nouns (e.g., *one children*). Although *a(n)* is no longer a numeral, the struc-tural property of incompatibility with plural head nouns has survived its develop-ment into an indefinite article. For obvious reasons, such constraints were absent in the genesis of the English definite article, which is thus compatible with both singu-lar and plural nouns (see chapter 4 for more details). Examples like this suggest that what surfaces in synchronic structure is just the tip of the iceberg of what makes up the dynamics of language use.

Assumption D does not mean that explanations based on a synchronic perspec-tive are not meaningful. It does imply, however, that before proceeding to synchronic explanations it is both easier and more efficient to establish to what extent the facts to be explained are due to historical forces. Thus, explaining the said asymmetry in the behavior of the English definite and indefinite article in terms of a synchronic analysis before proceeding to a diachronic analysis is likely to make the task of ex-planation unnecessarily complicated.

Assumption E rests on the observation that there is no such thing as synchronic or diachronic language or language use: There is just language use. Students of lan-guage usually divide their subject matter into synchronic and diachronic linguistics, and this division has turned out to be extremely useful. But for those involved in an individual act of communication—the speaker and the hearer—the distinction is hardly relevant. Whether we adopt a synchronic or a diachronic perspective depends on the goals we want to pursue, not on the subject matter concerned (see section 1.2.1).

Assumption F is by now commonplace in linguistics: The development of grammatical forms proceeds from less grammatical to more grammatical; from open-class to closed-class categories; and from concrete, or less abstract, to less concrete and more abstract meanings (see, e.g., Heine, Claudi, & Hünnemeyer 1991; Traugott & Heine 1991a; Bybee, Perkins, & Pagliuca 1994). A number of exceptions to the unidirectionality principle have been claimed (e.g., Campbell 1991; Greenberg 1991; Ramat 1992), but they have either been refuted or are said to involve processes other than grammaticalization (Hopper & Traugott 1993).

These assumptions will accompany us in the chapters to follow; they will induce us to adopt a perspective on language that differs in a number of ways from that assumed in most works of contemporary linguistics.

1.2   Methodological issues

As may have become apparent in the preceding section, my approach here requires that we look at language structure from a perspective that is not normally found in canonical treatments of language in contemporary linguistics. This means, for example, that theoretical notions that have been crucial in previous accounts are considered here to be epiphenomenal or marginal, while others that have been outside the scope of previous accounts are now interpreted as being central. This perspective also raises problems, however. Some of these are briefly discussed in this chapter, and subsequent chapters provide further details.

1.2.1   Conceptual transfer

The methodology used in this volume rests on the following observation: The presence of one linguistic form with several different meanings may suggest conceptual transfer patterns in which the form was first used to denote one meaning before it was extended to designate one or more additional meanings. Thus, we observed that the English item *keep* has at least two meanings, as illustrated in (1), reprinted here for convenience.

(1)   a. They keep the money.
       b. They keep complaining.

This fact can be explained as being due to conceptual transfer of the following kind: *Keep* was first used as a main verb in contexts such as (1a); later its use was extended to contexts like (1b), in which it is no longer a main verb but an auxiliary. This transfer has the following properties in particular:

1. It is unidirectional—that is, we do not normally expect a development in the opposite direction, where an auxiliary like *keep* in (1b) develops into a main verb.
2. Unidirectionality leads from concrete, or less abstract, meanings to more abstract meanings. With reference to our example in (1), this means, for example, that *keep* in (1a) is compatible with complements that are visible and tangible, like money, whereas in (1b), complements like *complaining* are more abstract in that, for example, one cannot touch them.
3. The transfer is a historical process and can be accounted for with reference to the principles of diachronic linguistics.

Our *keep*-example concerns the unidirectional transfer leading from lexical items that have a fairly concrete semantics to grammatical categories that express schematic meanings; these latter typically have to do with the relative time, boundary structure, and modality of events.

Conceptual transfer patterns like the one just looked at, as well as many others discussed in the following chapters, have been described variously as involving either figures of speech such as metaphor (e.g., Heine, Claudi, & Hünnemeyer 1991; Sweetser 1990; Stolz 1991, 1994b) and metonymy (Traugott & König 1991) or context-induced processes such as invited inferences, conversational implicatures, and the like. All these notions are relevant for understanding the process concerned, but I will not attempt an evaluation of them here (however, see section 7.4). Following Heine, Claudi, and Hünnemeyer (1991) I argue that the process has both a discontinuous and a continuous component—that is, it can be described variously in terms of both discrete jumps and gradual context-dependent extension of meaning.

1.2.2   On polysemy

The perspective sketched here also suggests an alternative way of dealing with an old and as yet unresolved linguistic issue—how to decide whether two meanings associated with one linguistic form are suggestive of polysemy, rather than monosemy or homonymy. Finding a satisfactory answer to this question is both a central and a controversial problem of linguistics. The answer proposed here is in line with the general theme of this book: In much the same way as we distinguished between three kinds of motivations, we may also distinguish between structural, psychological, and genetic polysemy. The distinction can be illustrated again by means of example (1).

(1)   a. They keep the money.
       b. They keep complaining.

Leaving aside various problems, one may say that polysemy has normally been defined by means of a set of three criteria:

1. There are two or more different but related meanings.
2. These meanings are associated with one linguistic form only.
3. The linguistic form belongs to one and the same morphosyntactic category in all its uses.

Whether the item *keep* in (1) is an instance of structural polysemy is not easy to establish; the problems are essentially the same as those mentioned in section 1.1 with reference to structural motivation. Accordingly, while the item appears to comply with criterion no. 2, one may argue, for instance, that criterion no. 1 does not apply. But how the semantic relationship between an auxiliary and the main verb from which it is derived should be defined is hard to answer independent of the theoretical position one decides to adopt. And the same applies to criterion no. 3: Some linguists would argue that *keep* belongs to more than one syntactic category since it is a main verb in (1a) but an auxiliary (or a catenative) in (1b); others claim that auxiliaries and main verbs belong to the same syntactic category (see Heine 1993 for more details). The former would be forced to say that on the basis of the above criteria, *keep* in (1) is not polysemous, while the latter might say that it is a case of polysemy (provided they can find sufficient formal criteria that allow them to define *keep* in (1) as having "different but related meanings"). Thus, determining structural polysemy is not an easy task. To put it perhaps more seriously, once one has found a convenient way of defining structural polysemy, the question arises as to what one has actually achieved by doing so.

Different problems arise in connection with psychological polysemy. Take, for instance, the following: How does one determine the native speaker's intuitions or awareness of a relatedness of meaning in (1)? Some might say that this question is not within the scope of the linguist's methodology and hence should be left to the psychologist, for example, to answer. Others believe this question can essentially be answered by means of linguistic evidence, though that evidence may not be available as yet (cf. Lyons 1977:552).

Such problems do not exist in the case of genetic polysemy: (1) is unambiguously an instance of genetic polysemy since *keep* in (1a) and (1b) can be traced back historically to one and the same item.

In a number of more recent works, the term *polysemy* is largely used in the sense of genetic polysemy. In such works, polysemy tends to be described as the synchronic reflection of semantic change (Geeraerts 1992:183). What these works appear to have in common is that they do not require polysemy criterion no. 3 to apply—that is, polysemy is not necessarily confined to instances that involve only one morphosyntactic category (cf. Brugman 1984; Traugott 1986; Norvig & Lakoff 1987; Lakoff 1987; Emanatian 1992). Brugman (1984), for example, observes that the English lexeme *over* is an instance of polysemy even if it has prepositional, adverbial, and derivational uses and hence is associated with different morphosyntactic categories.

To avoid such problems surrounding orthodox definitions of polysemy, Lichtenberk introduces the term *heterosemy*. With this term he refers "to cases (within a single language) where two or more meanings or functions that are historically related, in the sense of deriving from the same ultimate source, are borne by reflexes of the common source element that belong in different morphosyntactic categories" (1991:476). Heterosemy as used by Lichtenberk thus is a special case of genetic polysemy: special, since it is confined to instances of genetic polysemy that violate criterion no. 3. Note further that heterosemy is also said to be present when the items concerned are not phonologically identical—that is, when criterion no. 2 is violated. Thus, the English items *have* and *'ve* in (4) are also instances of heterosemy, even if they are not phonologically the same. This is in accordance with the notion of genetic polysemy, which is not confined to cases of linguistic forms observing criterion no. 2.

(4) a. They have two children.
     b. They have to come.
     c. They've come.

The notion of genetic polysemy is also material for understanding the significance of what has become known as the Typological Convergence criterion (see Croft 1991:166–7; Hopper & Traugott 1993:71). The latter can be illustrated with the following example: The fact that directional *to* (as in 'I drove to Chicago') and recipi-ent *to* ('I gave the package to you yesterday') are frequently expressed by the same form crosslinguistically is taken as evidence that they are polysemous in English. English *two* and *too*, on the other hand, do not satisfy the Typological Convergence criterion and, hence, are treated as an instance of homonymy. As this example sug-gests, whenever the Typological Convergence criterion applies, it is likely that we are dealing with an instance of genetic polysemy. Conversely, whenever there is no genetic polysemy, as appears to be the case with English *two*, *to*, and *too*, we may not expect the Typological Convergence criterion to apply.

Two objections have been raised against making genetic motivation the primary objective of study. First, it is argued that, more often than not, we lack reliable evi-dence to prove that an instance of genetic relationship actually exists. We do not think this is a valid objection since it is probably equally hard, and probably even more controversial, to prove structural or psychological relationships. Thanks to recent work on the evolution of grammatical categories, we now have a sizable knowledge of the main patterns of grammaticalization, which allows for fairly reliable linguistic recon-structions and hypotheses on genetic motivation.

Second, one might argue that establishing nongenetic, structural relationship is often an indispensable first step in defining genetic relationship. While this may be so in a specific case, it usually is not. Take example (4): a number of authors argue that the item *have* in (4a) and (4b) (as well as in (4c)) is structurally the same (= the "main verb hypothesis"). Others again claim that the two instances of *have* are struc-turally not the same (= the "autonomy hypothesis"; see Heine 1993:8ff. for details). Each of these positions is equally legitimate and is supported by substantial theoreti-cal arguments and bodies of evidence. But whether *have* shares genetic relationship in (4a) and (4b) is essentially a matter not of theories or models but rather of histori-cal facts: The two instances of *have* either are or are not genetically related, irrespec-tive of the theoretical standing one wishes to adopt. To conclude, it would seem that structural and genetic phenomena are of an entirely different nature and hence should be kept apart.

1.2.3   Universalism versus relativism

Frustrated by the diversity of linguistic forms they are confronted with, some lin-guists have decided that language is a mess and that structure can only be discovered and described when language is reduced to its "simpler" underlying functions or cognitive patterns. Cognitive linguistics thus tends to be viewed as a convenient means of reducing linguistic diversity to unity, be that diversity language-internal or crosslinguistic.

Such a view may appear somewhat naive, considering that cognition does not seem to belong to those phenomena that one would be inclined to classify as lacking complexity. Nevertheless, I believe that much of what languages offer in terms of structural complexity and diversity can be described and explained with reference to the extralinguistic forces that determine the shape languages take, most of all with reference to cognition. And there is an obvious reason for such a belief. The assump-tions made in the previous section are based essentially on the observation that human beings, irrespective of whether they live in Siberia or the Kalahari Desert, have the same intellectual, perceptual, and physical equipment; are exposed to the same general kinds of experiences; and have the same communicative needs. One therefore will expect their languages and the way their languages are used to be the same across geographical and cultural boundaries. One of the major goals of this book is to substantiate this point.

At the same time, the belief that linguistic complexity can invariably be reduced to cognitive simplicity is, in fact, unduly naive. This is especially so because there are considerable differences across cultures in the way the environment is conceptualized and communication is achieved. One therefore also expects to find divergences in the way languages are structured and language use takes place. Thus, in addition to a universalist perspective, there is also need for a relativist perspective.

Evidence in favor of the universalist perspective is massive and has come from all major camps of modern linguistics. The relativist position is much harder to defend. The work of its main proponent, Benjamin Lee Whorf (1956), is not uncontroversial, to put it mildly; even fervent adherents of this position take care not to be associated too closely with Whorf's main thesis. Nevertheless, some intriguing evidence in favor of the relativist position has more recently become available. This evidence suggests that there are salient alternatives of conceptualization which human beings have developed and which influence the way languages are used and language is structured.

A couple of examples may suffice to illustrate this point. There are considerable differences in the world's cultures with regard to the way spatial orientation is conceptualized. For the purpose of the present work, the following basic systems of spatial orientation or reference can be distinguished (see also chapter 3):

1. *Deictic orientation.* In this system, items are typically located within immediate reach of the speaker, the hearer, or both. Almost invariably, deictic orientation is speaker-deictic—that is, spatial orientation is described with reference to the location and perspective assumed by the speaker. In special cases, however, it may shift, for instance, to the hearer. Since speaker and hearer typically face each other when they interact linguistically, they have contrasting deictic coordinates and, hence, contrasting spatial reference. This system is associated above all with notions such as 'up', 'down', 'front', 'back', 'in', 'left', and 'right'. Note that these constitute only a small range of the deictic concepts that are normally distinguished conceptually and nomenclaturally. Instead of deictic orientation, the term "relative system" has been used by other authors.

2. *Object-deictic orientation.* Rather than the speaker (or the hearer), the deictic center may be some inanimate item, like a car or a chair, in which case we propose to speak of object-deictic orientation. The concepts figuring in this system are in most cases the same as those appearing in deictic orientation, but other reference points can be found as well, for example, *at the facade of the cathedral* (Levinson 1996a, 1996b). This system has also been referred to as an "intrinsic system" or "intrinsic frame of reference."

3. *Landmark orientation.* In addition to deictic concepts like 'front' or 'left', some reference points and structures are rooted in the particular physical environment of the people concerned. These points are used to describe locations with reference to environmental landmarks such as rivers, mountains, and the sea. Common concepts expressed via landmark orientation are 'away from the river' (versus 'toward the river'), 'facing the mountain', and the like. Landmark orientation is highly culture-specific and depends to some extent on the presence of significant geographical features as stimuli. Particularly salient features are, for example, the Nile for the ancient Egyptians or the land/sea division for Polynesian fishermen (see chapter 3 for examples).

4. *Cardinal orientation.* This domain includes items that lie outside the scope of typical face-to-face interaction. It is defined in terms of *absolute* or *fixed* reference points that are independent of the position assumed by the speaker, the hearer, or a particular object. The system of cardinal directions is perhaps the most salient, though not the only, subsystem within this domain. It is not always the case, however, that 'north', 'south', and other concepts figuring in this domain are defined in exactly the same way as we would define them.

One piece of evidence in favor of the relativist perspective relates to deictic orientation. According to Hill (1974, 1982, forthcoming), there is a distinction between what he calls the closed and the open systems of orientation, and what I propose to refer to as the face-to-face model and the single-file model, respectively. The two models are distinguished by their contrasting perspectives of spatial front-back orientation. This contrast is illustrated in figure 1-1: If the speaker (A) belongs to a culture using the face-to-face model, he or she would say that the box (B) is *in front of* the hill (C). People used to the single-file model, on the other hand, would say that the box (B) is *behind* the hill (C). In the face-to-face model, the landmark hill (C) of figure 1-1 is conceived of as facing the speaker (A); in the single-file model, it is conceived of as facing the same direction as the speaker—that is, as turning its back to the speaker (and, hence, also to the box).

Although the face-to-face model is the only one to be found throughout the Western world, it is also widespread in other parts of the world. The single-file model has been described in detail for the Hausa of northern Nigeria, but it has also been reported to be common in a number of other African and non-African societies.

Object-deictic orientation can also exhibit interesting cross-cultural variation. In all societies known to me there is a basic distinction between physical items that have an intrinsic (or inherent) reference frame—that is, that are consistently associated with a front and a back subregion—and items without intrinsic fronts and backs, that is, "frontless" or "nonfeatured" items (cf. Svorou 1994:21). The front region of a house, for example, is located where the main entrance is; that of a computer is located where the person using it is seated. Trees, mountains, and stones normally lack an intrinsic reference frame in Western societies: Where their fronts and backs are located is determined situationally by the relative location of the speaker and/or the hearer, rather than by inherent properties of the items concerned. In some cul-

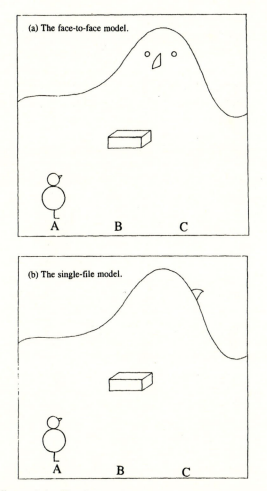

(a) The face-to-face model.

(b) The single-file model.

Figure 1-1   The face-to-face and the single-file models.

tures, however, trees and mountains do have inherent fronts and backs. For the Chamus of Kenya, for example, the front of a tree is located on the side toward which its trunk is inclined, and if the trunk is perceived as being absolutely vertical, then the front is in the direction of either the biggest branch or where the largest number of branches is found, in that order. Similarly, for the Kikuyu and other Bantu-speaking peoples living in and around the Kenyan Rift Valley, the steeper side of a mountain is conceived of as the back of the mountain and the opposite side as its front (Mathias Schladt, personal communication).

In some cultures, an even more elaborate system of object-deictic orientation is found. A particularly spectacular system appears to have been developed by the Mayan Tzeltal of Mexico. In this society, items such as knives, pots, leaves, feathers, and planks are construed as having an object-deictic organization (cf. Levinson 1994:816ff.); I will examine this structure in more detail in Chapter 7.

But perhaps the most dramatic piece of evidence in favor of the relativist hypothesis is provided by cardinal orientation. A speaker of English might say something like "The key is behind the phone" or "Canada is to the north of the United States," rather than "The key is to the north of the phone" or "Canada is behind the United States." This seems to suggest that we tend to describe location with reference to contrasting conceptual templates: The relative location of a key triggers the system of deictic orientation, while the location of a country is more likely to be described in terms of cardinal orientation.

Now, while many cultures do in fact distinguish between deictic and cardinal orientation, some are claimed to lack such a distinction—that is, these cultures are said to have no deictic orientation and/or no terminology for it. Rather, such cultures use cardinal orientation as a template, utilizing fixed angles or directions similar to our cardinal directions north, south, west, and east to refer even to spatial concepts that are described by means of deictic or landmark orientation in other cultures. Thus, in societies making use of cardinal orientation only, one may expect people to say something like "The key is to the north of the phone"; instead of "John is in front of the post office," "My glass is to the left of the bottle," and "There's a bug on your left leg," we find expressions that may be glossed as "John is north of the post office," "My glass is west of the bottle," and "There's a bug on your eastern leg" (Levinson 1992; Brown & Levinson 1993a:2, 1993b).

Such findings are remarkable: They give an impression of the wealth of cognitive patterns that can be observed in the cultures of the world. No doubt, such differences must have an impact on the structure of the languages concerned. It would seem, however, that this diversity does not pose an insurmountable problem for a theoretical framework like the present one, which is based on the claim that the major patterns of human conceptualization are universal in nature. As chapter 3 in particular shows, many examples suggest that human conceptualization, like the way it shapes language structure, is far from uniform across cultures; rather, it may offer various solutions to the problems it is meant to solve. At the same time, however, both the number and the kind of solutions developed to cope with a given problem are limited. What this means is that there is both diversity and unity: The human species, irrespective of whether it is located in Siberia or the Kalahari Desert, has essentially the same pool of options for conceptualization.

1.2.4   On communication

The way people in Siberia or the Kalahari Desert experience the world around them can immediately be held responsible for the way they shape their grammars. Although conceptualization strategies are perhaps the main driving force for linguistic categorization, conceptualization is not the only force that can be held responsible for why grammar is structured the way it is (see the discussion in later chapters of this book). Another, equally important, force is communication. While my concern here is with conceptualization and its effects on grammar, we have to be aware that essentially the only way language is accessible to the analyst is in the form of products resulting from acts of communication.

Linguistic communication takes place under specific conditions. These conditions concern, inter alia, the role relationship typically involved in speaker-hearer interaction. In many kinds of interaction, the speaker tends to portray himself as a humble, modest human being, as someone who is inferior to the hearer in intellectual capabilities, social status, and the like. The result is a situation of pretended status asymmetry between speaker and hearer, and this situation is likely to be reflected in linguistic discourse in some way or other. One way this asymmetry tends to surface in linguistic interaction is in the repertoire of expressions used by the speaker to describe himself as opposed to the hearer. For example, it is perfectly acceptable in most contexts to say "I am stupid," but much less so to say "You are stupid," as the latter might violate commonly accepted norms of social interaction.

Frequently this asymmetry has only a limited impact on language structure. In quite a number of languages, however, it gives rise to conventionalized patterns of language use in which the speaker is expected to refer to himself by using terms that suggest a socially inferior status while referring to the hearer as a socially superior being. One way of marking this distinction is by introducing plural pronouns to refer to the hearer: Apparently, in a number of European and other languages, the grammatical concept of plurality has been exploited to symbolize higher social status. Alternatively, personal pronouns are derived from nouns that are associated with specific social status characteristics, as has been observed, inter alia, in some East Asian languages (see especially Cooke 1968). In Burmese, for example, lexical sources such as those listed in (5) have been identified for first and second person singular pronouns:

(5) Burmese (Tibeto-Burman; Cooke 1968:74–6; Stolz 1994b:78–9)

First person lexical source pronoun		*Second person lexical source pronoun*	
kowv	'body'	kowv-dov	'efficient body'
tyunv-	'slave'	minx	'king'
dabeq-	'disciple'	hyinv	'master'

However, the nature of a canonical speaker-hearer relationship is but one of the factors that influence the structure of communication and language use; other factors are the cultural, religious, and sociopolitical forces. The way these forces contribute to structuring linguistic communication and grammar is a topic that is beyond the scope of this study. Suffice it to emphasize here that, rather than aiming at a comprehensive theory of grammar, I am merely drawing attention to one of the factors that must be considered when launching such a theory.

1.3   This volume

The approach used here is not new: It continues the tradition of what is sometimes referred to as Typological Universal Grammar, a direction in general linguistics that aims to establish crosslinguistic regularities based on worldwide samples of languages; the reader is referred to summary treatments—Ferguson (1978), Comrie (1981), Mallinson and Blake (1981), Bybee (1985), and Bybee, Perkins, and Pagliuca (1994) —for more details on this type of linguistic research.

At the same time, our approach differs from other works written in the Typological Universal Grammar paradigm in that it rests on the claim that language structure in many of its manifestations can be best understood with reference to the conceptual foundations on which it rests. The main reason for adopting this procedure is that some linguistic forms are meaningless if taken literally, but they can be accounted for if reference is made to the cognitive factors that can be held responsible for their growth. For example, in a number of languages we find that the cardinal direction 'west' is expressed by terms meaning 'it falls', 'the descent', 'going down', and the like. The reason for such terms becomes obvious once we note that cardinal 'west' is almost invariably expressed in the languages of the world in some way or other by means of the notion of sunset—that is, in terms of expressions referring to the descending sun. Quite likely in such languages terms for 'east' will resemble expressions for something like 'it rises', 'ascends', 'goes up', 'emerges', and so on (see Brown 1983 and section 3.2). Thus, our primary concern here, rather than the particular linguistic form or literal meaning, is the underlying concepts that can be held responsible for selecting that form or meaning.

A number of positions have been maintained regarding the relationship between language and cognition. The following have perhaps been particularly influential:

1. Language is the main shaper of mental and other activities. This position has been advocated at least since the 18th century, more recent proponents being Sapir (1921, 1949) and Whorf (1956:213–14).
2. Language is based on an innate stock of human endowment. This approach has been propagated in generativist lines of tradition (e.g., Chomsky 1986), but it can also be seen in the work of Wierzbicka on universal semantic primitives (Wierzbicka 1972, 1988, 1992:11).
3. Language equals cognition (Langacker 1987, 1991).
4. Language mirrors human conceptualization (Lakoff & Johnson 1980; Lakoff 1987).

Position 4 is the one adopted in this book. Language structure, I argue, reflects patterns of human conceptualization because it is shaped by them. An approach that includes information on conceptual organization and conceptual transfer must have a higher explanatory potential than one that ignores such information. Information on conceptual organization enables one to account for systematic links that exist between different linguistic expressions—for instance, between such different notions as cardinal point and sunset. More important, it allows one to explain language structure with reference to human experience and the way this experience is used in communication. Thus, as discussed in chapter 3, the location and movement of the sun provide the most important cognitive template for conceptualizing and naming cardinal orientation. It would be hard to explain the nomenclature used for cardinal directions like west and east in the languages of the world without reference to this template.

The main purpose of this book is to substantiate the assumptions made in the introductory section by applying evidence from many different languages, using topics that have turned out to be notoriously cumbersome in previous accounts of grammatical description. Such topics have to do with notions that extend from strictly grammatical concepts, like the marking of referential identity, to concepts that are located around the borderline between the lexical and the grammatical domains, like those relating to possessive and comparative notions.

The book is divided into eight chapters. This chapter, 1, discusses some basic assumptions and introduces the theoretical background on which the following treatment rests. Chapter 2 is devoted to the study of cardinal numerals, a topic that has enjoyed remarkable popularity over the course of the past decades. Our interest is with one specific issue—the question whether, or to what extent, the structure of numerals can be shown to be motivated. Chapter 3 deals with the domain of spatial orientation—in particular, with the question of how adverbs and adpositions like *behind* and *in front of* evolve and how their structure is to be explained.

While spatial orientation is portrayed as a domain of universal significance, chapter 4 is devoted to a grammatical category that is not found in all languages of the world. This is the category of indefinite articles, which exhibit some properties that distinguish them from definite articles; some of these properties are discussed in chapter 4. Possession is the subject of chapter 5. There is a bewildering variety of linguistic forms in the languages of the world that express as simple a statement as 'I have no money'; the main purpose of chapter 5 is to explain this variety. My discussion includes both attributive (or nominal) and predicative (or verbal) possession.

Another domain of grammar that appears to be consistently distinguished in the languages of the world is comparison. Chapter 6 focuses on comparisons of inequality—that is, expressions of the form 'Linda is smarter than Bill'. The linguistic means for encoding comparison are remarkably diverse, while the conceptual sources from which these encodings are derived are severely limited. That the generalizations presented in the preceding chapters do not apply only to grammatical forms but extend also to the domain of the lexicon is argued in chapter 7, where a few examples of unidirectional evolution within the lexicon are discussed. Finally, some conclusions from the foregoing discussion are drawn in chapter 8.

2

NUMERALS

Numeral systems have received a remarkable amount of scholarly attention, and many generalizations have been proposed by linguists, mathematicians, and other students of the subject. My goal in the following paragraphs is a modest one: to draw attention to some crosslinguistic regularities in the structure of numerals and to account for these regularities. In doing this, my main interest is not with description but with explanation.

Of central importance in the present, as well as in subsequent, discussions is the human body, for various reasons: First, because it represents a well-studied semantic domain for which a wider range of research findings is available; second, because it is a conceptually rich domain that is used as a source for structuring numerous other domains; and third, because the human body also serves as a conceptual template for the development of grammatical categories.

Like many other authors studying numerals (e.g., Stampe 1976; Greenberg 1978c; Seiler 1989), I confine myself to cardinal numerals in attributive construction—that is, to the use of numerals such as '2' or '3' in expressions like 'two apples' and 'three horses', rather than ordinal numerals (e.g., 'the second') or numerals as used in counting ('one–two–three–four–five').

Let us consider a few details before proceeding to the question why numerals are arranged and expressed the way they are. Most of all, we need to know what strategies are commonly used to express numeral values.

As is suggested by the many works that have become available on the subject, there are only a small number of strategies that can be reconstructed on the basis of lexical distinctions underlying numeral systems. One relates to the way in which operations in the sense of Western arithmetic—that is, addition, subtraction, multiplication, and division—are pressed into service for designating number values in a given language. Another relates to the patterns that can be reconstructed on the basis of linguistic analyis. According to a worldwide survey carried out by Schmidt (1926: 357ff.), for example, three major conceptual principles have been instrumental in shaping numeral systems. The first is "counting without system," according to which there are conceptually independent terms for '1', '2', '3', and so on, without there being any numeral base used to simplify the act of counting. Apparently, no society in the world has exploited this principle to the extent that numeral values like '13' or '29' are or may be expressed exclusively in terms of this principle. The second is what Schmidt calls pairing ("das Paarsystem"), whereby the smallest quantity serves as a base for further counting: '3' is expressed as '2 + 1', '4' as '2 + 2', and so on. Note, however, that addition is not the only arithmetic operation underlying pairing; pairing is also said to be present in languages that express, for instance, '6' as '2 times 3', '8' as '2 times 4', and '9' as '(2 times 4) + 1' (see below). Schmidt adds that there are various extensions of these two principles. The only alternative principle of major import, however, the third, is based on the fact that a human hand or foot has five digits. Virtually all remaining numeral structures in some way or other involve these body-parts as conceptual templates.

2.1 The body-part model

In accordance with the general theme of this book, I claim that numeral systems across languages are motivated—that is, they are nonarbitrary. As pointed out in section 1.1, my concern here is exclusively with genetic motivation. Not infrequently, motivation is no longer accessible to the native speaker, nor even to the historical linguist. But this does not mean there is no motivation—it simply means there is a gap in our knowledge that remains to be filled. I will return to this issue further after discussion of some of the diversity that exists in the world's languages for expressing numeral concepts.

Consider the following example. Mamvu, a central African Nilo-Saharan language, has the paradigm of cardinal numerals as sketched in table 2-1. These are not the only forms cardinal numerals may take; however, there is some variation in forms that is not relevant for our purposes. No numerals beyond 100 appear to exist.

Five of the numerals—that is, '1' to '5' (plus the item *màdyà* figuring in the numeral '16')—are etymologically opaque; no information on their genesis exists. For the rest of the numerals, the motivation is known; they appear to be derived from domains of conceptualization that do not immediately relate to counting. The source concepts involved are:

1. Concrete items: 'hand', 'foot', and 'person'
2. Actions: 'seize', 'spare'
3. Location: 'above'

In addition, three arithmetic concepts are involved in the construction of Mamvu numerals:

Table 2-1 Mamvu (Central Sudanic, Nilo-Saharan); orthography simplified (Vorbichler 1971:231–2)

Numeral	Meaning	Literal meaning
relí	1	
juè	2	
jenò	3	
jetò	4	
jimbu	5	
elí qodè relí	6	'the hand seizes one'
elí qodè juè	7	'the hand seizes two'
jetò. jetò	8	'four. four'
elí qoбò relí	9	'the hand spares one'
elí бòsí	10	'all hands'
qarú qodè relí	11	'the foot seizes one'
qarú qodè juè	12	'the foot seizes two'
qarú qodè jimbu	15	'the foot seizes five'
qarú qodè màdyà	16	'the foot seizes six'
múdo ngburú relí	20	'one whole person'
múdo ngburú relí, íjuní qa relí	21	'one whole person, above there is one'
múdo ngburú relí, múdo-ná-qiqà elí бòsí	30	'one whole person, another person, all hands'
múdo ngburú juè	40	'two whole persons'
múdo ngburú jimbu	100	'five whole persons'

1. Addition, as is suggested by such numerals as '6', '7', and '8'
2. Subtraction, as in '9'
3. Multiplication, as in '40' or '100'

In fact, these are the kinds of concepts that we will meet time and again in the following sections. They may be regarded as the building blocks of numeral systems. The following structural characteristics of the Mamvu system of cardinal numerals can be derived from these source structures:

- Since the human hand provides the most salient source model in Mamvu, numerals are divided into quinary blocks—that is, '5' constitutes the base number, and counting starts anew after each block of five entities.
- A second numeral base is '20', which is conceptually derived from the sum total of fingers and toes, or of hands and feet, the result being a vigesimal system—that is, a system having '20' as its primary numeral base.

The structure exemplified by Mamvu is widespread in the languages of the world. Following Stampe, we may call it the "one-hand, two-hand, one-foot, whole-man variety" (1976:596), even if there is some variation in the particular expressions employed; for example, instead of 'a whole man/person' one may find, for instance, an expression of the kind 'both hands and feet' that provides the source for the word for '20'.

The body-part model is in fact ubiquitous. Its effects can be observed in some way or another in most languages, even if it is merely in the form of a decimal system, for instance, as in English. Even if in a given language there are terms for numerals that do not look as if they could be related to the body-part model, it frequently turns out that they nevertheless are. For example, Meinhof (1948:118) reports that in Sotho, the verb form *selɛla!* or *taβɛla!* 'jump!' serves to denote '6'. The source of these forms appears to be an expression in which 'six' is conceptually rendered as 'jump over from one hand to the other!'

To summarize, there are a number of linguistic properties that tend to be associated with numeral systems, and these properties can be understood meaningfully only with reference to the conceptual templates that are employed for structuring numerals. The main templates and their linguistic implications follow.

1. The human hand provides the most important model for structuring the numeral system. Accordingly, the numeral '5' constitutes crosslinguistically the smallest recurrent base number, where "base number" is that number from which counting starts over (cf. Majewicz 1981). Note, however, that even if the human hand provides a widespread source for terms for '5' as a base number, more often than not the word for 'hand' is not mentioned in such expressions, frequently because its presence is implied rather than expressed. Speakers of the Api language of the New Hebrides, for example, do not need to express the notion of a hand in the numerals from '6' through '9' because this notion is already implied in the presence of the morpheme for 'new', as can be seen in table 2-2.

2. The most common structure of numeral systems appears to be one in which '5' is derived from 'hand', '10' from 'two hands', and '20' from either something like 'hands and feet' or 'whole person'. Since the perceptual difference is larger between hands and feet than between one hand and another, the numeral '10' appears to constitute a more salient base than '5'. This again means that there are more languages that have '10' as their base number than '5' (see section 2.5).

3. Numerals from '6' to '9', whenever their motivation is still transparent, are likely to refer to individual fingers and to have a propositional structure. The reason can be sought in the fact that these numerals are likely to be created as predications about fingers and hands. The linguistic implications of this fact are considerable: Not infrequently, numerals between '6' and '9' have a clausal morphosyntax, whereas numerals for '5', '10', and '20', for instance, are highly likely to be nominal rather

Table 2-2   Api, unknown affiliation
(Seiler 1989:10, based on Dantzig 1940:25)

tai	1	otai	'new one'	6
lua	2	olua	'new two'	7
tolu	3	otolu	'new three'	8
vari	4	ovari	'new four'	9
luna 'hand'	5	lua luna	'two hands'	10

than clausal in their structure. Our Mamvu example illustrates this situation. Another example, involving Zulu, is given in section 2.3.

4. That the human hand in particular and body-parts in general provide the most important conceptual source for structuring numeral systems is probably due to the important role played by body movements in expressing numerals. Greenberg reports that in parts of New Guinea, "gesture methods based on body parts starting with the fingers of one hand and then going up to wrist, elbow, etc., and around back to the other hand provide a way of expressing numbers as high as 20 at a point where the spoken language does not go beyond three or four" (1978c:291–2).

5. A characteristic of numeral systems that has been pointed out by several students of the subject (Stampe 1976:598–9; Greenberg 1978c:268–9, 276) concerns the construction of numerals above ten, for instance, of the numeral '30', where the multiplicand ('10') is often treated like a noun and the multiplier ('3') like a noun modifier. Thus, Greenberg observes that the Wolof numeral *nyar-i temer* (two-of hundred) '200' has the same structure as the construction *nyar-i nag* (two-of cow) 'two cows'. There appears to be an obvious reason for this similarity: That the multiplicand is treated like a noun appears to be due to the fact that it *is* historically a noun and has retained some of its nominal properties, like those that are at issue here. This means, for example, that the multipliers tend to behave like nominal modifiers. If such higher nominals modify nouns, they form the head of genitival constructions where the "actual" head noun appears as a genitival modifier, as in the Latin example (1). Compare also English *three ears of corn* (Stampe 1976:599).

(1)   Latin
       tres cent-   i   puer- orum
       3   hundred- M:PL:NOM boy-   M:PL:GEN
       'three hundred boys' (Lit.: 'three hundreds of boys')

One might expect this to apply to the numeral '5' as well, at least in those cases where it is derived from 'hand'. This is in fact sometimes also the case, but to a much lesser extent than it is with numerals above '10', for the following reason: The numeral '5' is used much more frequently and is more strongly adapted to the structure of the other lower numerals. Accordingly, it is likely to lose more of its nominal properties. If, nevertheless, we find a numeral '5' that still behaves like a noun, then we may predict that the development from noun to numeral is a recent one.

6. Numerals tend to be made up of combinations in which larger numerals precede smaller ones. Following Greenberg, we will assume that there is a cognitive principle at work here that has to do with requirements of efficient communication (ignoring less common patterns as found, for instance, in German *einundzwanzig* 'one and twenty' or '21':

> If I express a large number, say 10,253 in the order 10,000; 200; 50; 3; the very first element gives me a reasonably close approximation to the final result, and every successive item gives a further approximation. The opposite order leaves the hearer in the dark till the last item is reached. (Greenberg 1978c:274)

An alternative explanation is proposed by Stampe (1976:603). He argues that the order higher numeral–lower numeral is suggestive of a well-known principle according to which old information is placed before new information—since in counting the lower numbers change more rapidly than the higher ones, he says, they are the new material and are therefore ordered later. There is not much point in evaluating these two hypotheses in the absence of further information; in any case, both are in accordance with the facts considered.

7. In languages whose numeral system consists of less than five numerals, the highest numeral is likely to be derived from an approximate quantifier such as 'many', 'a few', or 'a couple' (Stampe 1976:597; see the discussion in 2.2).

8. Among the various operations used for constructing numerals, addition is the most widespread. But a number of numeral systems include subtraction as a minor operation. A perhaps extreme case has been observed in the Japanese language Ainu, in which all numerals from '6' to '9' are constructed by means of subtraction: *i-wan* (4-10) '6', *ar-wan* (3-10) '7', *tu-pesan* (2-down) '8', and *shine-pesan* (1-down) '9' (Stampe 1976:602).

Addition and subtraction are not the only operations that are involved in the construction of numeral systems: Instances of multiplication and even division can be observed crosslinguistically, even if there are societies, like the Australian Aranda and Walbiri (Stampe 1976:605), or the traditional Kxoé hunter-gatherers of northern Namibia, that do without multiplication. The way multiplication arises is easy to reconstruct once 'hand' has been introduced as a numerical concept: "Two hands are two fives, and (leaving anatomy) three hands are three fives. Here are sums of sums, and multiplication is born" (Stampe 1976:604).

The following observations on the behavior of arithmetic operations appear to hold true crosslinguistically (cf. Greenberg 1978c:257–8):

1. Addition and multiplication are the most common means for building numerals, in that order.
2. The existence of multiplication implies that of addition.
3. The presence of either subtraction or division implies that of both addition and multiplication.

An analysis of the strategies employed for the expression of the various operations would be beyond the scope of the present study; suffice it to conclude with a few general remarks on the most frequently used operation—addition. Addition is encoded by means of a number of formal means, such as word order, prosodic phenomena, inflection, or some combination of these. The crosslinguistic evidence available so far (see, e.g., Greenberg 1978c; Hurford 1987:237) suggests that the most common sources are either comitative markers ('with'), which tend to be grammaticalized to conjunctions and addition markers ('and', 'plus'), and location markers, where morphemes for 'on' and 'upon' (called the "superessive link" by Greenberg) are used in a metaphorical fashion: "If we add three items to ten, then the three are put on the heap of ten and not vice versa" (Greenberg 1978c:265). As we saw, in Mamvu the superessive marker *íjuní* 'above' is used for addition with numerals above '20', while in Swahili the comitative marker *na* 'with, and' has been generalized as an addition marker throughout the numeral system. In literary Welsh, location appears to have been drawn on for numbers up to '39', the connective used being *ar* 'on', while for all higher numbers the connective *ac* 'and' is used (Hurford 1987:53). Occasionally, other means are recruited. In (2), for example, there is a possessive structure serving as a source for addition, where '10' appears as the possessor and '1' appears as the possessee. Nevertheless, the most frequently employed sources for addition markers appear to be comitative and locative markers.

(2)   Quechua (Greenberg 1978c:265)
       anka ukni- yuk
       ten   one-   having
       '11'

2.2   Variation

In spite of the ubiquity of the body-part model in the creation of numeral systems, we also find structures that suggest alternative models. While the patterns sketched in the preceding section appear to be statistically predominant in the languages of the world, we nevertheless find numerals, or even entire numeral systems, that cannot be explained with reference to the body-part model. Such systems may have any of the numerals '3', '4', '6', or '9' as their base and, accordingly, may be called ternary, quaternary, senary, and nonary systems, respectively. Examples of a quaternary system can be found in Salinan-Chumash languages (Turner 1988), while senary system languages have been described by Beeler with reference to the Wintun stock in languages such as Patwin, Wintu, and Nomlaki (Beeler 1961:2).

That there are systems of numerals, or individual numerals, that are not based on the human hand—that is, that are not quinary, decimal, or vigesimal—can be due to a number of different factors. First, some societies appear to "have no need of numbers," as Stampe (1976:596) puts it. The Andamanese are said to count no higher than '2'; Botocudo, a Macro-Ge language in Brazil, is said to have only the terms 'one' and 'many'; and the Worora language of Australia has only a single numeral root which means 'one' in the singular (*iaruŋ*), 'two' in the dual (*iaruŋandu*), and 'three' or more in the plural (*iaruŋuri*) (Stampe 1976:596; Greenberg 1978c:256). Aboriginal Australian societies appear to have been particularly reluctant to develop more extended numeral systems. Thus, Dixon concludes, "The one obvious gap in Australian vocabularies is the lack of any system of numbers. It is usually said that there are only numbers 'one', 'two', 'several' and 'many'; some languages appear also to have 'three' although this is frequently a compound form" (Dixon 1980:107–8). This does not mean that Australians lacked or lack the ability to distinguish numerical concepts. For example, they did have ways of measuring and indicating the days remaining until some planned social event by pointing at different points on the palm of the hand. Furthermore, they never seem to have experienced major difficulties in learning to use English numerals (cf. Dixon 1980:108).

Second, there are culture-specific forces such as economic transactions and business strategies that may influence the structure of numeral systems:

The source for the reinterpretation of the Indo-European decimal 'hundred' as 120 seems to be geographically located around the North Atlantic and the Baltic Sea, and the primary use seems to have to do with trading fish and other goods that come 'by the dozen' or by the 'Grosshundert', where the remaining 2 or 20, respectively, represent a margin for discount (cf. "cheaper by the dozen", i.e. "12 for the price of 10"). (Seiler 1989:11)

Third, numeral expansion occurs. It may happen, for example, that in a traditional counting system the last number used for counting is then taken as a new base number from which counting starts over. Beeler reports that in some California Penutian languages the numeral '6' was used "as the end of a sequence and regarded as a general round number" (1961:2). Note also that the same numeral for '6' appears in Northern Nisenan as the word for '100'. Not surprisingly, therefore, some Penutian languages have developed a system in which '7' is expressed as '6 + 1', '8' as '7 + 1', and so on.

In addition, numeral systems that are not based on the human hand may arise as a result of the reanalysis of an existing system as something else. Stampe (1976:601) describes how in the Munda language Sora a canonical decimal-vigesimal system was supplemented by a duodecimal system (based on '12') via the erosion of constituents, which triggered the shift from '10' to '12' as a new numeral base.

The Sora development is a complex one, though probably not an uncommon one. It is summarized in table 2-3: At Stage I, we are dealing with a decimal-vigesimal system (based on '10' and '20'). With the reinterpretation of '12' as a new base, a duodecimal structure enters the old system, at least for the numerals from '12' to

Table 2-3 The rise of a duodecimal structure in Sora (according to Stampe 1976:601)

	Stage I	
*gəl		'10'
*mi'-gəl-muy	1-10-1	'11'
*mi'-gəl-bar	1-10-2	'12'
	Stage II	
gəlji		'10'
gəl-muy	10-1	'11'
miggəl		'12'
miggəl-bɔy	12-1	'13'
miggəl-bagu	12-2	'14'
miggəl-gulji	12-7	'19'
bɔ-koRi	1 × 20	'20'
bɔ-koRi-miggəl-bagu	(1 × 20)-12-2	'34'
bɔ-koRi-miggəl-gulji	(1 × 20)-12-7	'39'
ba-koRi	2 × 20	'40'

'19', from '32' to '39', and so on. The result is described by Stampe as "a Stravinskian alternation of twelves and eights unparalleled in any known language" (1976:601).

Reanalyzing an existing numeral as another numeral is perhaps more common than one might be inclined to believe. In Danish, the numeral base *tyve* '20' appears to have received the value '10' in the numerals *tredive* '30' (< *'3 × 20') and *fyrretyve* '40' (< *'4 × 20'; Seiler 1989:11, 17–18). Among the Matapato Maasai on the northern slopes of Mt. Kilimanjaro, all decade values have been doubled—that is, the numerals *tomon* and *tíkítam* mean not '10' and '20' as they do in all other Maasai dialects but '20' and '40'. It may not be coincidental that among all Maasai sections, it is the Matapato who are most strongly exposed to tourism.

In quite a number of languages it is not a matter of choosing between, say, a decimal or a quaternary system; rather, what we observe is a combination of the properties of more than one system. More precisely, what we are likely to be confronted with is the fact that in addition to the body-part model, some alternative secondary model appears to have been developed. If we find such a situation, then the latter is likely to be confined to what Schmidt (1926) calls the pairing principle (see the beginning of this chapter), or what Seiler (1989:8) refers to as "irregularities"—that is, to a few numerals (frequently only one) that interrupt an otherwise regular series.

Such irregularities are likely to be confined to lower numerals, even if they may exceed '10'. The numerals from '15' to '19' of Welsh and Breton, for example, are described by Seiler (1989:8) as in table 2-4, where '18' presents an instance of "irregularity": '18', which is based on a multiplicative pattern, interrupts an otherwise additive series of numerals. Irregularities of this kind are widespread. The dual form of the word for '8' in Indo-European is one example. A similar situation is found in many Bantu languages: Swahili, for example, has a decimal system, but the numeral for '8' (*-nane*) appears to be historically derived from an expression meaning 'four plus four' (cf. *-na* 'and', *-ne* '4'), an observation made already more than a century ago by Pott (1868:45).

Similarly, in the Penutian languages Wintu, Nomlaki, and Patwin, '5' is derived from 'hand'—that is, we are dealing with an instance of the body-part model based on the concept 'hand', while '6' is derived from a ternary model, or a notional basis 'two times three'. In one recording of Northern Wintu, a nonary system is found,

Table 2-4   The structure of some numerals in Welsh and Breton (based on Seiler 1989:8)

Number value	Pattern employed in	
	Welsh	Breton
15	'5 + 10'	
16	'1 on (5 + 10)'	'6 + 10'
17	'2 on (5 + 10)'	'7 + 10'
18	'2 × 9'	'3 × 6'
19	'4 on (5 + 10)'	'9 + 10'

where '11', '12', '13', and '14' contain the words for '2', '3', '4', and '5', respectively (Beeler 1961:2, 3).

One might predict that counting systems other than the decimal one will lose out in the long run, considering the ubiquity of the body-part model, on the one hand, and the global evolution of world culture and the role played worldwide by English, French, Spanish, Russian, and other Western languages on the other. Nevertheless, alternative models are still in use, and some of them are dynamic and progressive rather than recessive. For example, Beeler reports:

> In NE Maidu, the numerals recorded by Dixon at the beginning of the present century are the same as those obtained by Shipley some fifty years later, with one striking exception: the words for *7, 8,* and *9* given by Dixon are replaced in Shipley's record by expressions translatable 6 + 1, 6 + 2 and 6 + 3. (Beeler 1961:2)

Thus, rather than being a historically restricted source pattern, the senary structure recorded by Shipley turns out to be an active and replacive one. On the whole, however, modern evolution of numeral systems proceeds the other way round. In the Plateau languages of northern Nigeria, for example, a traditional duodecimal system (having '12' as a numerical base) is increasingly being replaced by a decimal system. Both English, the official language of Nigeria, and Hausa, the local lingua franca, are decimal, even if Gerhardt (1987) says that this fact cannot immediately be held responsible for this process. The transition from a duodecimal to a decimal system that can be observed in these languages involves the following patterns: Either the traditional numeral '12' was reinterpreted as meaning '10', or else the words for '11' and '12' of the duodecimal system were replaced, respectively, by '10 + 1' and '10 + 2'.

To conclude, there are usually explanations whenever cardinal numerals or numeral systems are found that cannot be reconciled with the body-part model. But there are a few other peculiarities that can be observed in the structure of numerals. One of these concerns the fact that one and the same number unit may receive different expressions in a given language. We noticed above that in Mamvu there are two different terms for 'six': one (*elí qodè relí* 'the hand seizes one') that is derived from the body-part model and another (*màdyà*) that occurs only in the numeral '16' and is etymologically opaque. Furthermore, English has three different items all denoting '10'—*'ten', '-teen'* (e.g., *eighteen*), and *'-ty'* (e.g., *eighty*). Why is it that such doublets or triplets exist, and why are they especially common when base numbers like '10', '20', '100', and the like are involved?

There are a number of possible answers, and the problem requires a more detailed analysis; suffice it to mention three possible answers. First, it may happen that an older system is superseded by a new one. In such a case it is to be expected that, at least for some time, a given number may be expressed simultaneously by means of items taken from both the older and the younger system.

Second, an expression for a numerical base can undergo phonological change in environment X but not in environment Y. In the course of time, this phonological change may have the effect that that expression comes to be associated with two different forms occurring in mutually exclusive environments: one form in X and the other in Y.

Third, another possible answer has to do with the choice of source models. As we saw above, the body-part model provides by far the most popular template for creating numeral bases. Since this model takes the human fingers and toes as counting units, it is most effective for creating numerals up to '20'. While the model may be extended by multiplication to higher numerals, alternative models may be recruited for numerals having '10', '20', or higher numeral bases. If that is the case, then a given base number has two different terms, where one is derived from the body-part model and another is derived from some alternative model, whereby inanimate collective items such as 'heap', 'sack', 'group', 'bundle', and the like are used as terms for base numbers. In the following example from So, a Ugandan language, lower numerals are suggestive of a quinary system, where the noun *an*, pl. *én-ek* 'hand' is part of the expression for the base number. For decades from '20' onwards, on the other hand, the base number is *îr-kon* 'tens', which is derived from the noun *îr*, pl. *îr-kon* 'house'. The number '20' is located in the intersection of the two systems—that is, it has two contrasting expressions, as can be seen in (3).

(3)   So (Kuliak, Nilo-Saharan; Carlin 1993:110)
       tud en- ek nɛbɛc   *or*   ir- kon in   nɛbɛc   '20'
       five hand- PL 2   house- PL   REL.PL 2

Eastern Pomo of California has a vigesimal system. But there appear to be no expressions relating to the body-part model; rather, '20' is expressed as *xai-di-lema-tek* 'a full stick' and multiples of '20' are referred to as so many 'sticks' (Farris 1990:179).

In the Balese language of eastern Zaire, the number value '100' marks the intersection between the two contrasting systems (Vorbichler 1965:94–6). The nontransparent noun *àbùcí* 'tenness' is used as a decimal base number to form the item *ábúcí àbùcí* 'ten tens' or '100'; at the same time, the collective model is used, based on the noun *ubvu* '100' which is used as a base number from '100' upward. The original meaning of *ubvu* was apparently 'liana', from which it came to acquire the additional meaning 'string of one hundred cowrie shells', and ultimately '100'. Note that cowrie shells were the main precolonial monetary currency; *ubvu* is also located at the intersection of the numeral system and the money-counting paradigm, the latter consisting of the items listed in (4).

(4)   Balese (Central Sudanic, Nilo-Saharan; Vorbichler 1965:96)
       wádí   'string of money consisting of forty cowrie shells'
       ubvu   'string of money consisting of one hundred cowrie shells'
       bomu   'fifty *wádí*–strings'

While the use of the body-part model tends to be confined to lower numerals, there are languages in which the model is extended to higher numerals. In Aztec, for example, the numerals '5' (*ma-cuil-li*) and '10' (*mà-tlae-tli*) have 'hand' (*ma*) as a conceptual source, while for higher numerals, another body-part has been recruited—namely *tzon-* 'hair', which appears to have given rise to the numeral *cen-tzon-tli* '400' (lit.: 'one-hair'; Stolz 1994b:83).

2.3   Morphosyntax

As the observations made here suggest, the way the morphology and syntax of grammatical categories are structured can largely be explained once we know the conceptual sources from which they are derived. Accordingly, the structure of cardinal numerals can be accounted for on the basis of what has been said in the preceding sections.

Perhaps one of the most noteworthy properties of cardinal numerals is that they behave to some extent like adjectives and to some extent like nouns (Greenberg 1978c; Corbett 1978a, 1978b). Adjectival properties would be, for example, agreement in number, gender, and/or case with the noun they modify, and occurrence in the same syntactic slot as "canonical" adjectives. Nominal properties are present, for example, if the numeral governs the noun it modifies, where the latter is likely to be encoded as a genitive plural constituent (see the following discussion).

But it has also been pointed out by the authors just mentioned that there is a dramatic difference between lower and higher numerals. According to a study by Corbett (1978a:358), the Russian cardinals *odin* '1', *dva* '2', and *tri* '3' have adjectival but no nominal features, while *sto* '100', *tysjača* '1,000', and *million* '1,000,000' have nominal but no adjectival features. After a careful crosslinguistic survey, Corbett proposes the following "candidate universals":

1. The syntactic behavior of simple cardinal numerals will always fall between that of adjectives and nouns.
2. If the simple cardinal numerals of a given language vary in their syntactic behavior, the numerals showing nounier behaviour will denote higher numerals than those with less nouny behaviour. (1978a:363)

That higher value numerals behave like nouns or have nounlike features is explained by Corbett in the following way:

> Thus the higher numerals are nouns pressed into service as numerals. An example would be Old Church Slavonic *t'ma* 'multitude' which came to mean '10,000'. As in the course of cultural development new numerals are introduced, naturally at the top of the earlier system, the previously highest numeral may be further integrated into the system and lose some noun-like features. (Corbett 1983:245–6)

Ignoring a few minor observations, like the fact that in some languages simple cardinal numerals behave like verbs rather than nouns or adjectives (Orin Gensler, personal communication; cf. Robins 1985), we have nothing to add to this account, which applies not only to Slavic languages but also to many languages across the world: While the body-part model provides the predominant source for lower numeral bases, higher numeral values are most likely derived from collective nouns. As we will see in the coming chapters, we are dealing here with instances of a more general process of conceptual transfer according to which concrete nouns provide perhaps the most common source for the development of closed-class items like adpositions, conjunctions, and the like.

That this development also leads from nouns to adjective-like words can be illustrated with examples from the color domain. One of the most common conceptual sources for new color terms is provided by the plant domain, most of all by plant parts like flowers and fruit. Now, what happens as a lexeme denoting a plant part develops into one denoting a color term (e.g., 'orange', 'violet') is that the noun increasingly loses nominal properties and acquires features that are characteristic of items whose main function is to express qualities and to modify other nouns. The process concerned has been described by Heine, Claudi, & Hünnemeyer (1991, chapter 2) with reference to a categorial metaphor whereby a concept belonging to the domain of concrete items— the OBJECT domain in their terminology—serves as a structural template to express concepts belonging to the QUALITY domain. The implications of this conceptual transfer are that the relevant terms for plant parts lose nominal properties and increasingly acquire properties linking them with the category of adjectives. With reference to numerals, the morphosyntactic consequences of this process are summarized by Hurford in the following way: "The meanings of numerals make 'nominal modifier' (adjective) the primary most natural syntactic category for them" (1987:197).

Corbett (1983:236) observes that in Slavic the numerals '5–10', '100', and '1,000' have lost some of their nounlike properties. Still, it is not just higher numerals that are of nominal origin—even lower numerals tend to go back to nouns (but see the following discussion). This is actually to be expected, since it is body-part nouns like 'hand', 'foot', and 'person' that are among the main sources for numerals like '5', '10', and '20'. Hurford interprets the process concerned in the following way:

> Thus, for example, in Melamela—a language of New Britain . . . —the form *lima-* denotes the set of hands (that is means 'hand'), but, pressed into use as a numeral, *lima* denotes the set of collections of five things (that is means '5'). With such a large difference in meaning, one would not expect the borrowed form necessarily to retain aspects of its former morphosyntactic behaviour. (Hurford 1987:200)

But what accounts for the adjectival properties of lower numerals, as opposed to the less adjective-like behavior of higher numerals? There are at least two main contributing factors. First, while nouns are essentially the only source for higher numerals, the situation is different in the case of lower numerals. Looking back at the list of Mamvu numerals presented in section 2.1, we notice a number of descriptive expressions that have developed into terms for numerals, like "the hand spares one" for '9' or "the foot seizes one" for '11'. Obviously, such expressions have a propositional form and a clausal, rather than a nominal, morphosyntax. Numerals derived from such expressions are therefore hardly likely to have nominal properties. In Zulu, for example, the numerals '6' through '9' are derived from concrete expressions that describe the conventionalized pattern of counting by using fingers, as can be seen in table 2-5. The numeral forms in the table suggest that while the conceptual sources of '6' and '7' are nominal, those of '8' and '9' are nominalized verb phrases. Accordingly, one will expect that the former two numerals are likely to have more nominal properties than the latter two. Furthermore, it may happen that lower numerals go back to categories such as adjectives (see the

Table 2-5   Some Zulu numerals (Bantu, Niger-Congo; Doke 1930:326)

Term	Meaning	Literal meaning
isithupha	6	'the thumb'
isikhombisa	7	'the index finger'
isishiyagalombili	8	'the leaving behind two fingers'
isishiyagalolunye	9	'the leaving behind one finger'

following discussion). Obviously in such cases one does not expect the resulting numerals to have nominal properties.

The second factor has to do with frequency of use. The lower the number value, the more frequently the corresponding numeral is likely to be used (Hurford 1987). Now, as has been argued by a number of students of grammaticalization, frequency of use correlates positively with degree of grammaticalization: The more frequently an item is employed, the more likely it is to lose properties characteristic of its category and to develop into some other category. Accordingly, the development from noun to adjective is more likely to affect lower numerals than higher numerals.

2.4   On transparency

Cardinal numerals were one of the paradigm examples used by Ferdinand de Saussure (1922) to argue that the meaning of linguistic forms is arbitrary or unmotivated. "Simple signs," such as the French numerals *neuf* '9', *dix* '10', or *vingt* '20', are said to be wholly arbitrary (or unmotivated), while "syntagms" like *dix-neuf* '19' are "relatively motivated" (Saussure 1922:180–4): The motivation of the latter consists in the fact that each such syntagm is related syntagmatically to its components and associatively to other syntagms having the same pattern (Saussure 1922:180–4). Ignoring "marginal exceptions" like onomatopoeia or instances like French *dix-neuf*, which are relatively motivated and hence are arbitrary to a certain degree only, Saussure says that a name reveals nothing about the nature of the entity named.

Among the basic assumptions on which the present work rests is the following: The forms used for expressing meaning are not introduced arbitrarily but rather are motivated (see section 1.1). This is an important assumption but, as many will agree, also a controversial one. It becomes less controversial if one adds, as we did in chapter 1, that our concern is exclusively with *genetic* motivation—that is, no claim is made here regarding either structural or psychological motivation. Still, even in this reduced form, the claim remains a strong one. Essentially it means that, first, seemingly meaningless linguistic forms are often historically derived from meaningful forms; second, in order to fully understand such present-day forms, it is essential to reconstruct the motivation that was responsible for their creation. There are a couple of problems with the reconstruction of genetic motivation, however.

Saussure was arguing in terms of either structural or psychological motivation— or, more likely, in terms of both. Our problem is the following: How to prove that numerals such as French *neuf* '9', *dix* '10', and the like are genetically motivated? As we saw in the preceding discussion, it is possible to reconstruct part of the genetic motivation underlying the form of numerals with reference to such source structures as the body-part model. But this model does not seem to take care of cases like French *neuf* and *dix*.

Two main positions can be taken vis-à-vis this issue. According to the first, which is not uncommon among linguists, one would say that since it has not been possible so far to reconstruct the genetic motivation underlying these numerals, there is no genetic motivation. This position apparently rests on the tacit assumption that, since I do not know X, X does not exist.

The second position, which is the one adopted here, can be phrased thus: There appear to be no examples where numerals have been invented arbitrarily, while many examples can be adduced to show that the introduction of numerals was motivated, as we saw in the preceding sections. One is therefore led to posit that genetic motivation is the expected case, while cases where no motivation has been discovered yet are in need of explanation. Accordingly, we will distinguish between *transparent* linguistic forms, where genetic motivation has already been reconstructed, and nontransparent or *opaque* forms, where it has not yet been reconstructed. For example, the cardinal numerals /x'oá 'three' and thíyà 'four' of Kxoé, a Central Khoisan language of northern Namibia, are transparent since their lexical sources (/x'oá 'few' and thíyà 'many', respectively) are still fully recoverable. In a similar fashion, transparency also obtains when Mamvu speakers use the numeral elí ɓòsí '10' (lit.: 'all hands'). French *neuf* and *dix*, by contrast, or their English equivalents, are opaque.

Not seldom, however, it happens that the etymology of the linguistic forms is buried in the darkness of prehistory, while the structural characteristics on which these forms are built are still recoverable. In such cases we propose to speak of *pattern transparency*. Pattern transparency can relate to syntactic or conceptual properties of the construction concerned. A paradigm example of the latter can be seen in the presence of a base number like '5', '10', or '20': Whenever we find a language that makes use of these numbers as bases for constructing numerals, very likely we are dealing with an instance of pattern transparency which ultimately is suggestive of the body-part model, as we saw in the preceding discussion.

The distinction between (semantic) transparency and pattern transparency is of secondary import to the purposes of the present work: Both are manifestations of genetic motivation. Whether we are dealing with the former or the latter can be simply a matter of historical depth: The presence of semantic transparency suggests a relatively young development, while the presence of pattern transparency that is no longer accompanied by semantic transparency is likely to signal a relatively old pattern of conceptual transfer.

2.5   Summary

A number of problems discussed in the preceding paragraphs have been concerned especially with the following questions:

1. Why are quinary, decimal, or vigesimal systems—that is, systems
    having, respectively, '5', '10', and '20' as their numeral base—
    statistically predominant in the languages of the world?
2. Why is it that decimal systems—that is, numeral systems based on the
    number '10'—are apparently crosslinguistically the most widespread
    ones?
3. Why is it that various numerals—in particular, base numbers like
    '10', '20', '100', etc.—may have more than one expression in some
    languages?
4. Why are cardinal numerals treated morphosyntactically as having
    both nominal and adjectival properties?
5. In the same vein, why is it that lower numerals are likely to have
    many characteristics in common with adjectives, while higher
    numerals tend to be more nounlike?
6. Why do markers used for the arithmetical operation of addition (i.e.,
    'plus') in complex numerals frequently resemble function words used
    for the expression of either accompaniment ('with') or superessive
    location ('on, upon'; see Greenberg 1978c:265; Hurford 1987:237)?

We have answered these questions over the course of this chapter. Here is a brief
summary. Questions (1) and (2) can be answered with reference to the body-part
model. Since this model is virtually the only conceptual source for lower base numbers, numerals having the value of the digits found on human hands and feet are those
that are most likely to occur as base numbers. And it would seem that by far the most
popular numerical entity cross-culturally consists of the two hands: As has been
pointed out by several researchers (e.g., Greenberg 1978c; see section 2.1 here),
counting plays an important role in the evolution of numeral systems, and counting
is likely to involve the two hands as a visual aid. Compared to hands, feet are considerably less convenient for this purpose, especially in societies that use footwear.

There are several possible answers to question (3). One answer has to do with
the fact that base numbers may be located at the border of contrasting conceptual
number domains and hence may be derived from different source models. Thus, '20'
can be of the "one-hand, two-hand, one-foot, whole-man variety" (Stampe 1976:596)
—that is, it may be derived from the body-part model. At the same time, it may have
a collective item such as 'bundle', 'heap', or the like as its source. In such a case we
may not be surprised to have synonymous terms for this number, with each term being
derived from a different model. An alternative answer would be that an inherited base
numeral is supplemented by a younger base numeral built on the same conceptual
pattern, or by a base numeral borrowed from another language.

Questions (4) and (5) were the subject of section 2.3: What we observed there
was essentially that the morphosyntactic shape of cardinal numerals depends on the
nature of the category of the source concepts involved. For example, higher value
numerals are more likely to have nouns as their source; hence these numerals can be
expected to exhibit more nominal properties than lower numerals do. That numerals
derived from nouns tend to lose their nominal structure and acquire properties that

relate them to nominal modifiers such as adjectives can be accounted for in a number of different ways. According to Heine, Claudi, & Hünnemeyer (1991), for example, this evolution has to do with a shift from one ontological domain to another: In the same way as nouns giving rise to numerals lose their association with the OB-JECT domain, they acquire the properties of the domain of QUALITY—that is, they tend to acquire the morphosyntactic properties of nominal qualifiers or modifiers.

An answer to question (6) can be given meaningfully only when we have dealt with the content of chapters 5 and 6: As we will see there, accompaniment (referred to as the Companion Schema) and location (Location Schema) belong to a small pool of source domains that are used time and again as prominent templates for expressing more abstract relational concepts.

Our discussion in the preceding sections was confined to a few issues that are relevant to explaining the structure of numeral systems. We had to leave aside issues that are culture-specific or of regional significance—for example, notions such as "overcounting" (Hurford 1975:235–9). Furthermore, the detailed correlations between body-parts and numeral expressions that can be observed in some societies could not be treated here; the reader is referred, for instance, to the description of the counting system of the Oksapmin of the West Sepik Province of Papua New Guinea for a particularly spectacular example of the relationship between human body and numeral system (Saxe 1981:306ff.).

After a detailed study, the main goal of which was a synchronic description of numerals within the framework of generative grammar, Hurford concludes that the "packaging strategy" underlying numeral systems "cannot be explained by appeal to innate mental structuring of the language acquirer" (1987:242), and instead offers an explanation in terms of social interaction and the way these systems evolve diachronically. This applies not only to numerals but also, in much the same way, to other domains of grammar.

The main purpose of this chapter was to demonstrate that cardinal numerals are shaped by extralinguistic factors such as anatomic characteristics of the human body. But while numerals thus are derived from other domains of human experience, they themselves may contribute to shaping other grammatical paradigms, as we will see in chapter 4.

3

SPATIAL ORIENTATION

In Lugbara, a language spoken in northeastern Zaire and northwestern Uganda, the traditional terms for spatial orientation are as shown in table 3-1. These Lugbara terms differ from corresponding terms in European languages in that they are all transparent (see section 2.4)—that is, in all cases, the motivation of the terms is still fully recoverable, as suggested by the literal meanings provided. At the same time, the motivation is similar to that found in many other languages. For example, quite a number of languages worldwide have derived their terms for 'east' and 'west' (if such terms exist at all) from expressions that relate to the rising and the setting sun, respectively (see section 3.2). Moreover, a common source of terms for 'right hand' is provided by such concepts as 'the male/strong hand', 'the eating hand', but also by 'the real/true hand' (see, e.g., Werner 1904). Thus, while Lugbara differs from English and other European languages, it has much in common with many languages elsewhere in the world.

Table 3-1 Lugbara (Central Sudan, Nilo-Saharan; Barr 1965:66)

Expression	Meaning	Literal meaning
andr-aleru	'north'	'down'
uru-leru	'south'	'up'
etuni cfuri-aleru	'east'	'where the sun comes out'
etuni 'deri-aleru	'west'	'where the sun falls'
dri ndi-aleru	'to the right'	cf. ndi 'real, true'
dri eji-aleru	'to the left'	cf. eji 'to carry'

At the same time, Lugbara also differs from other languages. The Lugbara people live close to the Nile, and the terms for 'north' and 'south' appear to owe their existence to the fact that the river flows north and water flows down. Obviously, one will not necessarily expect words for 'north' and 'south' to be etymologically related to 'down' and 'up', respectively, in societies that do not live close to the Nile. Similarly, the Lugbara traditionally carry their bows in their left hand; accordingly, 'left side' came to be expressed as the side where the bow is carried (Barr 1965:66). Again, we might be surprised to find the word for 'to the left' to be historically related to the verb 'to carry' in societies where bows are not carried in the left hand or where people do not normally carry bows.

The observations just made in the Lugbara language suggest that both cross-culturally stable ("universal") models and culture-specific models exist for creating linguistic items for spatial orientation. As we will see in the present chapter, both kinds of models are commonly recruited for creating the grammar of space, and we will try to explain why both are used and why they are used the way they are. Once again, our main interest is with the human body and its significance for shaping conceptualization and communication. But once more, we will not be confined to the body and its parts; alternative templates are also considered where they are found to determine the structure of spatial orientation.

The process looked at here is the same as the one observed in the preceding chapter: Concrete meanings serve as structural templates to denote more abstract meanings. But the result is different: Once the items used to designate concrete meanings come to be regularly associated with abstract meanings, such as expressing relations between items rather than denoting the items themselves, they lose properties that link them with the lexicon and gradually develop into grammatical forms. This has the following implications in particular:

1. Such items turn from open-class categories into closed-class categories. Nouns and verbs are open-class categories with a large membership; demonstratives, articles, and the like, by contrast, are closed-class categories with a small membership.
2. They lose in lexical meaning and acquire grammatical meaning.
3. They shift from autosemantic to synsemantic items, where "autosemantic" means that they have a meaning that is largely independent of that of other items figuring in the same sentence, while "synsemantic" items depend on the meaning of other items for their realization.
4. They tend to develop into invariable forms that, for instance, may no longer receive affixes.
5. They themselves tend to become clitics and eventually affixes on other words.
6. They are likely to lose in phonetic substance—that is, they become shorter.

In the first chapter I proposed a distinction between four systems of spatial orientation:

Deictic orientation

Object-deictic orientation

Landmark orientation

Cardinal orientation.

This distinction not only concerns different kinds of reference points, it also correlates with contrasting ways of conceptual derivation. I will now look at two of these systems in more detail. Deictic orientation is the subject of section 3.1, and section 3.2 is devoted to cardinal orientation—though what we have to say about these two systems has a bearing on the other two as well. Some characteristics of object-deictic orientation will be discussed in section 7.3.

3.1   Deictic orientation

In Yucatec, a Mayan language of Mexico, a number of terms for spatial orientation resemble expressions for body-parts. For example, similarities such as those listed in table 3-2 have been recorded. The similarity between the two types of words in table 3-2 is unlikely to be coincidental; as the analysis by Goldap (1992) and Stolz (1994b:60ff.) suggests, we are dealing with the result of a historical process whereby Yucatec speakers extended the use of some body-part items to also refer to certain spatial reference points, as the table illustrates.

The situation found in Yucatec is far from unusual; comparable situations can be found in many languages spoken in various parts of the world and belonging to different language families. The study of transfer patterns from concrete concepts to spatial concepts has received some scholarly attention since the 1980s, and a number of insights have been gathered in the course of that research (see especially Brugman 1983; Brugman & Macaulay 1986; Svorou 1986, 1987, 1988, 1994; MacLaury 1989). In 1989, a survey of 125 African languages was carried out to study the way in which some basic reference points of spatial orientation are expressed (Heine 1989). In this survey, five reference points were selected that are likely to receive a distinct linguistic coding and to be consistently distinguished conceptually across cultures (but see the following discussion). These reference points, which are typically encoded as locative nouns, adverbs, or adpositions (i.e., prepositions or postpositions), are listed in table 3-3. Subsequently, John Bowden (1991) conducted

Table 3-2   Yucatec (Mayan; Goldap 1992:613; Stolz 1994b:61)

Body-part term		Locative marker	
pàach	'back'	pàach(il)	'behind'
táan	'front'	táan(il)	'in front (of)'
ich	'eye'	ich-il	'inside'
		ich	'in'
ts'u'	'marrow'	ts'u'	'in'

Table 3-3   Five reference points of deictic orientation

Reference point	Spatial relation	Typical linguistic expression
'Up'	Top, superior	above, up, on, on top (of)
'Down'	Base, inferior	below, down, under, underneath
'Front'	Anterior	before, in front (of)
'Back'	Posterior	behind, back, in back of
'In'	Interior	inside, within, in

a similar survey in 104 Oceanic languages. In addition to the reference points listed in table 3-3, Bowden studied 'out', 'sea', and 'land', which he found were equally relevant to Oceanic languages. On the basis of these, as well as a number of other works (see especially Svorou 1994), we have a fairly good picture of how the conceptualization of space may affect the grammar of spatial orientation.

While the reference points listed in table 3-3 can be said to be universal to the extent that a given language is likely to have conventionalized expressions for them, it has been claimed that there are also languages that lack the notion of deictic orientation and hence have no conceptual and/or linguistic distinctions of the kind listed in table 3-3 (see, e.g., Brown & Levinson 1993a, 1993b). Instead of saying, for instance, 'Your car is in front of the house', a corresponding utterance made by speakers of such a language would be 'Your car is north of the house'. We have summarized this line of research in chapter 1 (section 1.2).

The research on conceptual transfer has established that there are three main source domains for the expression of the reference points presented in table 3-3, as well as various other points of spatial orientation. These domains are listed in table 3-4 (cf. Svorou 1994:70). Of all these source models, body-parts are by far the most important, and most of what we have to say in this section relates to them. As we shall see, in addition to the human body, bodies of animals may also serve as a reference domain.

Next to body-parts, there are what we refer to, following Svorou (1994:79), as environmental landmarks or, in short, simply landmarks. Particular items belonging to this domain are 'earth, ground', 'sky', 'mountain', 'river', 'road', and the like. The most common landmark sources and the resulting spatial target concepts are summarized in table 3-5. Landmarks are less important than body-parts as a source for the spatial concepts discussed in this chapter. In some cases, however, they are employed more frequently than body-parts are. As we will see in the following discussion, for example, the spatial reference point 'down' is more likely to have a landmark source than is any other conceptual source.

Table 3-4   Common source models for expressions of spatial orientation

Source models	Expressions of spatial orientation
Body-parts	Uses parts of the human body in its upright position as a model
Landmarks	Uses environmental landmarks
Dynamic concepts	Uses activities

Table 3-5 Common landmark models for
spatial orientation (cf. Svorou 1994:80ff.)

Source concept	Target concept
'sky', 'heaven', 'summit'	'up'
'earth', 'ground'	'down'
'field', 'doorway'	'front'
'track', 'trace'	'back'
'house', 'shore', 'land'	'in'
'field', 'doorway'	'out'

Much less commonly, the sources for spatial points of orientation may include dynamic concepts, primarily concepts typically expressed by motion verbs like 'come', 'go', 'follow', 'precede', 'pass', and 'descend' or by verbs of static location such as 'remain', 'stay', 'sit', and the like. These dynamic concepts relate almost invariably to activities or actions (see section 3.2). Verbs that serve as sources may be encoded as infinitival, participial, or other nonfinite items, or even as finite verbs. In addition to motion verbs, a number of other verbs may be used. Note the following example presented by Svorou (1994), where the Halia verb *tara* 'see' appears to have been grammaticalized to a directional marker 'to'.

(1) Halia (Oceanic; Svorou 1994:68)
     ara e   soata- mena- liyleyen tara tarak
     we PM carry- 1.PL- it   see truck
     'We (INCL) carried it to the truck.'

Frequently in such cases, the verb is presented as a nominal item rather than as a verb. Hill (1994:3), for example, observes that in the Longgu language of the Solomon Islands, expressions for 'front' (*na'ova-*) and 'down' (*orova-*) are derived from verbs. In fact, however, the two are actually nominals that are derived by means of the nominalizer *va-* from the verbs *na'o* 'to face' and *oro* 'to bend', respectively. The contribution of dynamic items to the concepts listed in table 3-3, however, is cross-linguistically negligible, and dynamic items will not be further looked at here. This leaves us with body-parts and landmarks as the primary source domains.

Mention should also be made of a fourth category of concepts that serves as a template for the spatial concepts 'up', 'down', and the like. These are what Svorou (1994:83ff.) calls relational object parts; following Heine, Claudi, and Hünnemeyer (1991:128), we will refer to them simply as relational concepts. This category includes items such as 'top', 'bottom', 'front(side)', 'back(side)', 'the interior or inside', and 'the exterior or outside'. This category is not treated here as a separate source domain for spatial orientation, for the following reasons:

First, wherever there is historical evidence, these relational concepts can be traced back to either body-part or landmark sources. Thus the diachronic chain involved has the following structure:

body-part or landmark → relational concept → spatial reference point

Second, these concepts do not exhibit any concrete physical contours, as, for instance, body-parts and landmarks do; they are highly schematic and in many cases hardly differ from spatial concepts like 'up' or 'down'. What distinguishes them from spatial reference points like the ones in table 3-3 in some languages is simply the fact that they have the morphosyntax of nouns, while those spatial reference points have more properties in common with adverbs and adpositions.

Third, while they have the morphosyntactic appearance of nouns, relational concepts are likely to be grammaticalized to the extent that they are no longer proto-typical nouns: they tend to lack some nominal properties such as encoding distinctions of number, case or definiteness, or taking modifiers like adjectives.

CONCEPTUALIZATION IS anthropocentric: Whenever possible, we use human categories to describe and understand nonhuman ones. Accordingly, the human body provides the most important model for expressing concepts of spatial orientation. But, as already indicated in the preceding discussion, there are other models—notably the zoomorphic model, which takes the bodies of animals as a structural template for spatial orientation. Instances of the zoomorphic model have been reported by a number of authors. Svorou (1994:75), for example, found that in Papago the concepts 'front', 'side', and 'inside' are derived from the anthropomorphic model, while 'back' is derived from the zoomorphic model. Brugman (1983) and Brugman and Macaulay (1986) observe that Chalcatongo Mixtec has different nouns for 'human back' and 'animal back' and that this difference affects the way certain items are conceptual-ized. A table, for instance, appears to be conceived as an animal whose back is the top and whose belly is the underside; the top of a wall is expressed with the noun for an animal back. Furthermore, in some African languages, certain spatial concepts are expressed in a way that suggests that the zoomorphic model was involved. This is the case in particular in languages where 'up' is expressed by means of the body-part term 'back', 'front' by means of 'head', and 'back' by means of 'buttocks' or 'anus' (Heine 1989), roughly as illustrated in figure 3-1.

Note, however, that there appears to be a clear cognitive preference principle according to which the zoomorphic model presupposes the anthropomorphic model, while the opposite does not apply: No languages have been found so far where the zoomorphic model constitutes the only model for structuring an entire cognitive domain. For example, in languages where some spatial concepts may have the ani-mal body as their source, at least some are based on the anthropomorphic model. Note also that in Chalcatongo Mixtec, a wall is generally based on the animal body as a template, but it may also take the human body instead (Brugman & Macaulay 1986; see also Svorou 1994:73–5).

We will now look at each of the orientation points listed in table 3-3 in turn, using the quantitative information contained in the surveys mentioned in the preced-ing discussion (especially Heine 1989; Bowden 1991; Svorou 1994).

3.1.1 'Up'

Of all possible source concepts, body-parts provide the most important source of expressions for the concept 'up'. There is only one body-part that is of noticeable

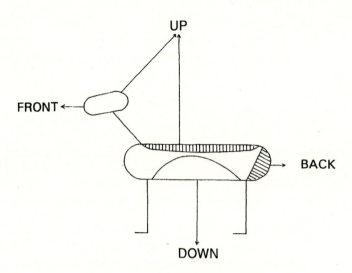

Figure 3-1 The zoomorphic model.

importance, which is 'head': 87% of all African and 61% of all Oceanic languages that were found to use body-part terms for 'up'-terms such as 'above', 'up', 'on', and the like have grammaticalized 'head' for this purpose. There appears to be no competitor to 'head', other body-parts being statistically negligible. The next most frequently used body-parts are 'face', which occurs in 4.3% of the African and 14.6% of the Oceanic languages, and 'shoulder', occurring in 4.3% of the African and 10% of the Oceanic languages having a body-part source for 'up'. The only other body-parts that have been recorded are 'hair' (7.3% of Oceanic languages), 'forehead' (7.3% of Oceanic languages), and 'back' (4.3% of African languages). The use of 'back' for the spatial concept 'up' might appear odd; as noted in the preceding discussion, however, it is probably due to the zoomorphic model, which appears to have been selected here instead of the otherwise generally preferred anthropomorphic model. In Svorou's (1994:70–2) worldwide sample of fifty-five languages, for example, there are eighteen instances of body-parts being used for 'up', of which fifteen derive from 'head' and three from 'back'. While body-parts provide the primary template for expressions for 'up', landmarks constitute a noteworthy secondary template (see the following discussion).

3.1.2 'Down'

Both in Africa and Oceania, 'down' is the only concept looked at here that has environmental landmarks ('earth', 'ground') as its primary source domain. Still, body-parts form an important secondary source domain in both areas. There is, however, no uniform behavior across the two continents. In Africa, 'buttocks' or 'anus' constitutes the outstanding body-part, providing the source in 84.6% of all languages having a grammaticalized body-part for 'down'. Note that also in Svorou's (1994:71) sample, 'buttocks' is the most common body-part source for 'down', even though there are only three examples of it in her fifty-five-language sample. This body-part appears to be irrelevant in Oceania, where 'foot/leg' is the primary body-part source. 'Foot/leg' also occurs in Africa (15.6%), but in Oceania it has been found to be the only relevant body-part template, to be found in 55.6% of the Oceanic languages using a body-part.

3.1.3 'Front'

Environmental landmarks are virtually absent as sources for 'front', the only conceptual template of importance being the body-part 'face': 52.8% of the African and 72.1% of the Oceanic sample languages make use of this source. The second most important African source is 'eye', which accounts for 15.7% of all body-part sources for 'front'. But since expressions for 'eye' are the most likely conceptual source for developing expressions for 'face' (see section 7.2), it is conceivable that some, or even most, of the 'eye'-sources must be added to the list of 'face'-sources. Compared to 'face', no other body-part is of comparable relevance, not even 'breast', which occurs in 6.7% of the African and 11.8% of the Oceanic languages. Another body-part that appears in both parts of the world is 'forehead', which accounts for 8.9% of the body-part sources for 'front' in Africa and 2.9% in Oceania. Some body-parts are confined essentially to one continent. Thus, while 'mouth' (6.7%) and 'head' (6.7%) are found in Africa, 'belly/stomach' (7.3%) appears to be largely restricted to Oceania; in Africa, by contrast, the latter body-part region is primarily associated with 'in' (see the following discussion). Note that 'mouth' is also a widespread source in Svorou's worldwide sample, even if clearly of secondary importance compared to 'face'.

3.1.4 'Back'

As in the case of 'front', environmental landmarks are irrelevant as source concepts. The universal source for 'back' expressions is the body-part 'back', which accounts for 77.7% of the African and 95% of the Oceanic expressions for the spatial concept 'back'. In Africa, however, there is a second source: 'buttocks/anus', which accounts for more than one-fifth (22.3%) of all expressions for 'back' in the African sample of 125 languages. To what extent this high figure, along with the fact that 'buttocks/anus' also provides the source for 'down', is due to the effect of the zoomorphic model (see the preceding discussion) remains to be investigated.

3.1.5 'In'

This concept shares with 'front' and 'back' the fact that landmark sources are virtually nonexistent. There is, however, a remarkable difference between Africa and Oceania. In Africa, 'belly/stomach' is the clearly predominant source, accounting for 92.1% of the expressions concerned, the only other body-parts being 'palm (of hand)' (4.8%) and 'heart' (3.1%). In Oceania a host of body-parts provide almost equally common templates, especially 'tooth' (26.7%), 'belly/stomach' (17.8%), 'heart' (13.3%), 'liver' (11.1%), and 'bowels' (11.1%). 'Heart' and 'stomach' are the only body-parts that appear more than once as sources for 'in' in Svorou's (1994:71) worldwide sample of 55 languages.

OF THE THREE MAJOR subregions of the human body (head, trunk, extremities), the extremities are virtually insignificant as a source for the spatial concepts considered: Neither in Africa nor in Oceania do extremities like 'hand' or 'arm' play a major role in expressing any of the spatial concepts looked at above, as is suggested by the quantitative data in table 3-6. An exception can be seen in the item 'foot, leg', which, at least in Oceania, constitutes an important source for 'down'.

According to table 3-6 there are remarkable areal differences in the relative weight given to the three major body regions. The trunk provides by far the most important source for developing expressions for spatial orientation in Africa but not in Oceania. On the basis of Svorou's (1994:71) crosslinguistic survey, it would seem that the situation in Oceania is much more in accordance with worldwide patternings: In her fifty-five-language sample, the head and the trunk each provide roughly 49% of the sources, while the extremities account for less than 2%. This observation might suggest that the belly is more prominent a source area for spatial orientation in Africa than elsewhere in the world. One may wonder why the extremities should constitute such an insignificant region for spatial orientation. Most likely, this is due to the particular target concepts looked at here. For example, if we had selected 'left' and 'right' instead of 'up' and 'down', then a rather different situation would have emerged since, worldwide, the human hand provides the primary locus for developing terms for left–right orientation (see, e.g., Werner 1904).

Regularities in conceptual shift like the ones we have just been dealing with are based on observations regarding probabilities of occurrence. This means that while the generalizations proposed hold true statistically, they may be contradicted in individual cases. The lexical concept 'breast', for example, constitutes one of the main sources for 'front', yet there is at least one language where 'breast' has given rise to a different spatial notion. In Baka, a Ubangi language spoken by some 35,000 pygmies in Cameroon, this body-part (*to-*), in combination with the locative preposition *à*, appears to have been responsible for the spatial marker *à to-* 'in' (Kilian-Hatz 1995:141).

A given spatial concept can be derived simultaneously from two different models within one and the same language. The concept 'on', for example, has two differ-

Table 3-6   The relative contribution of the head, the trunk, and the extremities as sources for the concepts 'up', 'down', 'front', 'back', and 'in' in African and Oceanic languages (Sources: Heine 1989; Bowden 1991)

	African languages		Oceanic languages	
	No. of instances	*Percentage*	*No. of instances*	*Percentage*
Head	123	38%	108	47%
Trunk	196	60%	107	46%
Extremities	8	2%	17	7%
Total	327	100%	232	100%

ent expressions in the Ewe language of West Africa: *dzí* and *ta´-me*. While *dzí* (<
'sky, the above') is derived from the landmark model, *ta´-me* (< 'in the head') has the
body-part model as its source. Furthermore, in languages that make use of the zoomorphic model (see the preceding discussion), there may in addition be corresponding expressions that are derived from the anthropomorphic model.

Conceptual development from source to target concept has two main components. The first has to do with the shift from concrete item to spatial relation or, to
use the framework proposed by Heine, Claudi, and Hünnemeyer (1991:123ff.), from
the OBJECT domain to the domain of SPACE. With regard to this component, the body-
part and the landmark models behave the same. The second component relates to the
spatial region expressed, and here the models behave in drastically different ways.
When a body-part noun like 'back' is recruited for the expression of the concept
'back', it is likely to refer first to the body-part region concerned before its use is
extended to denote the back region of inanimate objects. A new stage is reached when
the body-part term refers to the region immediately adjacent to that object and, finally, the term denotes the space adjacent to, but detached from, the object. Thus,
the evolution appears to proceed via the following four stages, which are illustrated
in figure 3-2:

> *From body-part to spatial concept: A four-stage scenario*
> 1. Stage 1—a region of the human body
> 2. Stage 2—a region of an (inanimate) object
> 3. Stage 3—a region in contact with an object
> 4. Stage 4—a region detached from the object

While the evolution can be assumed to proceed from stage 1 to stage 4 when the body-
part model is involved, it is likely to have a reversed directionality in the case of the
landmark model. Thus, if the landmark recruited for the expression of 'up' is the noun
for 'sky', then the spatial region first expressed is stage 4, and only subsequently is
the use of the noun 'sky' extended to stage 3, 2, and eventually 1. An illustration of
this scenario is found in figure 3-3.

We have confined ourselves to only five spatial reference points and their conceptual sources, but what we have observed about them applies essentially also to
other reference points. Thus, according to Svorou (1994), the same kinds of source
templates are employed in the languages of the world when other spatial concepts
are involved. As just discussed, there are usually systematic correlations between

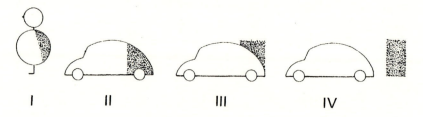

I   II   III   IV

Figure 3-2   A scenario of conceptual shift from body-part to spatial region.

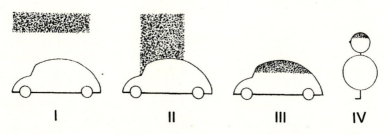

Figure 3-3 A scenario of conceptual shift from landmark to spatial region.

source and target concepts. Svorou (1994:204) discovered, for example, that what she calls the side-region ('beside', 'next to', etc.) and the medial-region ('in the middle of', 'between', 'among', etc.) have the body-part model as their most common source, while expressions for directional ('to', 'toward', etc.) and path concepts ('across', 'along', 'via', 'through', etc.) are invariably associated with the landmark model.

In fact, spatial terms derived from body-parts concern almost invariably static concepts, such as 'on', 'front', and the like. Occasionally, however, they may be dynamic concepts as well. Thus, Svorou (1994:78) observes examples in which the body-part noun for 'eye' develops into an allative marker ('to, toward'), or 'hand' develops into an ablative marker ('from'). The mechanism that underlies such evolutions is not entirely clear, but there is no doubt that it has to do with the inferential background associated with the use of body-parts in certain contexts. An account of such cases probably must take care of observations such as the following, which relates to the development of Papago *wui* 'eye' to a directional marker 'toward, movement to':

> We could explain this development, if we accept the following: eyesight, in a naive view, emanates from within the human body, and is directed towards the outside world. The eyes, as the organ of vision, may be metonymically used for eyesight. In fact, phrases such as "She could see no living soul as far as her eyes could reach" are not uncommon. Thus, the conceived directedness of eyesight makes eye terms eligible as lexical sources of directional grams. (Svorou 1994:78)

Still, the relationship between dynamic concepts like that of an allative or a path role and static concepts like 'up' and 'in' is far from clear, and the same applies to the correlations that exist between these two kinds of concepts and their respective source domains.

TYPICALLY, THERE IS a close conceptual association between a given body-part and the corresponding spatial concept. Such an association exists, for example, between the body-part 'back' and the spatial concept 'back', between 'face' and 'front', or between 'head' and 'up' since in all these cases the former item is the most probable diachronic source for the latter, as just discussed. Not infrequently, however, one of the spatial concepts discussed here is derived from two different body-part regions, be it crosslinguistically or even within one and the same language. There are two possible explanations for this fact. First, it may be that the language concerned makes simultaneous use of both the anthropomorphic and the zoomorphic models. In such a language one might not be surprised to find two expressions for 'on', one derived from 'head', in accordance with the anthropomorphic model, and one derived from the body-part 'back', in accordance with the zoomorphic model. Second, such a situation may be due to the fact that some of the spatial concepts can be interpreted alternatively with reference to two different body-parts—that is, that one spatial concept invites inferences relating to two different body-parts. What is located behind, for example, may be expressed in terms of what is located at or around the body-part back, but it may also be located in the buttocks region.

Conversely, a comparable relationship can hold between one body-part and two (or even more) spatial regions for which that body-part provides a structural template. The body-part head is likely to provide the source for the concept 'up'—that is, for items to be translated as 'above', 'on', 'up', and the like. In some languages, however, it may also lead to linguistic items for 'front'—that is, to expressions translatable by 'in front (of)', 'ahead', 'before', and the like. Similarly, in African (though not in Oceanic) languages, the body-part 'buttocks' is treated alternatively as the 'back'- or the 'down'-region—that is, it has given rise to expressions both for 'behind', 'after', etc., and for 'below', 'down', and so on.

To summarize, there is a salient pattern of transfer according to which either 'up' and 'front', or 'back' and 'down', derive from the same body-part source, while 'up' and 'back', 'up' and 'down', 'down' and 'front', or 'front' and 'back' do not. These findings are illustrated graphically in figure 3-4. It remains to be investigated how the facts illustrated in figure 3-4 are to be explained. Two hypotheses seem to suggest themselves. One has to do with the way the human body is perceived. That the up/front and the back/down regions tend to be associated with the same source concepts might suggest that the human body in its upright position is not perceived as being absolutely vertical but rather as leaning forward—that is, the way it is situated when one is running or walking, rather than when one is standing. This would explain why 'up' and 'front', or 'back' and 'down', are conceived as being spatially more closely interrelated than any of the other pairs of reference points are.

According to the second hypothesis, certain body-parts are perceived as having a dual locative potential. With regard to the body-parts in question, this would mean that the head can be interpreted alternatively as being located above and in front of

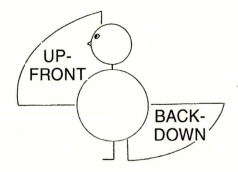

Figure 3-4   Basic points of spatial orientation that may be derived from two different body-part items.

other parts, while the buttocks tend to be associated with both the location behind and the location below the rest of the body.

These two hypotheses do not contradict each other, but conceivably there is yet another one. As we will see in chapter 7 (section 7.2), there is a regular conceptual transfer from one part of the body to another, based on what appears to be a universal strategy to conceptualize the lower half of the body in terms of the upper half. In particular, the front part of the upper half tends to serve as a structural template for the lower regions of the body. Andersen (1978:343) therefore says that 'up' and 'front' cover the optimally perceptible space and that these are therefore "positive" directions. Note that this is exactly the region where the organs of perception are concentrated.

A question that may have arisen in the course of the foregoing discussion is the following: What induces people worldwide to decide that a body-part like face, rather than navel or kneecap, provides the favorite model for developing expressions for the spatial concept 'front'? And why not the body-part nose? Why, in fact, is the nose notoriously ignored as a source concept for spatial orientation? To answer these questions, more research on the nature of transfer from the OBJECT to the SPACE domain, and of the notion of conceptual similarity, is urgently required.

The findings arrived at in the preceding discussion on the concepts 'up', 'down', 'front', 'back', and 'in' and their cognitive sources in African and Oceanic languages can be summarized in the following way:

1. Of all the source domains considered, the body-parts constitute the main domain, followed by environmental landmarks. Heine, Claudi, & Hünnemeyer (1991:129) observe, for example, that there appears to be no African language that derives all five concepts from landmarks, while a number of African languages have been found that rely exclusively on the body-part model—that is, that derive all five concepts from this model.
2. The spatial reference points looked at in the preceding discussion differ considerably with regard to the source models they are associated with. 'Up' and 'down' involve both the body-part and the landmark models, while 'front', 'back', and 'in' are associated almost entirely with the body-part model only (see the following discussion).
3. With regard to their relative degree of association with the two source domains, an implicational scale of the kind presented in (2) is proposed by Heine, Claudi, & Hünnemeyer (1991:130). This scale is to be interpreted in the following way: If any one of the five concepts figuring in (2) is derived from the body-part model, then none of the concepts to its right may be derived from the landmark or any other model.

(2)   DOWN   →   UP, IN   →   FRONT   →   BACK

On the basis of (2) one would not expect a language to use a body-part, say 'buttocks' or 'foot', for 'down' and a landmark for either 'up', 'in', 'front', and/or 'back', as, for

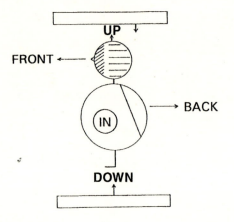

Figure 3-5   The primary body-part sources for 'up', 'down', 'front', 'back', and 'in'.

instance, 'sky' for 'on'. Similarly, if 'front' and 'back' are derived from the landmark model, then the body-part model is unlikely to be made use of in that language.

According to the generalizations just made, the most likely situation of conceptual derivation to be met within the languages of the world is that illustrated in figure 3-5. There are considerable variations on this basic pattern, however. Figure 3-6, for example, illustrates two variants to be found in Africa—one (A) that is characteristic of the majority of 300–plus Bantu languages, hence referred to as the Bantu Model, and another (B) that is found, for example, in Western Nilotic languages. What distinguishes the two is mainly the fact that whereas the Western Nilotic Model relies entirely on body-parts, the Bantu Model does not: In the latter the reference points 'up' and 'down' are derived, respectively, from the landmarks 'sky' and 'earth'.

IN THIS SECTION we have been concerned with a limited range of evolutions leading from concrete concepts to spatial concepts. We observed that it is only specific domains, and within each domain only specific items, that are exploited for conceptual transfer. For example, while the head and the trunk of the human body present a rich pool of templates for expressing spatial distinctions, the contribution of the body's extremities is highly limited. There is one noteworthy exception: The reference points 'left' and 'right' are very likely to have the body-part 'hand' as a conceptual model. A survey carried out nearly a century ago by Alice Werner on the 300–plus Bantu languages yielded a number of results that can be summarized thus (Werner 1904:427f.):

1. The notion 'right' is likely to be designated by means of any of the concepts 'hand used for eating', 'male hand', 'strong hand', or 'great hand'—or simply by some expression equivalent to '*the* hand'. This catalogue does not exhaust the range of concepts employed; related source items include expressions like 'the throwing hand' (Zulu *isandhla sokuponsa*) or 'straight hand' (Tswana *se siamen*).
2. The notion 'left' is frequently etymologically opaque. Wherever a conceptual source can be reconstructed, however, that source is either

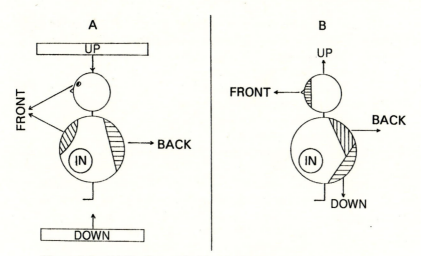

Figure 3-6   (A) The Bantu Model and (B) the Western Nilotic Model.

'female hand' or else an expression denoting some entity or quality judged to be of inferior status.

It would seem that there are good reasons for drawing on hands (and arms) as conceptual sources for 'left' and 'right': It is the location of hands vis-à-vis the rest of the body that makes them eligible for expressions for 'left' and 'right', but not necessarily for 'up' and 'down'. We saw in chapter 2 that the human hand also provides a salient conceptual template for the evolution of numeral systems. 'Left' and 'right' do not seem to have much in common with cardinal numerals, yet they nevertheless share the same source. Obviously, it is different properties of the hand that can be held responsible for this fact: In the former case it is the location; in the second, it is the fact that the fingers of a hand provide convenient units for counting.

3.2   Cardinal orientation

In a number of languages there is a word that means both 'midday' and 'south'. Some of these languages, like Hungarian, Polish, and Latvian, may be genetically and/or areally related; others again have no recognizable genetic or areal link (Brown 1983:131). Furthermore, the Proto-Oceanic root *raki* has a large number of semantically diverse reflexes, meaning, for instance, 'northeast or northeast wind' in Lou, 'southwest wind' in Pukapukan, 'southeast or southwest wind' in Eastern Uvean, 'southwest veering to northwest' in Samoan, 'south, summer' in Marshallese, and simply 'wind' in Tigak and 'weather' in Eastern Fijian (Ross 1995:9–10). This evokes several questions:

1. Why is it that one and the same term serves to designate both the time of day and a cardinal direction, or a wind and a cardinal direction, or a season and a cardinal direction?

2. Why is it that one and the same term has come to refer to virtually any cardinal direction in closely related languages? Are we dealing with cases of coincidence?
3. Furthermore, how is the fact to be explained that in Hawaiian, for instance, the word *hema* denotes both 'left' and 'south', while in Cornish there is a word *clēth* that means 'left' and 'north'?
4. Why are terms for cardinal directions frequently polysemous?

In the present section we will try to answer these questions. That we are not dealing with isolated instances of homonymy is suggested by the fact that there are a number of languages where quite different concepts—one being a cardinal direction—are regularly associated with one and the same form, where terms for 'up' and 'down' or 'right' and 'left', for instance, are also employed to express the cardinal points 'west', 'east', 'north', and 'south'. We will first deal with questions (1) and (4) and then proceed to the remaining questions.

In a worldwide survey of 127 languages, Cecil Brown has attempted to determine the conceptual sources of cardinal directions. A summary of his quantitative data is presented in table 3-7. As table 3-7 suggests, the movement or position of the sun clearly provides the predominant model for developing terms for cardinal directions. Compared to this source, other templates are of limited significance, the next most important source being the domain of deictic orientation ('up', 'down', 'right', 'left', etc.; see section 3.1) with 20.1% altogether, and wind directions and landmarks (environment-specific features including upstream and downstream) with 9.2% each. The fact that in more than half of all cases involving cardinal directions the sun-model (relating to the movement or position of the sun) is involved allows us to formulate at least the following prediction:

If in a given language a term for a cardinal direction is introduced, then the sun provides the most likely model to be selected.

The significance of this model becomes even more obvious once we confine ourselves to the cardinal directions 'west' and 'east': According to Brown's (1983) data, the sun-model has been chosen, respectively, in 84% (fifty-nine out of seventy)

Table 3-7   The main source domains for cardinal direction terms in 127 languages (based on Brown 1983)

Conceptual source	Cardinal direction				Total	Percentage
	West	East	North	South		
Sun	59	58	1	13	131	57.2%
Deictic orientation	9	12	12	13	46	20.1%
Wind			17	4	21	9.2%
Landmarks	2	2	7	10	21	9.2%
Other domains		1	6	3	10	4.3%
Total of occurrences	70	73	43	43	229	100.0%

and 79% (fifty-eight out of seventy-three) of all languages considered where a term for 'west' or 'east' was developed. The significance of this model is also underscored by the fact that, as we saw in the preceding discussion, wind provides one of the most important alternative models to the sun, but wind is unlikely to be used for the expression of 'west' and 'east'—that is, the wind-model is ignored whenever it would be in immediate competition with the sun-model.

While the sun provides such a salient template for cardinal directions, other celestial bodies are virtually irrelevant. The moon, for example, never appears as a source, and for good reason: Unlike the sun or certain wind types, the moon is not constantly associated with some specific cardinal reference point.

The existing linguistic data suggest that the description of source schemas for cardinal directions in Brown's (1983) account is biased in favor of languages of the Northern Hemisphere. For example, the sun-model is suggestive of a conceptualization of space that one would expect north of the equator but not south of it. In Czech and Polish, for example, 'north' is related to the middle of the night or midnight (Brown 1983:132), while 'south' is associated with midday in some European languages. Obviously, such correlations are unlikely to obtain anywhere south of the equator.

While the sun is a universally stable phenomenon—that is, its position is predictable irrespective of whether I move two hundred kilometers away from where I am—wind is more susceptible to local geographical influence: What turns out to be a west wind here may be a north or a south wind not too far away from where I am now. As we will see in the following discussion, this observation is of fundamental importance for the nomenclature of spatial orientation in some regions of the world.

Eskimo speakers of western Greenland, for example, may experience problems when communicating with their compatriots from eastern Greenland. The nomenclature for cardinal directions is the same on both sides of Greenland, but rather than being absolute, it is based on geographical landmarks such as the riverine system (upriver versus downriver), prevailing winds, and one's position on the coast (up versus down). Since it is likely for rivers to flow and for winds to blow in opposite directions on the two sides of Greenland, this means that what is north for a western Eskimo is south for an easterner, and vice versa (Fortescue 1988).

What we call here landmark orientation subsumes Brown's notions of upriver, downriver, and his environment-specific features. The following appear to be the main kinds of landmarks figuring as sources for cardinal directions (Brown 1983:138):

1. Rivers
2. Mountains and/or rocky places
3. Sea vs. mainland
4. Trees and other vegetational properties

Deictic orientation in terms of the landmark distinction 'toward the sea' versus 'away from the sea' is likely to be prominent in societies that inhabit smaller islands. Redfield (1930:57), for example, observes that in Polynesian islands, "directions are not given in terms of the compass points but rather as 'toward the sea' or 'away from the sea.'"

That the landmark model is not only a cross-culturally relevant one but also one that is used *instead* of the cardinal system is suggested by numerous descriptive remarks, such as the following, in the anthropological and related literature:

> The Yurok lack the idea of cardinal directions. They orient themselves by their principal geographical feature, the Klamath, and speak of directions as upstream or downstream. Since the river is crooked, upstream and downstream may designate almost all points of the compass. Yet the predominant trend of the river is clearly recognized: it bisects their world. The sense of cardinal directions is not necessary to the conception of a symmetrical world. (Tuan 1974:36)

While landmarks account for less than one-tenth (9.2%) of all sources for cardinal directions, they nevertheless seem to be of universal distribution.

The significance of deictic orientation in structuring cardinal orientation may be illustrated by the following quotation by Margaret Mead on the Manus of the Admiralty Islands:

> The known world was the world in which they lived—the South Coast of the Admiralty Islands, each small creek mouth and bay accurately known. When people spoke, they spoke of going either *up*—toward the open sea—or going *down*—toward the nearby shore—or going *along*—parallel to the shore. (Mead 1956:67)

Strikingly similar situations are described by other authors in other parts of the world, as, for example, by Fortescue (1984, 1988) on the Eskimos, by Abraham (1933:49–50) on the Tiv of southeastern Nigeria, and by Redfield (1930:57) on the Mexican Tepoztlan (see Brown 1983:134).

Brown (1983:135ff.) observes that crosslinguistically, 'north' and 'south' are nomenclaturally associated predominantly with 'up' and 'down', respectively, and 'east' and 'west', with 'front' and 'back'; we will return to this point in the following discussion.

Table 3-8 provides a more detailed breakdown of the figures presented in table 3-7. What is obvious from the data summarized in table 3-8 is that body-parts, which are the main conceptual source for deictic orientation, are absent: We know of no single instance where a body-part has given rise to a term for cardinal orientation.

WHILE THERE IS a clear-cut correlation between the east-west axis and sunrise-sunset, the conceptual sources for 'north' and 'south' are more difficult to interpret. What is clear is that 'north' is most strongly associated with the wind-model, while 'south' is closer to the sun-model. Note, however, that the data on which these observations are based appear to be biased in favor of languages spoken in the Northern Hemisphere, a fact we have already drawn attention to (see also Brown 1983). Conceivably, the situation would be different if more languages of the Southern Hemisphere were considered.

The data presented in table 3-8 also seem to suggest that the source domains that we met in the preceding discussion when dealing with deictic orientation are essentially different from those we are faced with when dealing with cardinal orientation. While this is essentially so, two clarifying remarks seem in order. First, there

Table 3-8 Salient source concepts for cardinal direction terms in
127 languages (based on Brown 1983)

Conceptual source	Cardinal direction				
	West	East	North	South	Total
Sun	59	58	1	13	131
Other celestial bodies			2		2
Darkness or nighttime			4		4
Wind			17	4	21
Weather conditions		1			1
'Up'	5	3	6	2	16
'Down'	1	3	2	7	13
'Front'		4			4
'Back'	3	1		1	5
'Right'		1	1	2	4
'Left'			3	1	4
'Upstream'		1	1	2	4
'Downstream'			1	3	4
Environment-specific features	2	1	5	5	13
Others				3	3
Total number of occurrences	70	73	43	43	229

is one source domain that is shared by both systems of orientation—namely, that of
landmarks: Environment-specific features are relevant in the development of both
systems. Second, a link between the two can also be seen in the following generalization: One of the source domains for cardinal orientation consists of basic points
like 'up', 'down', and the like. The opposite does not seem to hold—that is, terms for
cardinal orientation do not provide templates for deictic orientation. Thus, both systems are in a clear-cut unidirectional relationship of conceptual derivation; we will
return to this point in the following discussion.

There is some correlation between 'west' and 'east' on the one hand, and 'back'
and 'front' on the other. 'Back' is less likely to provide a model for 'east' than for
'west' and, conversely, 'front' serves only as a model for 'east', not 'west' (see table
3-8). Brown comments on this fact in the following way: "The most canonical posture for humans involves an east-west axis and . . . an eastward orientation is usually
preferred over a westward one. This almost certainly relates to the fact that the east is
often of great salience for people since it is the place of the sun's rising" (Brown
1983:136). Furthermore, Brown (1983:135ff.) observes that crosslinguistically, 'north'
and 'south' are nomenclaturally associated predominantly with 'up' and 'down'. Thus,
in his sample, the proportion between 'up':'down' and 'north':'south' is 7:1—that is,
it is seven times more likely that 'up' expresses 'north' than 'south'. What such observations might suggest is that there is a kind of cross-culturally preferred correlation between deictic and cardinal orientation, essentially as sketched in figure 3-7.

There are several problems with reference to these correlations between the two
kinds of spatial orientation. The first concerns what we propose to call the *map-model*
and relates to Western techniques of describing cardinal orientation. Schoolchil-
dren, irrespective of whether they live in the Amazon basin or the Himalayas, learn

N
UP

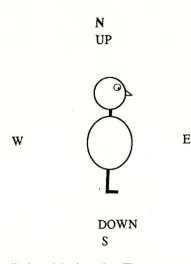

W   E

DOWN
S

Figure 3-7   Deictic and cardinal spatial orientation: The most canonical human posture (based on Brown 1983:135ff.)

that macro-space is conveniently represented graphically on a blackboard or a sheet of paper in terms of a generally agreed on schema according to which cardinal concepts like 'west', 'east', 'north', and 'south' are not expressed in terms of macro-orientation— that is, in terms of distinctions such as that between sunrise and sunset—but rather in terms of a micro-model introduced in connection with the spread of western formal education. According to this model, cardinal directions are referred to not in terms of celestial or atmospheric phenomena but in terms of a symbolic presentation that specifies that left, right, up, and down symbolize the cardinal points 'west', 'east', 'north', and 'south', respectively. It remains unclear whether, or to what extent, the map-model influences the linguistic expression of cardinal directions in Western or any other societies. Brown recognizes the possible relevance of this model (note that the figures he gives in the following quotation differ from the ones found in table 3-8):

> North is nomenclaturally related to an upwardness referent seven times while it is related to a downwardness referent only once. Conversely, south is nomenclaturally connected to a downwardness referent eleven times while it is connected to an upwardness referent only one time. This finding may be indicative of an innate human predisposition for such associations but it is equally plausible that it reflects diffusion of a western prejudice, i.e. the ubiquitous aligning of north with the top of maps. (Brown 1983:135)

Second, one may wonder what the empirical relevance of such structures is, considering the small quantity of instances on which these structures are based. Note, for example, that in Ambrym (or Lonwolwol), an Oceanic language, 'east' and 'west' appear to be derived, canonically, from 'front' and 'back', respectively—that is, the model employed would seem to be that of a human being facing east—but 'north' clearly goes back to 'down', and 'south', to 'up' (Brown 1983:135–6). Similarly, in

Ewe, a Niger-Congo language of Togo and Ghana, 'north' is conceptually derived from 'down', and 'south', from 'up'. The east-west axis, on the other hand, is encoded in terms of the sunrise-sunset dichotomy. A geographically meaningful interpretation of such situations is urgently required.

Third, in addition to the "up versus down model," there is also the "right versus left model" serving the expression of the cardinal points 'north' and 'south'. In Hawaiian, for example, an orientation system as proposed in figure 3-8 can be reconstructed on the basis of the data provided by Brown (1983).

THE IMPRESSION CONVEYED so far may have been that the transition from source to target domain—that is, from deictic orientation or wind direction to cardinal orientation—is a discrete one. As a matter of fact, it is not: The transition is gradual and involves an overlap in meaning, where a given expression refers simultaneously to the source and the target concept, or to the source in some contexts and the target in others. The Eskimo "demonstrative" *qav-* (also: *kujat-*) illustrates the transition from the landmark domain to that of cardinal orientation: This item is used everywhere in Greenland, both for landmark-space and for cardinal macro-space orientation. With regard to its landmark-space use, *qav-* refers to the "direction to the left along the coast when facing out to sea." This means that the "demonstrative" can refer to just about any point of the compass, depending on the exact position of a settlement on a fjord, island, or the like. With regard to macro-space orientation, on the other hand, *qav-* refers to approximate cardinal south, irrespective of indentations and outcroppings of the coastline (Fortescue 1988:5).

In this Eskimo example, the variable nature of the landmark-model is responsible for the many possible cardinal points that one and the same source item may be associated with. That a given source item is conventionalized in contrasting ways in accordance with different experiential contexts can be illustrated with the following

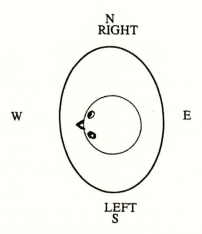

Figure 3-8 Deictic and cardinal spatial orientation: A reconstruction of the Hawaiian posture (based on Brown 1983:28–36).

Polynesian examples volunteered by Brown (1983:138ff.). Brown is surprised to note that, in spite of the detailed knowledge Polynesians as seafarers have of celestial bodies and events, they have only rarely drawn on celestial bodies in innovating labels for cardinal directions. Brown observes that the sun-model is recruited less frequently than elsewhere to develop labels for 'east' and 'west', while 'north' and 'south' are hardly ever, if at all, derived from experiences associated with the movement or position of the sun. It would seem, in fact, that Polynesian languages appear to have drawn much less on the sun-model than other languages have.

Perhaps the main source domain for cardinal directions in Polynesia is that of winds. But wind, or specific kinds of wind, has a different significance depending on the location concerned. The following example illustrates the pragmatic association between source and target concept and the resulting linguistic output:

> For example, the word *tiu* denotes *north/northwest wind* in Marquesan and *north/ north wind* in Maori, but labels *west/west wind* in Mangareva. In other languages it has no association with cardinal directions and designates several different winds: e.g., Tahitian *southeast by east wind*, Rarotongan *west southwest wind quarter*, and Tikopian *northwest wind, west wind.* (Brown 1983:140)

Probably as prominent as the wind-model in Polynesia is the deictic orientation-model. 'Up', 'down', 'left', 'right', and the like are concepts that appear as sources for cardinal directions in a number of Polynesian languages. The Proto-Polynesian lexeme **lalo* 'down, below, under' has been grammaticalized as a term for a range of different cardinal directions like 'north', 'south', and 'west' (note that the figures mentioned by Brown in the following quotation are not identical with those found in his statistical account):

> Reflexes of **lalo* which denote cardinal directions are invariably polysemous, also designating a more general direction having the property of downwardness, e.g., *down, beneath, under, below, the lower part*, and so on. These occur in eight languages: Niuean *below/west*, Rennellese *below, under/west*, Maori *the bottom, under/ north*, Anutan *down, below/west*, Rarotongan *beneath, under, below, down/west*, and Tuamotuan *below, under/west* in one dialect and *down, under/south* in another. The form occurs in virtually all remaining Polynesian languages where it is restricted in application to a "downwardness" referent. In at least one case a **lalo* reflex has figured into an overt marking construction labeling a cardinal direction. (Brown 1983:141; see Ross 1995 for more examples)

The landmark-model can be illustrated with the development of the Proto-Polynesian lexemes **'uta* 'toward inland' and **tahi* 'toward the sea': **'uta* has acquired the additional meaning 'east' in Niuean, and in Kapingamarangi the item **tahi* 'toward the sea' has been extended to also designate 'west' (Brown 1983).

What the examples just presented show is that the transition from source domain to target domain creates a transitional structure where both the source and the target meanings coexist in a given language, thereby giving rise to polysemy, or where the source meaning of deictic or landmark orientation is found in one language, while the target meaning of cardinal orientation occurs in another language. To conclude, seemingly complex issues like the semantics of the terminology for cardinal directions in Polynesian languages lose much of their complexity once we analyze them with reference to universal principles of conceptual evolution.

3.3 Some principles of spatial orientation

In the course of this chapter we have distinguished a number of patterns of spatial orientation. We are now in a position to determine how these patterns are conceptually and diachronically interrelated. On the basis of the evidence available so far, a number of correlations between source and target systems emerge, such as the following:

1. Expressions for deictic orientation may derive from terms for body-parts or environmental landmarks but never from terms for celestial or atmospheric phenomena.
2. Terms for deictic orientation may themselves serve as models for developing nomenclatures for cardinal orientation, but not vice versa.
3. Sun and wind provide important templates for expressions for cardinal orientation but apparently never for deictic orientation.

The conceptual relationship between source and target domains is described in table 3-9, and the transfer patterns from source to target domain are illustrated in figure 3-9. As figure 3-9 shows, conceptual transfer leads from the ontological category OBJECT, the domain of physically perceptible items, to the category of SPACE.

While the various concepts figuring in the development of spatial orientation differ in their overall significance, the question of which of them is the most salient also depends on the particular culture-specific situation in which they are employed. For example, the sun provides the most salient source for structuring cardinal orientation, as discussed here. Nevertheless, in a country dominated by the presence of an outstanding geographical landmark such as a mountain or a river, the sun may be of secondary importance. Such a situation appears to have existed in ancient Egypt: "The course of the Nile exerted a powerful influence on the Egyptian's sense of direction. The word 'to go north' meant also 'to go downstream,' and the word 'to go south' meant 'to go upstream' or against the current" (Tuan 1974:86).

Table 3-9   The main sources for spatial orientation (n.a. = not applicable)

	Target domain		
Main source models	*Deictic orientation*	*Landmark orientation*	*Cardinal orientation*
Sun	–	–	+
Wind	–	–	+
Deictic orientation	n.a.	+	+
Landmarks	+	+	+
Body-parts	+	–	–

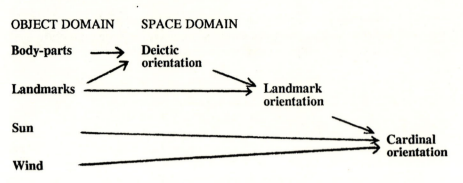

Figure 3-9 Cognitive sources for expressions of spatial orientation.

An equally relevant example of the predominance of the landmark-model, where the landmark again is a river, is provided by Henry and Henry on the Northern Athapaskan Koyukon of central Alaska:

> The cardinal directions are not pertinent as points of reference; of primary importance is the alignment of the location with respect to the river's flow (whether it be location of village, lake, open area or general hunting/trapping/fishing area). It is interesting to note that when an Indian is in an unfamiliar village or area he will try to determine the course of an adjacent main river before using specific locationals. . . . River orientation is reflected in the Indians' usage of English. When referring to the four sides of a house one often hears: 'the up side' (upriver side); 'the down side' (downriver side); 'the back side' (away from the river side); and 'the front side' (the riverward side). Directions involving long distances may reflect more acculturation on the part of the speaker, usually being oriented to the cardinal points of the compass. (Henry & Henry 1969:136–7)

The findings made above also shed light on some other problems of linguistic encoding. Our discussion of deictic orientation suggested, for example, that the primary domain used for expressions for 'up' is body-parts—above all, the concept 'head'. For 'down', on the other hand, it is not a body-part but rather a landmark that is recruited most frequently. The reason for this difference appears to be the following: The primary alternative to a body-part for the notion 'up' is the landmark 'sky', while for 'down' it is 'ground'. Now, 'sky' is neither a tangible item nor is it clearly delineated. Neither objection applies to 'ground', which is tangible and can be delimited vis-à-vis non-ground. Thus, there are obvious reasons that within a given source domain, certain concepts are more salient than others.

3.4   Notes on grammar

Once nouns denoting body-parts or landmarks are pressed into service for the expression of spatial orientation, their morphosyntactic status is likely to change: Linguistic items that refer to spatial orientation are typically found as adverbial material—that is, they are likely to belong to the adverbial phrase. Thus, concepts of deictic orientation, like 'up', 'down', and the like, almost invariably occur as either adverbs or adpositions (prepositions, postpositions, or ambipositions). Our concern in the preceding discussion was primarily with one particular type of adpositions, which are called *N-adpositions*: These are grammatical forms that owe their genesis to the grammaticalization of head nouns in genitive constructions. But there are two other common types of adpositions, which are called A-adpositions and V-adpositions. The former are derived from adverbs; the latter are derived from verbs.

V-adpositions have dynamic concepts as their source. The particular linguistic form they take differs from one language to another. In many languages, the verb must appear in a nonfinite form to be eligible for adpositional use. The nonfinite form may be an infinitival, a participial, a gerundival, or any other verb form. The pattern favored by English speakers is to use the verb in its gerund form, as exemplified by 'preceding' in (3a) and 'following' in (3c), which are largely equivalent to the adpositional items 'before' and 'after', respectively, in (3b) and (3d).

(3) English (Svorou 1994:113)
  a. Preceding the parade, there will be a famous New Orleans band.
  b. Before the parade, there will be a famous New Orleans band.
  c. A big crowd came following the funeral procession.
  d. A big crowd came after the funeral procession.

In other languages again, the verb is simply used in its most unmarked form without any derivative or other trappings. Such a situation is encountered typically in analytic-isolating languages like Chinese or Ewe, but it is by no means confined to languages of this type. The following example is taken from Thai, where the verb *càak* 'depart, leave' appears to function as an adposition.

(4) Thai (Austro-Tai; Kölver 1984:17)
  khǎw maa càak rooŋrian
  he   come depart school
  'He comes from school.'

The evolution of *A-adpositions*, whereby adverbs develop into adpositions, can be illustrated with the following example from German. Example (5a) illustrates the initial stage I, where there is an orthodox adposition like 'in', 'on', 'at', or the like. At this stage, the locative expression refers to the normal or unmarked position of the item concerned. In (5b), at stage II, an adverb *hinauf* 'up' is added. In (5c), at stage III, the orthodox preposition *auf* 'on' is omitted, and the erstwhile adverb now functions exclusively as an adposition.

(5) German
  a. Er stieg   auf den Berg
     he climbed on the mountain
     'He climbed on the hill'.

  b. Er stieg   auf den Berg   hinauf
     he climbed on the mountain up
     'He climbed up on the hill'.

c. Er stieg   den Berg   hinauf
   he climbed the mountain up
'He climbed up the hill'.

The purpose of adding an adverb is typically to specify in more detail the locative contours expressed by the orthodox construction and/or to lay emphasis on the locative notion. Reh describes a similar situation in Krongo, a Kordofanian language of the Republic of Sudan, in the following way: "Thus I suggest that Krongo post-positions developed not from genitival constructions but from locative adjuncts or adverbials. They have the function of further specifying the necessarily vague location indicated by the PP [prepositional phrase]" (Reh 1983:54).

There are, in fact, good reasons why Krongo, like German, has developed post-positions rather than prepositions. The evolution involved in Krongo can be illustrated with the three examples in (6). Example (6a) is suggestive of the initial stage, where the noun occurs either in the locative-directional (LOC) or the ablative (ABL) case, and where no postposition is used. In (6b), the location is further specified by the adverbial *kàtì* 'beside', which functions as a postposition and adds emphasis to the location marked by the case prefix. When specifying human beings, as in (6c), then the use of the postposition is obligatory (see chapter 8).

(6)   Krongo (Kordofanian, Niger-Kordofanian; Reh 1983:53)
   a. k- áfì   kí-   jòorì
      PL- be. at LOC- house
     'They are in the house.'

   b. k- áfì   kádú ki-   jòorì kàtì.
      PL- be. at people LOC- house beside
     'They are beside the house.'

   c. m-òmì sárrà kà-   dí kàtì.
      F-sit   Sarra LOC- me beside
     'Sarra is sitting beside me.'

It may happen that in a given language there is only one etymological type of adposition. More likely, however, two, or even three, types can be found in one and the same language. The three types occurring in English are exemplified in (7), where (7a) is suggestive of N-, (7b) of V-, and (7c) of A-adpositions.

(7)   English
   a. because of, instead of, in front of, on account of, in back of, etc.
   b. following, preceding, concerning, considering, given, etc.
   c. off, up, down, through, etc.

Note that this does not exhaust the catalogue of sources for adpositions: There are occasionally other sources in addition. English, for example, also has prepositions derived from adjectives (König & Kortmann 1991:109). As a rule, however, such sources are statistically insignificant.

The fact that there are three different types of adpositions in English has implications for the structure of the items concerned. The monosyllabic prepositions of

English, for example, are almost invariably A-adpositions, while English prepositions that are themselves accompanied by one or two monosyllabic prepositions (e.g.,
'thanks to', 'in front of') are N-adpositions, and V-adpositions are likely to bear the
gerund ending '-ing' (see König & Kortland 1991:110). In other languages, each type
may be associated with a different syntax, with the result that the morphosyntax of
adverbial phrases can turn out to be rather complicated. In Ewe, for example,
V-adpositions are prepositions, while N-adpositions are postpositions, and each of
these two classes exhibits a distinct morphosyntactic behavior that can be explained
with reference to their respective lexical sources. Since the verb precedes its complement in Ewe, the evolution of V-adpositions can be sketched as in (8a), while the
fact that the head noun precedes the genitival modifier leads to a syntactic reinterpretation of head nouns as postpositions, as sketched in (8b) (see Heine, Claudi, &
Hünnemeyer 1991:140–42 for details).

(8) Morphosyntactic reinterpretation processes in Ewe
     a. Verb – nominal complement → preposition – noun
     b. Genitive noun – head noun → noun – postposition

The data on transfer patterns presented here enable us to answer a few questions
that arise when one studies the morphosyntax of adpositions. For example, why is it
that English prepositions like 'on top of', 'in front of', 'because of', and the like
have the marker 'of'? In a similar fashion, why do many Swahili prepositions contain the Genitive marker *ya*, as in (9), or why are certain postpositions in Indo-Aryan
languages preceded by the Genitive marker *ke*, as in (10)?

(9) Swahili (Bantu, Niger-Congo)
     juu   ya   meza
     above GEN   table
     'on the table'

(10) Hindi (Indo-Aryan, Indo-European; Blake 1994:10–11)
     lərkə ke   sath
     boy   GEN   with
     'with the boy'

The question of why adpositions worldwide frequently carry genitival morphology
can be answered with reference to their genesis. Many of these adpositions go back
to head nouns in genitive constructions, and the genitive morphology is retained even
if the body-part or landmark item that served as the head noun is now interpreted
exclusively as a grammatical marker.

Predictably, not all adpositions exhibit genitival morphology. Only N-adpositions
do, while A-adpositions and V-adpositions can be expected to exhibit different effects of their respective conceptual sources. Moreover, even if there had been a
genitive marker at the time when the construction arose, that marker may have disappeared in the course of history.

Linguistic forms for spatial markers frequently look different from the items from
which they are conceptually and historically derived. Most likely they are shorter
than the latter, in that they have undergone *erosion* (see Heine 1993). Erosion may

be phonological or morphological; in the former case, it involves shortening the phonetic material employed for the expression of the item concerned; in the latter case, it entails elision of entire morphemes (see Heine & Reh 1984:21–5, 27). An example of phonological erosion is provided in table 3-10, and of morphological erosion, in table 3-11: In Maasai it is the entire gender prefix (whose basic form is *ol-* masculine and *en-* feminine) that is elided in morphological erosion.

To summarize, the morphological and syntactic properties of linguistic items used for the expression of spatial orientation can largely be explained with reference to their respective conceptual sources.

3.5   Summary

In the introductory section (section 3.1), beginning with an analysis of Yucatec, we drew attention to the formal similarities that exist between certain terms for body-parts and locative markers. Following the analysis by Goldap (1992:613) and Stolz (1994b:61), we argued that the latter are historically derived from the former. In the course of this chapter, evidence from other languages, demonstrating that we are in fact dealing with a process of universal significance, was presented. Locative markers for 'behind' and 'in front' are not uncommonly derived from body-part terms like 'back' and 'face'/'front', respectively. However, the Yucatec data also showed that there are limits to the universality of the process. For example, while items denoting 'in' or 'inside' are quite commonly derived crosslinguistically from body-part terms, the number of languages using body-parts like 'marrow' or 'eye' for this purpose is probably quite limited. Thus, there are both universal and regionally restricted forces that account for the structure of conceptual transfer. The question of why 'eye', for instance, has ultimately given rise to terms for 'in front' in quite a number of languages, while in Yucatec (*ich*) it appears to have developed into an expression for 'in', is left to further research.

Another question that has been raised repeatedly in the literature is whether, or to what extent, systematic differences in the way spatial orientation is structured linguistically correlate with certain degrees of human evolution. For example, according to one position, cardinal orientation is a cognitive domain that evolved relatively late in human history. Such a position is perhaps most strongly associated with the work of Cecil Brown and associates. Brown has the following to say on this issue:

Table 3-10   Examples of phonological erosion in the evolution from body-part term to preposition in Acholi (Malandra 1955:127–8)

Body-part term	Meaning	Preposition	Function
ɪc	'belly'	ɪ	'in, inside, within'
ŋec	'back'	ŋe	'behind, after'
wic	'head'	wi	'on, upon, on the top'

Table 3-11 Examples of morphological erosion in the evolution from body-part term to adverb and/or preposition in Maasai (Tucker & Mpaayei 1955:43)

Body-part term	Meaning	Preposition	Function
en-korioŋ	'back, spine'	orioŋ	'behind'
en-dukuya	'head'	dukuya	'in front (of)'
o-siadi	'anus'	siadi	'behind'

That languages of the remote past generally lacked terms for cardinal points is not particularly surprising. By and large these languages were spoken by peoples of small scale societies who had little reason for formulating notions of location in terms of cardinal directionality. . . . The general increase in societal scale and complexity over the last several millennia of human history has no doubt promoted the lexical encoding of cardinal points in many of the world's languages. Technological advances accompanying increases in societal scale such as ocean-going vessels, the compass, maps, mathematics, and so on, obviously have contributed significantly to this development . . . In some instances cardinal point terms have been directly borrowed from Western languages. In others, native terms have been extended to borrowed concepts of cardinal directionality. (Brown 1983:122–3)

Such a position is hard to reconcile with other hypotheses that have been voiced—for instance, with the claim that cardinal orientation, or the "absolute system," is of worldwide distribution and of great antiquity (Brown & Levinson 1993a:3). It remains to be investigated how the two positions just sketched are to be reconciled—that is, whether cardinal orientation belongs to the earliest patterns in the human conceptualization of space or whether it is the result of a relatively late evolution.

Another topic concerns the relationship between the organization of source concepts and target concepts. The kind of questions we have in mind include the following: To what extent does the nature of the available source concepts determine that of the resulting target concepts?

We may illustrate the problem involved with reference to the structure and distribution of cardinal orientation. As we saw above (tables 3-7 and 3-8), the most salient source model for cardinal directions is provided by the sun—namely, sunrise and sunset—and these two concepts almost invariably give rise to labels for the cardinal directions 'east' and 'west', respectively. At the same time, the data provided by Brown (1983:143ff.) suggest that 'east' and 'west' are more commonly distinguished in the languages of the world than other directions. First, in his sample of 127 languages, terms for 'east' are found in 104 and for 'west' in 101 languages, while terms for 'north' and 'south' are found in only 89 and 91 languages, respectively. Second, there is a kind of implicational relationship between the two axes, which Brown describes in the following way:

Putting aside the 81 languages having terms for all four cardinal points and the 18 totally lacking them, 28 languages remain. These languages show implicational patterns. For example, 24 of the 28 have terms for east and/or west while only 14 have terms for north and/or south. This means that languages having north and/or south typically have east and/or west but not vice versa. (Brown 1983:144)

Such observations must be taken with care; nevertheless, they might suggest that the presence versus the absence, or the relative frequency of occurrence, of a given grammatical category in the languages of the world might be determined by the nature of the items that provide the conceptual templates for that category.

What the discussion of this section would seem to suggest is that the way we draw on basic templates for understanding the world around us, for communicating successfully, and for developing the kind of grammatical categories we do is determined crucially by "what the world around us" offers us. Salient landmarks, like mountains, lakes, or unusual vegetational phenomena such as rain forests or deserts, are likely to shape our patterns of conceptualization, and therefore inevitably also our patterns of using language and, hence, grammar.

The transfer patterns sketched here have a number of consequences for the way we relate the various experiences we are regularly exposed to to one another—in short, for the way we construe the world around us. Things that are believed to resemble each other are likely to be viewed as being causally connected, and in this way cosmologies and other folk categories arise. The following may be viewed as a typical example: It is said that there is a persistent structural motif in virtually all of Indonesia to be observed in art, religion, and nature, according to which there are two functionally antithetical social groups. In Amboina of the South Moluccas, for example, the village is divided into two parts, where each part "is not only a social unit but a category in cosmic classification comprising all objects and events around the villager" (Tuan 1974:20). The main parameters figuring in this cosmic classification are summarized in (11).

(11)   Conceptual antinomies associated with functionally antithetic groups in Amboina, South Moluccas (based on Tuan 1974)

Left	– Right	Peel	– Pit
Female	– Male	Exterior	– Interior
Seaside	– Mountainside	Behind	– In front
Below	– Above	West	– East
Earth	– Heaven or sky	Younger brother	– Older brother
Spiritual	– Worldly	New	– Old
Downward	– Upward		

Cosmic dichotomies comparable to those sketched in (11) are not uncommon in the traditional cultures of the world. The distinctions figuring in this particular classification relate to a number of different experiential domains. The majority belong to the domain of spatial orientation, in particular to deictic orientation (Left–Right, Below–Above, Downward–Upward, Exterior–Interior, Behind–In front); landmark orientation (Seaside–Mountainside, Earth–Heaven); and cardinal orientation (West–East). Others relate to social and religious structure, or to the domain of qualities. It would be pure conjecture to attempt, without any further information, to account for the fact that several distinct domains are combined in this instance of cosmological categorization or in the many comparable structures to be observed in other cultures. What we can safely assume is that the strategy employed for combining elements from different domains of cognition is the same as the one we have observed in the preceding paragraphs—that is, that the cluster of properties to be observed in (11) is the result of conceptual transfer patterns of the kind described in figure 3-9.

4

INDEFINITE ARTICLES

In chapters 2 and 3 we were concerned with the first step in the evolution from concrete concept to grammatical concept—for example, from body-part to locative marker or numeral. Here we deal with the subsequent evolution from grammatical concept to even more grammatical concept. In addition, we attempt to illustrate what this evolution means with reference to the structure of grammatical categories. The example chosen is that of indefinite articles, already touched upon briefly in the introductory chapter. The question raised there was the following: Why does the English definite article determine both singular and plural nouns, as can be seen in (1), whereas the indefinite article may not be used with plural nouns, as can be seen in (2)?

(1) a. I see the child.
     b. I see the children.

(2) a. I see a child.
     b. *I see a children.

Ignoring the fact that the unmarked plural form corresponding to (2a) is the one without an indefinite article ('I see children'), one might argue that English has a suppletive pattern of marking indefinite articles, where *a* is used in the singular, and *some* is used in the plural. So, instead of (2b), the plural of (2a) would then be (3) (Wally Chafe, personal communication).

(3) I see some children.

There is a problem with such an argument, however. Note that (4a) seems acceptable, while (4b) is not—that is, *some* can be used as both an attribute and a pronoun, whereas *a* cannot be used as a pronoun. As (4c) shows, the indefinite article shares this characteristic with the definite article—that is, *some* differs in its behavior from that of the two articles.

(4)   a. I see some.
         b. *I see a.
         c. *I see the.

A general answer to the question raised here has already been sketched in chapter 1. I will now try to account for the asymmetry between definite and indefinite articles by looking at a larger sample of languages. The discussion will rely as much as possible on published sources, especially Moravcsik (1969). The data provided there is supplemented with our own data based on a survey of thirty-one languages (Heine et al. 1995).

4.1   Generalizations

In spite of the many treatments of indefinite articles over the course of the past decades, there is not much agreement on how they should be viewed, defined, or located in grammar. The problems associated with the definition, categorial status, and/or functions of indefinite articles are illustrated, for instance, by the way they are discussed in linguistic dictionaries. Rather than being of any real help, such "definitions" may be more of a burden to someone consulting these dictionaries. According to Pei and Gaynor, for example, an indefinite article is a "particle inserted before or prefixed to nouns to indicate that the noun is used as a generic term" (while the definite article denotes "a specific member of the class which it designates") (1954:53, 98). Similarly, Conrad says that the definite article denotes "a precisely marked single being" or a "genus," and the indefinite article denotes "some arbitrary being" (1988:31). Obviously, none of the characteristics that a student of linguistics normally associates with articles is addressed in such characterizations; rather, such characterizations are more likely to contradict present-day notions of what articles are all about.

For the present purposes, let us say that indefinite articles are nominal determiners whose functions include that of marking indefinite specific reference. Indefinite specific reference typically involves a speech act in which the referent of a noun phrase is identifiable for the speaker but is presented by the speaker in such a way that it is left unidentified for the hearer. For example, in 'I've seen a bunny rabbit', the rabbit is identifiable for the speaker but is left unidentified for the hearer.

Markers for indefinite specific reference are thus perhaps the most appropriate means of presenting first mentions of participants in discourse. Indefinite articles may be independent words, particles, clitics, or affixes; they may be segmental or suprasegmental; and they may precede or follow the noun they determine. This characterization is not meant to be a definition, but it may be helpful in distinguishing indefinite articles from other kinds of linguistic forms, such as indefinite pronouns.

Here I make an attempt to explain some of the properties of indefinite articles. To this end, I propose a catalogue of crosslinguistic regularities to be observed in the behavior of such articles, based on the surveys alluded to previously. On the basis of these regularities, some questions are posed, and answers are provided in section 4.3. My analysis is restricted in a number of ways. For example, I will only look at affirmative uses of indefinite articles (e.g., 'a car') and ignore negative uses (e.g., 'no car'), since the latter raise a number of problems that require a separate treatment.

Both Moravcsik's (1969) and Heine et al.'s (1995) surveys suggest a number of properties that are likely to be associated with indefinite articles in the languages of the world. As the qualifier "likely" indicates, we are dealing with statements about probabilities, rather than with exceptionless regularities. Nevertheless, it seems that the facts contained in these statements are not coincidental but, rather, need an explanation. Because only a minority of the languages of the world have grammaticalized indefinite articles, obviously the following list of properties relates only to them (see Heine et al. 1995 for details and references):

1. Indefinite articles are generally short—that is, they never have more than two syllables (Moravcsik 1969:86).
2. They are stressless.
3. They are likely to employ the same position in the clause as the numeral 'one'.
4. They tend to be confined to determining the singular of count nouns. Nevertheless, there may be exceptions where the article has been extended to nonsingular referents.
5. If the indefinite article determines mass nouns, then it is also used for plural nouns.
6. If it determines plural nouns, then it also determines singular nouns.

The last three statements are supported by the quantitative evidence of table 4-1, according to which singular nouns are statistically the most likely to be associated with indefinite articles, plural nouns less so, and mass nouns, the least likely.

Table 4-1   Crosslinguistic frequency of occurrence of indefinite articles with singular, plural, and mass nouns (sample: 31 languages; source: Heine et al. 1995)

Use of article	No. of languages (%) using an indefinite article with:		
	Singular nouns	Plural nouns	Mass nouns
Yes	81%	23%	10%
No	19%	71%	77%
No information	0%	6%	13%
Total	100%	100%	100%

7. The relationship between form and function is an asymmetric one in many languages: Presence of an indefinite (specific) marker does not mean that that marker is used for all instances of indefinite specific reference. Even if a given language has a grammaticalized indefinite article, that article is not necessarily used in all instances where indefinite reference is involved.

8. While the use of indefinite articles is likely to be confined to singular nouns, as we saw above, such a constraint does not exist in the case of definite articles, as table 4-2 suggests.

9. Indefinite and definite articles differ also in the fact that the former, but not the latter, may have a numeral function ('one') in some contexts, as appears to be the case in the following English examples, where *a* could be replaced by *one* without much change in meaning (Quirk et al. 1985:274).

(5)   a. The Wrights have *two* daughters and *a* son.
      b. *a* mile or *two*

10. If a language has a grammaticalized indefinite article, it is likely to also have a definite article, while the reverse does not necessarily hold true. Thus, the presence of an indefinite article is likely to be accompanied by that of a definite article, but not vice versa (see table 4-3).

Table 4-3 is based on Moravcsik's data, even though the calculation and interpretation are ours. As this table suggests, statement (10) is supported by 95 percent of the languages in Moravcsik's sample and contradicted by 5 percent. Compared to this observation, the reverse generalization—that languages with definite articles also have indefinite ones—is supported by less than 40 percent of the languages and, hence, is empirically hardly significant. Note that only 5 percent of the languages have an indefinite but no definite article.

THE ABOVE GENERALIZATIONS raise a number of questions, among them the following:

1. Why does the indefinite article in English and a number of other languages determine singular nouns (e.g., 'a child') but normally not plural nouns ('*a children')?

Table 4-2   Crosslinguistic frequency of occurrence of definite articles with singular, plural, and mass nouns (sample: 31 languages; source: Heine et al. 1995)

	No. of languages (%) having a definite article and using that article with:		
Use of article	*Singular nouns*	*Plural nouns*	*Mass nouns*
Yes	78%	71%	61%
No	16%	16%	23%
No information	6%	13%	16%
Total	100%	100%	100%

Table 4-3   Presence or absence of definite and indefinite markers in 104 languages (based on Moravcsik 1969)

Definite marker	Indefinite marker	No. of languages	Percentage of total
Yes	Yes	42	39%
Yes	No	61	56%
No	Yes	5	5%
No	No	0	0%
Total		108	100%

2. Why are there nevertheless languages such as Spanish, where indefinite articles are used in the plural?

3. Indefinite articles tend to be portrayed as markers for specific reference. Why does it nevertheless happen that they are also used in some languages, but not in others, to express nonspecific reference?

4. Why do indefinite articles resemble lexemes for the numeral 'one' in many languages?

5. Why do indefinite articles almost invariably occupy the same syntagmatic position as numerals?

6. If it is the case that indefinite articles tend to resemble the numeral 'one', then why is it also the case that not infrequently, the item used as an indefinite article is phonetically shorter or simplified vis-à-vis the item denoting 'one'?

7. More precisely, what accounts for the other phonetic properties alluded to in the preceding discussion—for example, the fact that indefinite articles never have more than two syllables and are stressless?

8. Definite and indefinite articles are usually portrayed as denoting mutually exclusive grammatical functions. Why, then, does it happen that in English and a number of other languages the two occur in some contexts as functionally largely equivalent items, as in (6)? Furthermore, why does it happen that the two can be replaced by "zero" in (6c) without any remarkable change in meaning?

(6)   English (Hawkins 1978:214)
    a. A lion is a noble beast.
    b. The lion is a noble beast.
    c. Lions are noble beasts.

9. Why does it happen that in some languages, definite and indefinite markers co-occur—for instance, that the presence of an item serving the function of an indefinite article presupposes the co-presence of a definite article, as in Ewe (7) or French (8), though not vice versa?

(7)   Ewe (Kwa, Niger-Congo)

ŋútsu- (l)á	ŋútsu-a-	ɖé
man- DEF	man- DEF-	INDEF
'the man'	'a man'	

(8)   French

la viande	de	la viande
DEF meat	PARTIT/INDEF	DEF meat
'the meat'	'meat'	

10. Finally, why are indefinite articles severely limited in the range of their syntactic functions? For example, why can the numeral *one* be used both as an attribute (e.g., 'one car') and as a pronoun ('I want one') while the indefinite article cannot be used as a pronoun (e.g., '*I want a')?

This is but a small subcollection of the questions that may have arisen in the course of this section, where we proposed some generalizations on the crosslinguistic behavior of indefinite articles. In the following sections an attempt will be made to answer them.

4.2   Evolution

As a rule, grammatical categories can be traced back to two, or even more, different concrete sources. We saw in chapter 3, for example, that locative adverbs or adpositions relating to meanings such as 'up', 'front', and the like tend to go back to either body-part or landmark concepts. In the case of indefinite articles, the situation is somewhat different: There is essentially only one conceptual source. While it is possible that in a given case some alternative source might be found, in the vast majority of languages that have developed an indefinite article it is the numeral 'one' that was recruited for this purpose. Thus, it is possible to predict with a high degree of probability that if we find an indefinite article in some unknown language, that article is historically derived from a numeral.

As mentioned in the preceding chapters, the evolution from lexical to grammatical structure is not discontinuous but proceeds gradually; it involves a large number of small, contextually defined extensions. For descriptive convenience, these extensions can be divided into a smaller number of more salient stages. With the following five-stage model, an attempt is made to account for the evolution of indefinite articles. The model can be interpreted in a dual way. On the one hand, it may be viewed as a synchronic implicational scale. This means, for example, that an indefinite article of a given stage also has, or may have, the properties of all preceding stages, but not vice versa. On the other hand, it is claimed to reflect diachronic evolution, where the initial stage represents the oldest and the final stage the most recent situation.

4.2.1 *Stage I*: The numeral

At this stage, there is an item for 'one' which functions exclusively as a numeral. A large number of languages belong to this stage—that is, all those languages that are said "to lack an indefinite article." In Swahili, for example, the item *moja* in (9a) is used exclusively as a numeral ('one'). If the noun *gari* 'car' has indefinite specific reference, then neither a numeral nor any other marker is used, as in (9b).

(9)   Swahili (Bantu, Niger-Congo)
    a. ni- na   gari moja
       I- have car   one
       'I have one car.'

    b. ni- na   gari
       I- have car
       'I have a car.'

4.2.2 *Stage II*: The presentative marker

This stage is reached when the article introduces a new participant presumed to be unknown to the hearer and this participant is taken up as definite in subsequent discourse—for example, when the article is used to refer to the phrase printed in italics in (10).

(10)   Russian (Tania Kuteva, personal communication)
     Zhyl da   byl *odin starik* . . .
     lived PARTICLE was one old. man
     'Once upon a time there was an old man . . .'

A number of languages are characteristic of this stage, including the Gurage language Soddo-Goggot of Ethiopia. Hetzron (1977:56) notes that in this language, a limited indefinite article is used "presentatively" for newly introduced items that are going to be talked about.

    An early stage II situation would obtain in a language where the article is confined to the beginning of a narrative discourse—for instance, where the main participants are introduced with the presentative article at the beginning of the tale. In the story "The Coyote and the Jackrabbit" of Western Tarahumara of the Uto-Aztecan family, for example, the indefinite marker *bilé* 'one, a' appears essentially only in the initial sentence (11); in the remainder of the text, specific reference is normally unmarked.

(11)   Western Tarahumara (Uto-Aztecan; Burgess 1984:145)
     bilé rawé bilé basačí 'wé e'lowí- le- ga- ra-   'e . . .
     one day   one coyote much hungry- PAST- STAT- QUOT-EMPH
     'One day, a coyote was very hungry, they say . . .'

4.2.3 *Stage III*: The specific marker

The article is no longer confined to presentative uses; it is extended typically to any participant in discourse known to the speaker but presumed to be unknown to the hearer, irrespective of whether or not the participant concerned is expected to be taken up in subsequent discourse. Nevertheless, the use of the article is still associated with subsequent mentions, even if much less so than at stage II. Almost invariably, the article is still confined to singular participants that are countable. Street Hebrew *exad* 'one, a', as used in (12a), may be an instance of a stage III marker. It is used in contexts like (12a) but not in contexts like (12b), where pragmatically the exact identity of the referent ('man') is incidental; what matters is its type membership (Givón 1981:36).

(12) Street Hebrew (Givón 1981:36)
   a. ba   hena ish- xad etmol   ve- hitxil le- daber ve- hu . . .
      came here man- one yesterday and- started to- talk   and- he
      'A man came in yesterday and started talking and he . . .'

   b. ba   hena ísh etmol,   lo isha!
      came here man yesterday not woman
      'A man came here yesterday, not a woman!'

4.2.4   *Stage IV*: The nonspecific marker

The article can now be used when a participant is introduced whose referential identity neither the hearer nor the speaker knows or cares to know. The examples in (13) illustrate situations that are likely to be associated with stage IV articles.

(13) a. Buy me *a newspaper*, please!
   b. Draw *a dog*!

While the article is no longer confined to marking specific reference at this stage, it is fairly regularly used whenever a singular count noun is presented as a specific participant.

   Examples of stage IV situations can be found in many European languages, including English, German, Dutch, and most Romance languages, or Punjabi and Chinese, among others.

4.2.5   *Stage V*: The generalized article

At this stage, the article can be expected to occur on all types of nouns, even if there may remain a number of exceptions—for instance, if the noun is marked for definiteness, or is a proper noun, or is a predicate noun defining members of an ethnic, professional, or some other class ('He is Swiss'). This means that the use of the article is no longer restricted to singular nouns but is extended to plural and mass nouns, as in the following example from Spanish.

(14) Spanish
   Un día ven- ían   un- o- s hombres . . .
   one day come- 3PL.PRET.IMPERF one- M- PL men
   'One day there came some men . . .'

As INDICATED HERE, the five stages present a kind of crosslinguistic implicational scale. This means, for example, that an indefinite article of stage IV can be expected to also have the properties of all preceding stages—that is, it may typically be used as a numeral, a presentative marker, or a marker of indefinite-specific reference, while it lacks the property that is characteristic of the subsequent stage V (but see the following discussion).

The various stages must not be viewed as discrete entities; rather, the evolution from stage I to V is continuous and involves overlaps of various kinds. In accordance with the Overlap Model of grammaticalization (Heine 1993), there is always an intermediate stage where the construction can be interpreted alternatively with reference to the earlier and the later structure. For example, at the initial stage the marker used as an indefinite article is still ambiguous as to whether it is to be interpreted as a numeral or as an article. Such a situation appears to exist in Tamil: The numeral *onru* 'one' has a special form *oru* when used as noun modifier in prenominal position, and it is this reduced form that serves as an indefinite article. However, *oru* is ambiguous between the numeral and the article readings:

(15)   Tamil (Dravidian; Lehmann 1989:112)
       oru   nalla patam
       one/a good movie
       'one/a good movie'

Similarly, in Kannada the item *ondu* 'one, a' is ambiguous between the numeral and the indefinite meaning. Note, however, that in its numeral use it is stressable—as, for instance, in (16a)—while as an indefinite marker it is not (16b). Furthermore, there are contextual constraints on the use of the indefinite marker: When used in postverbal position as an afterthought or in sentence-initial position, the article meaning is ruled out, and *ondu* can only have a numeral meaning serving a partitive function ('one of a definite set'), as, for example, in (16c).

(16)   Kannada (Dravidian; Bhat 1991:62)
       a. avanige ondu   pustaka   sikkide
          him. DAT one. STRESS book. ACC   got. is
          'He has got one of the books.'

       b. avanige ondu pustaka   sikkide
          him. DAT one   book. ACC. STRESS got. is
          'He has got a book.'

       c. ondu pustaka   me:jina me:le ide
          one   book. NOM table's   on   is
          'One of the books (*a book) is on the table.'

The historical development of the indefinite article in English illustrates some of the characteristics mentioned in this section. According to Hopper & Martin (1987), there were two indefinite articles in Old English, the two being in functional overlap as presentative markers. *Sum* appears as the typical stage II marker. It introduces into the discourse a thematic participant, and NPs introduced by *sum* have numerous subsequent mentions. The indefinite article *an* is also presentative, but the NP introduced by it is less salient for the discourse than one introduced by *sum* and supports subsequent references to a more limited degree than *sum*. Furthermore, *sum* almost always occurs at the beginning of an episode, while *an* may occur at any point. Thus, already at the stage of Old English, *an* appears to have proceeded beyond stage II.

Subsequent developments are characterized, first, by the encroachment of *an* onto the domain of "zero"—that is, *an* comes increasingly to be used where formerly there was no article, and *sum* is more likely to be used with plurals and generics. Second, *an* acquires the ability to occur with topics: While in the Old English period it was virtually nonexistent with topic NPs, Hopper & Martin (1987:300) estimate that 27% of NPs with *a(n)* in Modern English are subjects/topics. Third, the ability of NPs with *an* to stand alone, without subsequent mentions, increases even further: While in Old English 56% of the indefinite NPs with *an* have subsequent mentions, the proportion drops to 10% by the 20th century.

Underlying the evolution described in this section are a number of grammaticalization processes, which we will now look at briefly in turn. One of these concerns *bleaching*. This term refers to a process whereby in the development from lexical to grammatical item the semantic content of the item is "bleached out." Bleaching is at once a popular and a controversial notion in grammaticalization studies (see Heine, Claudi, & Hünnemeyer 1991, ch. 4). Nevertheless, if one would ever feel justified defending the relevance of this notion, then it is in the present case: The evolution of indefinite articles would seem to be a paradigm case of bleaching, as was pointed out already by Givón (1981:51); see Lessau (1994:74–8).

Givón proposes an evolutionary scale, as presented in (17). This scale is interpreted with reference to two complementary parameters—namely, implication and bleaching. With reference to implication, Givón says that quantification implies existence/reference, and existence/reference implies genericity/connotation; with reference to bleaching, he says that as a first step, quantification is bleached out, followed by the bleaching out of referentiality, the result of this double bleaching process being that in the end, only genericity/connotation survives.

(17)   quantification   →   referentiality/denotation   →   genericity/connotation

It goes without saying that this is only one perspective that grammaticalization theory offers to deal with the problem concerned. An alternative perspective would be that we are dealing with a transition from one ontological category to another—for example, from the domain of "real-world phenomena," which Frajzyngier (1991) refers to as the *domain de re*, to the world of linguistic discourse—that is, Frajzyngier's *domain de dicto*.

Givón's scale, which appears to be based on synchronic logic, can immediately be related to the evolutionary model sketched earlier: Our stage I largely corresponds to his "quantification" category, while our stages II, III, and IV are suggestive of a subclassification of his "referentiality," and our final stage V, of his "genericity" category.

Another process concerns *cliticization*. With this term we are referring to the general process whereby a lexical item loses in morphosyntactic autonomy and becomes increasingly associated with some adjacent word or phrase, turning into a clitic and eventually an affix. In the case under consideration, the erstwhile numeral 'one' gradually becomes an appendage of the noun or noun phrase it determines until it ceases to exist as a separate word unit, at least in its grammaticalized form as an indefinite marker. This process entails that the item concerned loses in properties that define a word unit, such as forming a tone- or stress-bearing unit of its own (see the following discussion).

Another common process that accompanies grammaticalization is erosion, whereby the phonetic substance of the item concerned is increasingly reduced, simplified, or both (Heine & Reh 1984; Pagliuca & Mowrey 1987; Heine 1993). The English indefinite article offers an instance of this process in that it has been reduced from *one* to *a(n)*. Similarly, the item *exad* 'one' of modern Street Hebrew is reduced to *-xad*, "where a *referential* interpretation of the indefinite is possible" (Givón 1981:42).

To summarize, the evolution from numeral to indefinite article entails a number of individual syntactic, morphological, and phonological processes; the main ones are listed in table 4-4. There exists a general correlation between these processes and the five stages discussed previously, which is of the following kind: The more stages an item has passed through on its way from numeral to indefinite article, the more it is affected by grammaticalization processes such as bleaching, cliticization, and erosion. However, languages do exhibit individual differences in the extent to which they realize this correlation.

4.3   Answers

We are now in a position to address the questions raised in section 4.1. Note that our analysis is confined to indefinite articles that are homophonous or phonologically similar to the numeral 'one'; nevertheless, for a more comprehensive discussion of the nature of indefinite articles, we will also have to include in this section a few remarks on alternative strategies for expressing indefiniteness.

The question of why the indefinite article in English and a number of other languages determines singular nouns but not normally plural or mass nouns (question (1)) can be answered with reference to the semantics of its conceptual source: The numeral 'one' inherently determines singular nouns and retains this property even in its grammaticalized form as an indefinite article.

Table 4-4   Canonical processes characterizing the evolution from numeral to indefinite article

Source item	Target item
Numeral 'one'	Indefinite article
Free word	Clitic > Affix
Full form	Phonologically reduced form

In the end, however, at stage V (and sometimes even earlier) (question (2)), the association with the numeral can get lost: The constraint on using the indefinite marker only with singular count nouns is lifted, as appears to have happened in languages like Catalan, Portuguese, and Spanish, where *uno/una* came to be extended to plural nouns (see the preceding discussion). Frequently, however, such a process does not take place; rather, people tend to use alternative strategies to introduce indefinite articles on plural and mass nouns. One such strategy is the use of some qualifying nominal that is morphologically singular and hence compatible with the use of the indefinite article, but that semantically introduces the notion of a plural or mass concept. Thus, what seems to be a plural use of the indefinite article is historically a singular use, in that the article modifies a singular item heading a plural noun (cf. English 'a few/a dozen/a million'). In the following Tamil example, the indefinite article *oru* would appear to modify the "numeral noun" *ampatu* 'fifty' rather than the plural noun *peer* 'people'.

(18) Tamil (Dravidian; Lehmann 1989:113)
      oru   ampatu peer
      INDEF fifty   people
      'some fifty people'

An alternative strategy is to use a partitive notion roughly meaning 'several out of X', where X is a definite noun. One peculiar side effect of this strategy is that the resulting indefinite article contains a definite article. This strategy appears to have been adopted in the Romance languages French and Italian, or in the Niger-Congo language Ewe, as we saw in the preceding discussion, but other examples are not hard to come by; Hetzron (1977:56) notes, for example, that in the Gurage language Soddo-Goggot of Ethiopia, the indefinite (*(a)at*) and the definite articles (*-i*) can be combined (*-att-i* 'a-the') to express 'one of them'.

It would seem that Italian is still in a transitional stage: There is disagreement among the experts about the status of the plural specific marker *dei* (see table 4-5)— whether it is (still) a partitive marker, as some traditional grammarians argue, thus making Italian a language without plural indefinite articles, or whether it is (already) an indefinite article, which would mean that Italian has two indefinite articles in the singular: one for count nouns, which is derived from the numeral 'one', and another for noncount nouns, which is derived from a partitive marker.

In spite of the fact that indefinite articles determining plural or mass nouns are not normally derived from numerals, there are nevertheless languages like Spanish

Table 4-5 The paradigm of Italian articles (according to Renzi 1989–91)

Article	Singular	Plural
Definite	il cane 'the dog'	i cani 'the dogs'
Specific	un cane 'a dog'	dei cani 'dogs'
Nonspecific	un cane 'a dog'	cani 'dogs'

where such indefinite articles (*uno, una*) are indeed used in the plural. This fact can be accounted for by appeal to "bleaching" or "generalization": The further grammaticalization progresses, the more likely it is that the lexical semantics of the erstwhile numeral is "bleached out." In extreme cases, this may mean that the numeral meaning becomes so attenuated that there is no longer felt to be any semantic incompatibility between 'one' and plurality.

The same general answer can be given with reference to question (3): The further the grammaticalization process proceeds, the more the indefinite article is extended to nonreferential uses. At a certain stage in its history, the article may modify both specific and nonspecific nouns in the same way.

Questions (4) and (5) can both be answered in the same way: Indefinite articles are likely to resemble lexemes for the numeral 'one' and are likely to occupy the same position as that numeral because historically they *are* the numeral.

In a similar vein, questions (6) and (7) can be answered with reference to one parameter of grammaticalization—that is, erosion. With increasing grammaticalization, grammatical markers lose in phonological substance and complexity: They tend to become shorter and to give up suprasegmental contrasts such as distinctions in tone or stress. Thus, their reduction to stressless mono- or disyllabic determiners is in line with exactly the same kinds of erosion observed in other parts of grammar (Heine & Reh 1984; Heine 1993).

Question (8) was why, in spite of their contrasting functions, definite and indefinite articles may occur as functionally largely equivalent items. The answer has once more to do with bleaching: With their increasing degree of grammaticalization, both definite and indefinite articles can be bleached out to the extent that they are no longer in functional contrast in certain contexts. In English there are such contexts, for instance, when count nouns are used generically; in this case, the two articles can be functionally largely equivalent, and they can even be replaced by "zero," as we saw in section 4.1.

Question (9) was why definite and indefinite markers obligatorily co-occur in some languages—that is, why indefinite articles in languages like Ewe (and, in the case of plural articles, for instance, also in French and Italian) contain a segment that is identical with the definite article. An answer to this question was proposed in the preceding discussion of question (2).

Finally, question (10), why indefinite articles are severely limited in their syntactic functions compared to their lexical source, can be answered redundantly in the following way: Since their specialization as an article is restricted to one syntactic environment—namely, that of noun phrase determination—they lose the ability to occur elsewhere and become fixed in that one environment only.

4.4   Discussion

This catalogue by no means exhausts the list of questions that arise with regard to the evolution and synchronic profile of indefinite articles. One may wonder, for example, what makes the numeral 'one' the primary candidate for serving as an indefinite article. An answer to this question may be sought in the discourse functions this numeral may fulfill. Dixon found that in Boumaa Fijian, the numeral *dua* 'one' accounts for "more than three-quarters of the occurrences of numbers in texts" (1988:141). Givón (1981:52) argues that the numeral is an ideal means for the speaker to perform two seemingly conflicting tasks: (a) to introduce a new argument as referential/existing ('There is X'), and (b) to identify it by its generic/type properties ('X is one of the members of Class C'). These two desiderata, Givón concludes, are exactly the requirements for introducing a referential-indefinite argument into discourse.

There are a number of other problems that I mentioned in section 4.1 but have not tackled here. For example, why are there more languages that have grammaticalized a definite marker than there are languages that have grammaticalized an indefinite marker? Why is it that only a limited number of the languages in the world have indefinite articles? Why is it that even in many of those languages that do have an indefinite article, that article is rarely made use of? Why do indefinite articles exist in the first place?

To answer these questions, much further research will be required. Suffice it here to add a few notes that might prove relevant to such research. One point concerns areal typology. Some of the questions raised in the preceding discussion can be answered more meaningfully if one takes into consideration linguistic geography in general and language contact in particular. Thus, one might expect with a certain degree of probability that a given language will have an indefinite article if the neighboring language or languages also have one. The older Germanic languages did not have a definite or indefinite article, in much the same way as the ancestor of the modern Romance languages did not. On the other hand, most modern European languages across genetic boundaries have both kinds of article. It goes without saying that such observations need to be tested against the background of a larger, genetically and areally balanced sample of languages.

Furthermore, a number of studies suggest that the functional yield of articles, both indefinite and definite, is low, if not minimal. Articles have been described as being largely or entirely superfluous. For Beckmann, for example, the article is "a redundant check morpheme," mainly for the following reasons: (a) Languages such as Latin, Czech, and Russian lack articles, yet there is no difficulty in communicating in these languages without their benefit; and (b) the article is "discarded as unnecessary and wasteful in newspaper headlines and telegrams, even when the grammar of the language would require its use" (Beckmann 1972:165–66).

While the point made by Beckmann and others is well taken, it does not answer the question of why we nevertheless find quite a number of languages that, independent of one another, indeed have grammaticalized indefinite articles.

Indefinite articles and numerals are different in virtually every respect, be it in their semantic, syntactic, or morphological behavior. Thus it is justified to treat them as belonging to different linguistic domains. This is what grammarians of European or other languages have done: Almost invariably, the two types of items are treated as unrelated linguistic units.

That indefinite articles and the numeral 'one' nevertheless have certain similarities has been observed independently by a number of authors, even if no major conclusions with reference to a theory of language have been drawn from such observations. A few proposals have attempted to account for this similarity. Rather than dealing with similarity, it is argued, we are dealing with *identity*; accordingly, rather than being similar to the numeral, the indefinite article *is* the cardinal numeral 'one'. Thus, Perlmutter (1968) is satisfied that English *a(n)* is an unstressed cardinal: First, he says, *a(n)* contrasts with cardinals; second, the collocational properties of *a(n)* "resemble" those of cardinals; and third, the phonological shape of the article has evolved from 'one'. Such a claim is supported by Moravcsik on the basis of cross-linguistic evidence: She says that the cardinal 'one' is an optional indefiniteness marker in all languages, and adds that "several properties of the indefinite article can be understood if we assume that it is a numeral." Crosslinguistically, she says, the difference between cardinal 'one' and the indefinite article "is basically one of stress" and almost all properties of an indefinite article can be derived from properties of numerals (1969:84). She defines the following properties that are shared by the cardinal numeral 'one' and indefinite articles:

1. Both mark count nouns.
2. Both usually have no plural.
3. Further pertinent criteria for testing the relationship of cardinals and indefinite articles "might be ordering and associated categories" (Moravcsik 1969:87).

Depending on the nature of the descriptive model adopted, both Perlmutter's and Moravcsik's claims are legitimate, and indeed are supported by a certain body of evidence: On account of the presence of some similarities between the numeral 'one' and the indefinite article on the one hand, and of the presence (or presumed presence) of some instances of complementary distribution on the other, it is possible to argue that the two are covariants of one and the same category. Since all linguistic models we are familiar with rest on generalizations involving probabilities, the Perlmutter/Moravcsik position, which does so as well, is a valid one: The two argue that there are "sufficient" criteria for postulating a single category only.

However, there are a number of problems with the Perlmutter/Moravcsik position. The first has to do with the fact that it ignores certain portions of evidence that would contradict the position. This concerns primarily languages where (1) the indefinite article is grammaticalized to the extent that it no longer contrasts with the numeral; where (2) the distinction stressed/unstressed is immaterial because stress is not distinctive in such languages; and/or where (3) the indefinite article is confined neither to count nouns nor to singular nouns.

The second problem concerns the fact that there remain a number of important questions that cannot be answered by the Perlmutter/Moravcsik framework. Among the questions discussed in section 4.3 are the following in particular:

1. Why are indefinite articles likely to be shorter and phonologically less complex than the numeral 'one'?
2. Why are indefinite articles syntactically more constrained in their co-occurrence with other constituents than the numeral 'one'; for example, why can the numeral be used both attributively (e.g., 'one

car') and pronominally ('I want one'), while the indefinite article cannot be used pronominally ('*I want a')?

The third problem has to do with explanation. These authors do not say *why* the similarities observed by them exist. Moravcsik (1969:84) at least goes as far as one can go within the limits of the framework used. Still, it remains unclear why almost all properties of indefinite articles can be derived from properties of numerals, why this derivation is unidirectional, and why indefinite articles and the numeral also have a number of contrasting properties, as we saw in section 4.2.

On the basis of such problems, one might decide to ignore the Perlmutter/ Moravcsik position and to argue that indefinite articles and numerals are different kinds of animals and should not be related to one another. This is, in fact, the position adopted in most models of modern mainstream linguistics. What such a position entails is that the many similarities that were pointed out in the course of this chapter are declared irrelevant or nonexistent. We are not aware of any serious arguments that might justify such a position.

WE THUS REMAIN in a situation where there is a problem of worldwide significance that is ignored by most contemporary linguists concerned with this issue. What is required for an appropriate descriptive and explanatory account of indefinite articles is a model that is able to explain a seeming contradiction: On account of their genesis, indefinite articles are likely to be confined to singular nouns. Nevertheless, it is possible to predict that there will be languages, like Spanish, where indefinite articles occur with plural nouns as well.

As we saw in the preceding discussion, this contradiction has to do with the relative degree of grammaticalization that an indefinite article has undergone. In its earlier stages, the article is still so strongly associated with the semantics of the numeral 'one' that its use is incompatible with nonsingular nouns. In a more advanced stage of development, however, one will expect that the use of the indefinite article is extended to all kinds of nouns, irrespective of whether they are singular or plural, count or mass nouns—with the effect that any number-specific behavior is bleached out.

Characteristics like these can be satisfactorily accounted for only, it seems, if one chooses a model that explains linguistic categories with reference to their genesis and evolution.

4.5 Summary

In this chapter we saw how a numeral turns into a relatively abstract grammatical marker—that is, how a linguistic item having a fairly concrete semantics gradually loses that semantics and assumes a function relating to the organization of texts. Thus, in our journey from concrete visible and tangible concepts like body-parts or environmental landmarks to relational concepts such as locative markers and numerals, we have arrived at an even more abstract domain where linguistic items have no use beyond that of highlighting referential properties of participants in discourse. This evolution leads (a) from open-class items like nouns and verbs to closed-class items like adverbs, adpositions, or numerals, and, further, to items belonging to paradigms having three, two, or one member(s) only; (b) from free words to clitics to affixes; and (c) from polysyllabic to monosyllabic (and even to nonsegmental) forms.

Indefinite articles, especially in their more advanced stages of development, are likely to be located toward the end point of this overall evolution—that is, they are likely to belong to grammatical paradigms that have perhaps no more than two members, are affixes rather than free forms, and are short (typically monosyllabic). Evolutionary patterns of the type discussed here have been described as involving metaphor, metonymy, conversational implicatures, invited inferences, and other notions (see Heine, Claudi, & Hünnemeyer 1991; Traugott & König 1991; Bybee, Perkins, & Pagliuca 1994 for further details; see also section 7.4). Most important for understanding the process concerned, it would seem, is the role played by context. As we saw in section 4.2, the genesis of indefinite articles appears to involve a situation of asymmetric information content roughly of the following kind: 'There is some*one* I know but you don't.' The use of the numeral 'one' in such a contextual frame provides the basis for the rise of a stage II use of the numeral, which subsequently may develop into a "full-fledged" indefinite article.

But this is only one out of many possible situational frames in which the numeral 'one' may be used. A second situation can be sketched thus: 'There is only *one* X.' Such a situation can be interpreted as implying that since there is only one X, X must have properties that other items do not have—that is, X is *unique*. English 'unique', as well as many similar examples in other languages, appears to be a conventionalized reflex of such a use of the numeral 'one'. An alternative interpretation of the same frame would be that X is a human being, and since there is only one X, X has no company and hence must feel *lonely*. English items like 'alone', 'lone', or 'lonely', as well as their equivalents in many other languages, appear to be conventionalized forms of this use of the numeral.

A third kind of frame can be sketched thus: 'They are all *one*.' The interpretation this frame may receive is that, since they are all one, they are united or belong together. Expressions found crosslinguistically corresponding to such English items as 'unity', 'be united', or 'unanimous' appear to be conventionalized forms of this use of 'one'.

These are but a few examples of the way the numeral 'one' tends to be manipulated in discourse, with the effect that new meanings and new words arise. The variousness of these examples suggests that there is no fixed relationship between source concepts and target concepts. What makes it possible for the numeral 'one' to assume the referential functions it does in many languages is that specific contextual frames exist, which enable numerals to be reinterpreted as something else and, hence, to be used for the expression of new lexical and grammatical functions.

SO FAR WE HAVE BEEN looking at simple conceptual phenomena, more particularly at objects such as body-parts and environmental landmarks. In the following chapters, we will discuss more complex items—phenomena that are propositional in form and that will be referred to as *event schemas*.

5

POSSESSION

In the foregoing chapters, we have been concerned with simple linguistic forms, such as lexical items that develop into grammatical items. However, it is possible to argue, as some in fact do, that this evolution involves entire constructions, rather than individual items. For our purposes, this issue is of minor importance. As we will see in this and the following chapter, however, there are, in fact, more complex structures that are equally relevant for understanding why grammar is structured the way it is. In section 5.3 we will see that there are certain domains of grammar that cannot be accounted for satisfactorily with reference to simple entities like words or morphemes but rather owe their genesis to schematic structures that have a propositional form; following Heine (1993) we will refer to these structures as *event schemas*. Possession is one such domain.

5.1   Concepts, constructions, and problems

Possession is a universal domain—that is, any human language can be expected to have conventionalized expressions for it. When working on the linguistic expression of possession, however, one is likely to be confronted with a number of problems.

Possession has occasionally been described as a vague concept, or one that is neither conceptually nor linguistically basic, or one that may not be of universal significance. Nevertheless, I am not aware of any language that would not dispose of some explicit means for expressing, for instance, "my children" or "I have a dog." But possessive expressions are used for a wide range of contents, and some authors therefore claim that linguistic expressions for possession are meaningless—that is, that English items like *have* or *of* are semantically vacuous (cf. Bach 1967). Furthermore, the wide range of meanings expressed by possessive constructions has induced some authors to propose fairly abstract descriptions of possession. For Langacker, for example, the various uses of the English genitive have in common that one entity "is invoked as a reference point for purposes of establishing mental contact with another" (1993:8). Some authors would go so far as to claim that possession simply involves any abstract relation between two entities.

Students of law, among others, have drawn a distinction between possession and ownership. This distinction is in fact a relevant one. I will not deal with it in any great detail, however, primarily because it appears to be highly culture-specific, and our interest is primarily with crosslinguistic regularities. Moreover, there are a number of quite divergent ways in which this distinction has been treated in the relevant literature. For example, while some authors argue that possession and ownership are clearly different things (e.g., Bickerton 1981), others treat the two as being essentially the same (cf. Gentner 1975:212). We will therefore avoid the term "ownership"; rather, we will propose a more detailed classification of possessive notions that will serve as a basis for further analysis (section 5.1.3).

Another problem concerns the crosslinguistic and cross-cultural significance of the possessive domain. Is it in fact a universal domain, as some argue, or is it culture-specific? That is, does it occur in certain parts of the world but not in others? Did it evolve during certain periods in the history of mankind but not during others? We noted here that the range of meanings expressed by possessive constructions is so wide that referring to all of these meanings as "possessive" would be misleading; in addition, possessive expressions are likely to have other, nonpossessive, meanings. For example, there is no doubt that (1a) is an instance of possession, but what about (1b)?

(1)   a. Ron has a cheetah.
      b. Ron has a cold.

To take care of cases like (1b), alternative terms such as "relational," "associative," and the like have been proposed to refer to concepts that include possession but are not confined to it (cf. Creissels 1979). Rather than offering a solution, such proposals are likely to sweep the problem under the rug: They do not seem to be of help in answering the question of whether there is something like an ontological category of possession that can be delimited and defined by means of linguistic methodology.

From such observations it follows that perhaps the most crucial problem is the definition of possession. For example, should one aim at a definition in terms of linguistic properties? While most linguists will probably answer in the affirmative, there are some who seek an extralinguistic definition. For Seiler (1983:4–7), for example, possession is essentially a conceptual relationship pattern: He defines possession as "the relationship between a human being and his kinsmen, his body-parts, his material belongings, his cultural and intellectual products." What distinguishes possession from other relational domains such as location, he observes, is that it is *bio-*

cultural. Furthermore, like location, he says, it is binary, in that it involves two items, the possessor and the item possessed (= the possessee).

5.1.1 Alienable and inalienable possession

A widespread distinction to be observed in the languages of the world concerns what is commonly referred to as inalienable versus alienable possession. A wealth of alternative terminologies and characterizations has been proposed; the inalienable category, for example, has also been called "intimate" or "inherent," or has been associated with part-whole relations (cf. Voeltz 1976; Ultan 1978a; Seiler 1983; Chappell & McGregor 1996). Nevertheless, we will use the traditional labels, even if they are not adequate in every respect.

Superficially, the distinction is a straightforward one: Items that cannot normally be separated from their owners are inalienable, while all others are alienable. Thus, items belonging to any of the following conceptual domains are likely to be treated as inalienable:

1. Kinship terms
2. Body-parts
3. Relational spatial concepts, like 'top', 'bottom', and 'interior'
4. Inherent parts of other items, like 'branch' and 'handle'
5. Physical and mental states, like 'strength' and 'fear'

In addition, there are a number of individual concepts in a given language that may also be treated inalienably, such as 'name', 'voice', 'smell', 'shadow', 'footprint', 'property', and 'home'.

The way inalienability is defined in a given case or in a given language is largely dependent on culture-specific conventions. In some languages, concepts like 'neighbor', 'house', 'bed', 'fire', 'clothes', and 'spear' belong to the inalienable category, while in others they do not. In fact, languages differ considerably with regard to where the boundary is traced between inalienably and alienably possessed items.

There are quite a number of languages, spoken in all major parts of the world, that mark a morphosyntactic distinction between an inalienable and an alienable category. This distinction tends to involve the following properties (see especially Nichols 1988, 1992:116ff.; Chappell & McGregor 1996):

1. It is confined to attributive possession.
2. It is likely to be associated with a number of marking features. For example, alienable nouns can be described as being marked and inalienable ones as unmarked. This means, for instance, that, as a rule, more phonological and/or morphological expenditure is employed to encode alienable, as opposed to inalienable, possession.
3. Inalienable possession involves a tighter structural bond between possessee and possessor (Nichols 1992:117).
4. Possessive markers on inalienable nouns are more "archaic"—that is, they look etymologically older than those used on alienable nouns (Nichols 1992:117).

5. The nouns belonging to the inalienable category include kin terms, body-part terms, or both, usually also some other groups of nouns.
6. The inalienable category consists of a closed set of nouns, while alienability is an open-class category; its membership is described by Nichols (1988:562) as "infinite."

This does not exhaust the list of properties associated with inalienability. A number of additional characteristics have been pointed out by Nichols (1988, 1992:116–23). On the basis of a survey of North American and other languages, she finds that there is a small range of main patterns for marking inalienability. The criterion employed by her is morphosyntactic in nature: Languages which have the grammatical element used for signaling a possessive relation placed on the head noun (= the possessee) are called head-marked (or head-marking), while in dependent-marked (or dependent-marking) languages the possession marker is found on the dependent noun (= the possessor). Rather than being head- or dependent-marked, languages may be double-marked (= having both kinds of marking in the same construction), or they may have no marking at all, or else they may have split patterns, where, for instance, the inalienable category is head-marked and the alienable one is dependent-marked.

5.1.2   Kinds of possessive constructions

Another issue concerns the classification of possession into two main types of linguistic constructions. All languages we are familiar with have a morphosyntactic distinction between what is variously called *attributive*, nominal, or adnominal possession on the one hand (e.g., 'my credit card'), and *predicative* or verbal possession on the other ('I have a credit card'). What the two kinds of possession have in common is, first, that both typically concern a relation between two nominals or between two thing-like items (cf. Seiler 1988:95), and, second, that both can be described with reference to a set of prototypical properties (see Taylor 1989:202–3). Attributive possession can be said to differ from predicative possession chiefly in the following ways:

1. It typically presents presupposed, rather than asserted, information.
2. It involves object-like, time-stable, rather than event-like, contents.
3. It has phrasal, rather than clausal, syntax.

Among the many different ways of expressing predicative possession, *have-constructions* provide the most salient pattern. What characterizes this pattern in English is the fact that the possessor appears as the clausal subject or topic, and the possessee appears as the complement (e.g., 'I have a car'). In other languages, again, have-constructions can take quite a different form; instead of a have-verb, there may be a copula or even no verb at all. We may say that the have-construction in a given language is that construction which is used canonically to express 'I have a car' or 'we have no money'.

In addition, there is a second pattern, in which the possessee is encoded as the clausal subject and/or topic, and the possessor is encoded as the complement or an oblique constituent (e.g., 'The car belongs to me'). We will call this pattern the *belong-construction*.

A number of descriptive devices have been employed to distinguish the two kinds of construction. In have-constructions, it is argued, there is "emphasis" on the possessor, or the possessor is "paramount," while in belong-constructions it is the possessee that receives "emphasis" or is "paramount" (Watkins 1967:2194). I will treat the distinction between the two kinds of construction as being pragmatically motivated. One exponent of this distinction is its association with discourse-pragmatic reference: The possessee is typically indefinite in the case of have-constructions but definite in the case of belong-constructions. The possessor, by contrast, is likely to be definite in both kinds of construction, although it may also be indefinite in the case of belong-constructions.

To conclude, there are essentially three different types of possessive constructions, summarized in (2). The distinction between these constructions is a basic one; all languages known to me have conventionalized means of expressing it.

(2) Attributive possession   e.g.: 'Ron's dog'
     Predicative possession
       a. Have-constructions   e.g.: 'Ron has a dog.'
       b. Belong-constructions   e.g.: 'The dog is Ron's.'

5.1.3   Possessive notions

Finally, the term "possession" appears to refer to a number of different concepts. On the basis of a wide range of languages one may distinguish a catalogue of possessive notions that are relevant to a cross-cultural understanding of possession. These notions are as follows:

Physical possession. This notion, which has also been referred to as momentary possession (Miller & Johnson-Laird 1976:565), is said to be present when the possessor and the possessee are physically associated with one another at reference time, as can be assumed to be the case with *have* in (3) below.

(3)   I want to fill in this form; do you have a pen?

Temporary possession. Alternative terms that have been used for this notion are accidental possession or temporary control (Miller & Johnson-Laird 1976:565). According to this notion, the possessor can dispose of the possessee for a limited time but cannot claim ownership to it, as in (4).

(4)   I have a car that I use to go to the office, but it belongs to Judy.

Permanent possession. Miller and Johnson-Laird (1976:565) call this inherent possession. The possessee is the property of the possessor, and typically the possessor has a legal title to the possessee, as can be assumed to be the case in (5).

(5)   Judy has a car, but I use it all the time.

Permanent possession may be said to correspond most closely to the legal notion of ownership as found in western societies.

Inalienable possession. The possessee is conceived of typically as being insepa- rable from the typically animate possessor—for instance, as a body-part or as a rela- tive, as in (6).

(6)   I have blue eyes/two sisters.

Abstract possession. In this kind of possession, the possessee is a concept that is not visible or tangible, like a disease, a feeling, or some other psychological state.

(7)   He has no time/no mercy.

Inanimate inalienable possession. This notion, which is frequently referred to as part-whole relationship, differs from inalienable possession in that the possessor is inanimate, and the possessee and the possessor are conceived of as being insepa- rable, as in (8).

(8)   That tree has few branches.
      My study has three windows.

Inanimate alienable possession. The possessor is inanimate and the possessee is separable from the possessor, as in (9).

(9)   That tree has crows on it.
      My study has a lot of useless books in it.

In English, all seven notions may be expressed somehow by using the item *have*, or else by genitive constructions, which means that these constructions are inherently "vague." An English sentence such as 'I have your book, but I have it at home', for example, suggests three different possessive notions: The first 'I have' involves tem- porary possession, the second 'I have' involves physical possession, and 'your book' involves permanent possession. In other languages, different expressions may be required for the various different possessive notions. On the basis of this notional distinction, we may propose the following definition: A possessive construction is one that is used habitually for the expression of any combination of the above notions.

5.1.4   Problems

In the course of the past decades a number of quasi-universal observations have been made on the behavior of predicative possession, such as the following (cf. Claudi (1986:4):

1. The clausal subject usually is the possessee (Clark 1978:102, 113; Ultan 1978a:34).
2. The possessor is usually encoded either in the clausal object or in some locative-based constituent (Ultan 1978a:34).

3. In spite of the previous two observations, the possessor precedes the possessee in the majority of languages. Clark (1978:101–2) attributes this to the preference for animate nominals to precede inanimate ones within a sentence (see the following discussion).

4. In many, and perhaps all, languages, existential and possessive constructions are related to locatives. Or, to take a slightly different perspective, possession belongs to the same general category as location. There are, however, a number of more specific views that have been expressed regarding the relationship between location and possession, such as the following:

   a. Possessive constructions are locational constructions. This view is held by Clark (1978:89), who argues that the possessor in constructions like 'Tom has a book' and 'The book is Tom's' "is simply an animate place."

   b. Possessive constructions are included in locational constructions. Lyons, for example, says it can be argued "that so-called possessive expressions are to be regarded as a subclass of locatives" (1977:474).

   c. Possessive constructions are derived from locative constructions, where the notion "derived" is not further specified. This is the position maintained by Lyons (1967), where it remains unclear whether he is concerned with diachronic or synchronic derivation, or with both. In a later paper (1968b), however, he argues that there should be some correlation between synchronic, diachronic, and ontogenetic derivation (cf. Clark 1978:90).

   d. Possessive constructions are historically derived from locative constructions.

Many of these statements are of doubtful value. For example, we are not aware of any substantial evidence that would support hypotheses (a) or (b). There are at least two reasons for separating possessive constructions from existential and locative constructions. First, the two show different morphosyntactic behavior; Clark (1978:97–8) observes, for example, that, unlike existential and locative constructions, possessive constructions do not show regular word order alternations depending on the definiteness of the possessed constituent. Second, and more important, they are simply different in meaning, and speakers usually are aware of this difference.

The preceding discussion has shown that a number of questions still need to be answered for a better understanding of what "possession" stands for. Thus, to understand have-constructions, questions such as the following must be addressed:

1. Why do expressions for predicative possession frequently resemble expressions for identification, description, existence, equation, and/or location?

2. Why do have-constructions frequently involve verbs having what Seiler (1988:94) calls a "marginal status," exhibiting, for instance,

systematic pardigmatic gaps in the inflectional and derivational morphology they are associated with? And why do so many languages employ "nonverbal" expressions for have-constructions (Welmers 1973:308ff.)?

3. Why does predicative possession exhibit such a large variety of different encodings in the languages of the world? For example, why is the possessor presented as the subject and the possessee as the complement in some languages or in some constructions of a given language, while in other languages or constructions the possessee appears as the subject and the possessor as a complement or oblique case expression?

4. In connection with (3): How can we explain the observation made by several authors (cf. Benveniste 1960:121; Bach 1967:479; Hopper 1972:119–200; Clark 1978:102, 111; Ultan 1978a:34) that the situation found in European languages (i.e., the presence of a verb 'have') is not typologically very common?

5. Why do quite a number of languages employ locative morphology for have-constructions?

6. If possessive expressions are to be regarded as a subclass of locatives (cf. Lyons 1977:474), what exactly does this mean?

7. Why is the syntax of have-constructions frequently highly idiosyncratic, in that it cannot be reconciled with rules operative elsewhere in the given language?

These questions are confined to the structure of have-constructions. A similar catalogue of questions could be added on other kinds of possessive constructions. With regard to attributive possession, for example, questions like the following may arise:

8. Why do markers of attributive possession frequently resemble markers of clausal case relations, such as locative, dative/benefactive, or ablative?

9. Why do possessive markers precede the possessor in some languages, like English, French, and many other European languages, but follow the possessor in other languages?

Finally, in more general terms, one may also wonder whether possession is a lexical or a grammatical concept—that is, whether it should be treated as being part of the lexicon or of grammar.

These are the kinds of questions that have been raised over the course of the past decades. We will now try to answer them.

5.2   Event schemas

Possession is a relatively abstract domain of human conceptualization, and, as we argue, expressions for it are derived from more concrete domains. These domains have to do with basic experiences relating to what one does (Action), where one is (Location), who one is accompanied by (Accompaniment), or what exists (Existence). Following Heine (1993), we will refer to stereotypical descriptions of such recurrent experiences as event schemas. An event schema has the properties commonly associated with schemas: It summarizes important attributes abstracted from a large number of related events, and it has to do with stereotyped situations with which we are constantly confronted (cf. Sanford 1985; Matlin 1989). The term roughly corresponds on the one hand to what Hengeveld (1992) calls a predication type and on the other hand to the notion of proposition as used by Langacker, who defines it as "a simple semantic unit consisting of a predicate and associated variables" (1978:857).

There are eight event schemas that account for the majority of possessive constructions in the languages of the world (see Claudi 1986; Heine 1997). These schemas are sketched in table 5-1. The schemas develop into possessive constructions, where X refers to the possessor and Y to the possessee. As we will see in the following discussion, not all of the schemas are used for all kinds of possessive constructions. Note further that two of these schemas (Genitive and Equation) are already possessive expressions, serving as sources for other possessive constructions.

We will now look at each of these schemas in turn. Note that whenever we use the expression "Y is derived from X" in the following paragraphs and chapters, we are referring to a diachronic process—more precisely, to a reconstruction according to which "X gave rise historically to Y." It goes without saying that there are languages whose have-constructions are synchronically opaque. Nevertheless, in a number of these languages there is evidence in the form of pattern transparency (see section 2.4) that allows us to reconstruct the schema involved.

5.2.1   The Action Schema

According to this schema, the notion of predicative possession is conceptually derived from a propositional structure that typically involves an agent, a patient, and some action or activity. In addition to 'take', a number of related action verbs can be employed, such as 'seize', 'grab', 'catch', and the like, but nondynamic and/or inactive verbs like 'hold', 'carry', 'get', 'find', 'obtain', 'acquire', or 'rule' can be used,

Table 5-1   A formulaic description of event schemas used as sources for possession (the target schema means invariably 'X has Y')

Source schema	Label of schema
X takes Y	Action
Y is located at X	Location
X is with Y	Companion
X's Y exists	Genitive
Y exists for/to X	Goal
Y exists from X	Source
As for X, Y exists	Topic
Y is X's (Y)	Equation

too. An example of the schema is found in (10); the have-constructions in European languages like English, German, or Spanish are further examples, involving earlier verbs meaning 'seize', 'hold', and the like as a predicate nucleus.

(10)   Nama (Central Khoisan, Khoisan; Heinz Roberg, personal communication)
        kxoe. p ke   'auto . sa 'uu hââ
        person. M TOP car   . F take PERF
        'The man has the car'. (Lit.: 'The man has taken a/the car.')

The Action Schema may give rise to have-constructions, as in (10), or to belong-constructions, but never to patterns of attributive possession.

5.2.2   The Location Schema

In accordance with its source form, the syntactic structure of possessive constructions derived from this schema is such that the possessee is encoded as the subject and the possessor as a locative complement, while the predicate is a locative copula or verb. The following example illustrates this schema as a source for have-constructions.

(11)   Estonian (Lehiste 1969:325)
        isal   on   raamat
        father. ADESSIVE 3. SG. be book. NOM
        'Father has (a) book.' (Lit.: 'The book is at father.')

Not infrequently, there is no, or no obligatory, verbal item as a predicate; the following example from Russian illustrates such a situation. As we will see in the following discussion, there are essentially two main explanations for this fact.

(12)   Russian (Lyons 1967:394)
        U menja kniga
        at me   book
        'I have a book.'

The Location Schema has two common subschemas involving formulas of the following kind:

(13)   a. Y is at X's home.
        b. Y is at X's body-part.

Examples of subschemas (13a) and (13b) are presented in (14), (15), and (16).

(14)   So (Kuliak, Nilo-Saharan; Carlin 1993:68)
        mek   Auca eo-   a   kus- in
        NEG. be : at Auca home- LOC skin- PL
        'Auca has no clothes.' (Lit.: 'Skins are not at Auca's home.')

(15)   Kpelle (Mande, Niger-Congo; Westermann 1924:20, 193ff.; see also Welmers 1973:316)
       sεŋkau   a n yee- i.
       money. PL be my hand- LOC
       'I have money.' (Lit.: 'Money is in my hand.')

(16)   Gisiga (Chadic, Afro-Asiatic; Lukas 1970:37)
       du   'a v'ə- ɗo
       millet at body- my
       'I have millet.' (Lit.: 'Millet [is] at my body.')

The body-part employed in (13b) is, in most cases, 'hand', as in (15), but it may also be 'head' or 'back' (see Claudi & Heine 1986; Claudi 1986). Instead of a body-part, it may be the entire body that serves as the nucleus of the locative phrase, as in (16).

The Location Schema forms one of the most frequently employed templates for expressing attributive possession: The possessor is conceptualized as the place where the possessee is located. The following is an example of attributive possession derived from Location (the possessive marker *pé* in (17) is derived from the relational noun **pé* 'place, area').

(17)   Ewe (Kwa, Niger-Congo)
       Kofí pé xɔ
       Kofi of house
       'Kofi's house' (Historically: 'The house at Kofi's place')

A more detailed treatment of Location as a source for attributive possession in African languages is found in Claudi & Heine (1989). What these authors observe is that when the Location Schema is grammaticalized to a kind of genitive construction, it is initially confined to the expression of alienable possession, with the effect that any preexisting pattern of attributive possession becomes reserved for inalienable possession (see the following discussion).

5.2.3   The Companion (or Accompaniment) Schema

Languages that use this pattern as a conceptual template for have-constructions are likely to encode the possessor as the subject and the possessee as a comitative complement. The example 'She is with child', at least as used in some dialects of English, illustrates the structure of this schema. The following are examples of Accompaniment:

(18)   a. Luo (Western Nilotic, Nilo-Saharan; Stafford 1967:18)
          Joluo   nɪ gɪ tɪm mabεyɔ.
          Luo : people COP with habit good. PL
          'The Luo have good customs.' (Lit.: 'The Luo are with good habits.')

       b. Mupun (Chadic, Afro-Asiatic; Frajzyngier 1993:264)
          war kə   siwol.
          3.F with money
          'She has money.' (Lit.: 'She with money')

The Companion Schema is largely confined to have-constructions, but a few instances of attributive possession do exist. The following is taken from Turkana, where it is confined to contexts where a kinship term (excluding *itòò* 'mother') functions as a possessor, as in the following examples (note that 'aunt' takes a masculine gender-prefix in Turkana, and 'father' a feminine prefix):

(19)   Turkana (Eastern Nilotic, Nilo-Saharan; Dimmendaal 1983:340)
    a. è- ya` kɛŋ` kà   à- pa`   kaŋ`
       M- aunt his   with F- father my
       'my father's aunt'

    b. a- mòtḭ kà   è- ya` kaŋ`
       F- pot   with M- aunt my
       'my aunt's pot'

5.2.4   The Genitive Schema

This schema is characterized by the fact that the possessor is encoded as a genitival modifier of the possessee. The schema exploits preexisting means of encoding possessive relations between thinglike entities—that is, attributive possession—for the encoding of propositional forms of possession. The schema involves a one-place propositional structure; examples are found in (20).

(20)   a. Turkish (Lyons 1967:395)
      Kitab- im var
      book-   my existent
      'I have a book.' (Lit.: 'My book exists.')

    b. Anywa (Western Nilotic, Nilo-Saharan; Reh 1994)
      dá   cí-   ɛ́.
      exist   wife : of- 3 : SG
      'He has a wife.' (Lit.: 'His wife exists.')

5.2.5   The Goal Schema

As a source for predicative possession, this schema typically consists of a verb of existence or of location, where the possessor is encoded as a dative/benefactive or goal case expression and the possessee typically is a subject. Since dative/benefactive markers are frequently derived from allative/directional markers, the latter functions may also be part of the case marking figuring in the Goal Schema. The following are examples of this schema:

(21)   a. Bolivian Quechua (Quechuan, Andean; Bills, Vallejo, & Troike 1969:186)
      waska tiya- puwan.
      rope   exist- for. me
      'I have a rope.'

b. Breton (Celtic, Indo-European; Orr 1992:252–3)

ur   velo c'hlas am   eus
a   bike blue   to : me   is
'I have a blue bike.'

The Goal Schema is not only widespread as a source for have-constructions, but it is also equally popular as a template for forming belong-constructions, as in (22), as well as for patterns of attributive possession, as in (23).

(22)   French
Le livre est à moi.
the book is to me
'The book belongs to me.'

(23)   Aranda (Pama-Nyungan; Wilkins 1989:135, 179)
Toby- ke   alere
Toby- DAT child
'Toby's child'

In the case of attributive possession, the possessor is introduced by means of some directional marker, usually an allative, dative, or benefactive adposition or case inflection. The following examples are taken from West African Pidgin English, where the possessive marker is the benefactive preposition *fo* (< English *for*), and from Diyari, which uses the dative inflection for this purpose. Diyari has a morphological distinction between alienable and inalienable possession, and the Goal Schema is used for both, as can be seen in (24b) and (24c), respectively.

(24)   a. West African Pidgin English (Schneider 1966:92)
aprántis fo kápenta   wok-tíng fo mésan
'an apprentice of the carpenter'   'tools of/for the mason'

b. Diyari (Pama-Nyungan; Austin 1981:137)
nhulu kuḍu   paku-yi wilha-ya wana-   li
he. A hole. ABS dig- PRES woman-DAT digging. stick- ERG
'He is digging a hole with a woman's digging stick.'

c. yini   thika- Ø-   mayi nhuwa yiŋkaṇa-   ya
you. S return- IMP- EMPH spouse 2. SG. DAT- ALL
'You go back to your husband.'

Isolated instances of the Goal Schema are also to be found in English (cf. 'secretary to the president').

5.2.6   The Source Schema

This schema is largely confined to attributive possession; it does not seem to provide a relevant source for have-constructions. The formal exponent of the schema is the use of an ablative or related morphological means for encoding the possessor.

Instances of the Source Schema are not difficult to come by; common examples can be found in European languages, including the English *of*-genitive, the German *von*-genitive, and the Romance *de*-genitives, all of which may be said to be historically derived from a structure where the prepositional element had an ablative or source function ('(away) from' or 'out of') as its focal, or one of its focal, senses.

The notion "Source Schema" must not be confused with "source schema" (lowercase); with the latter term, we refer to any schema that may serve as a structural template or source for a grammatical construction.

5.2.7   The Topic Schema

Another type of possessive construction has the possessor presented as a kind of theme: It appears as a topic or theme constituent in initial position but figures in addition as a possessive modifier of the possessee. An example of a have-construction derived from this schema is found in (25).

(25)   Lango (Western Nilotic, Nilo-Saharan; Noonan 1992:148)
    òkélò gwók'kérê pé
    Okelo dog.his   3. NEG. exist
    'Okelo doesn't have a dog.' (Lit.: 'As for Okelo, his dog does not exist')

Since the topicalized constituent tends to acquire properties of a subject and to be increasingly grammaticalized as a subject, the final result is a construction effectively having two subjects; Seiler (1983:60) therefore proposes the term "double subject strategy" for such cases.

The Topic Schema may not be very widespread as a source for have-constructions. As a source for attributive possession, however, it provides one of the most common templates. Examples of this schema include the following.

(26)   a. Afrikaans (Germanic, Indo-European)
      die boer se huis
      the farmer his house
      'the farmer's house'

    b. Kairiru (Oceanic, Austronesian; Lichtenberk 1985:99)
      Nur yaqal qajuo- ny
      Nur he   cousin- his
      'Nur's cousin'

5.2.8   The Equation Schema

Finally, there is a propositional structure that appears to be based on the partial or total equation of two different items. The formula that we proposed earlier for this schema was 'Y is X's (Y)' (where X is the possessor and Y the possessee); examples are found in (27).

(27)   a. English
      The car is mine.

b. Swahili (Bantu, Niger-Congo)
   Gari ni yangu
   car   is mine
   'The car is mine.'

In this schema, the possessor is presented as a genitival modifier, in the same way as in the case of the Genitive Schema, and the presence of a construction of attributive possession is presupposed. Apart from belong-constructions, no other possessive constructions are derived from the Equation Schema.

ONE OF THE MAIN findings arrived at in the preceding discussion is that predicative and attributive possession are built on the same general conceptual pattern. This means, in particular, that the sources from which they are derived are largely the same. The sources and the resulting possessive constructions are listed in table 5-2. The data summarized here involve fully grammaticalized patterns only. The data would seem to suggest that have-constructions are associated with the largest range of conceptual sources and belong-constructions with the smallest, with attributive possession being in between. There is only one source schema—namely, Goal—that gives rise to all three kinds of possessive constructions.

More research is required on the relationship between sources and targets. It seems that some correlations can be interpreted meaningfully—for example, the fact that the Action Schema is a source for both have- and belong-constructions but not for attributive possession. Whereas the latter is a static and time-stable concept, both the Action Schema and the two kinds of predicative possession typically involve dynamic situations. On the other hand, it remains unclear, for instance, why the Source Schema ('Y exists from X') is confined essentially to attributive possession.

While predicative and attributive possession involve the same pool of sources, more often than not they are derived from entirely different schemas in a given language. By contrast, it may happen that have-constructions and attributive possession are both derived historically from the same source schema in one and the same language. The southern African Kxoé language illustrates such a situation, where the Location Schema has been exploited for both predicative (28a) and attributive possession (28b).

Table 5-2   The main source schemas and the possessive constructions derived from them

Source schema	Have-constructions	Belong-constructions	Attributive possession
Action	+	+	−
Location	+	−	+
Companion	+	−	+
Genitive	+	−	−
Goal	+	+	+
Source	−	−	+
Topic	+	−	+
Equation	−	+	−

(28)   Kxoé (Central Khoisan; Köhler 1973:78, 94)
    a. bó 'à   tcá ò tìn ré.`káré
       axe ACC you at be QU
       'Do you have an axe?' (Lit.: 'Is there an axe at your place')

    b. tí 'ò /oán- djì
       I at child- F. PL
       'my daughters' (Lit.: 'female children at my place')

On the whole, however, situations like that found in Kxoé are not very common; in the majority of languages for which reliable information is available, different source schemas are recruited for attributive and for predicative possession (Heine 1997).

5.3   Morphosyntactic implications

We observed in the introductory section to this chapter that the syntax of have-constructions is frequently highly idiosyncratic in that it cannot be reconciled with syntactic patterns operative elsewhere in the language. The overall reason for this, it seems, is that the syntactic structure typically associated with source schemas like Location or Goal is not necessarily appropriate to encode possessive notions. This means that, whenever such a source schema is gradually reinterpreted as, for instance, a have-construction, this is likely to result in morphosyntactic restructuring of some kind. We will illustrate the process concerned with one example; the reader is referred to Heine (1997) for more exemplification.

    While the syntax of a given possessive construction can largely be predicted once we know the event schema from which it is derived, some additional factors also influence the shape of possessive constructions. Perhaps the most important concerns two discourse-pragmatic principles that may determine the linear arrangement of linguistic expressions for predicative possession. These are (cf. Clark 1978):

    1. Definite participants tend to precede indefinite ones.
    2. Animate participants tend to precede inanimate ones.

In the case of the Action and the Companion Schemas, no problems exist, since the syntax of these schemas is in accordance with the two principles. In the case of the other schemas, however, the principles are at variance with basic word order constraints, since in such schemas, typically inanimate and indefinite possessee arguments precede human and definite possessors, and the possessor is not the subject, as is suggested by the structure of source schemas summarized in table 5-3.

    Languages differ with regard to the way they resolve this conflict between word order constraints and discourse-pragmatic principles. One widespread strategy is to topicalize the possessor, with the effect that arguments having a locative or dative morphology appear in clause-initial position when they express possessors but not when they express other kinds of participants. The peculiar morphosyntactic structures that may arise as a result of the reinterpretation of source schemas like Location or Goal as possessive schemas have been discussed by Hagège (1993) and Heine (1997); the main effect is what may be called *transitivization*.

Table 5-3 Typical participant encoding in have-constructions according to source schema

Source schema	Target schema	
	Possessor	Possessee
Action	Subject	Object
Location	Locative complement	Subject
Companion	Subject	Comitative adjunct
Genitive	Genitive modifier	Subject
Goal	Dative adjunct	Subject
Topic	Theme, subject	Subject

The development from concrete source schema to possession is likely to activate forces that result in definite participants being placed before indefinite ones, and animate participants being placed before inanimate ones. The hypothetical end point of this process is a predication structure with the following characteristics:

1. The possessor precedes the possessee.
2. The possessor has properties of a subject, and the possessee has properties of a clausal object.
3. The possessor is definite and the possessee is indefinite.

Nevertheless, what we usually find are situations in which have-constructions retain some properties of their conceptual source but additionally acquire some properties characteristic of the "transitivization" process. The result is a structure that has been described by Heine, Claudi, and Hünnemeyer (1991:231–3) as a "hybrid form": The possessive construction concerned combines the properties of its nonpossessive conceptual source with the target properties listed in (1) through (3) above. I will now illustrate the nature of such hybrid forms with an example from Hungarian.

The major pattern of predicative possession in this language is provided by the Goal Schema '*Y* exists for/to *X*'. The structure that this pattern normally shows is sketched in (29a); an example is found in (29b).

(29)   Hungarian (Biermann 1985)
    a. Possessor- nak van Possessee-PRON
              DAT is

    b. a   férfi- nek van ház- a.
       the man- DAT is   house- 3. SG
       'The man has a house.'

The possessee noun phrase is encoded in the nominative case (marked by zero) and has an obligatory pronominal suffix (PRON) agreeing with the possessor in person, and optionally in number.

While the case morphology of (29a) exhibits a clause structure dative–verb––nominative, the actual use patterns are at variance with such a structure. Rather, these patterns suggest a process in which the dative-marked possessor noun phrase (henceforth: the possessor) has gained a number of subject properties, and, in a parallel fashion, the nominative-marked possessee noun phrase (the possessee) has lost some properties that one would expect of canonical subjects in Hungarian. This claim is based on the following observations made by Biermann (1985:96ff.):

1. Like canonical subjects in the nominative case, the possessor can be deleted if its reference has been established by the preceding discourse.
2. Like subjects, the possessor is normally referred to in the following discourse by means of zero anaphora, while the formal subject—that is, the possessee—is likely to use a demonstrative (*az*) for anaphoric reference, as do nonsubject participants.
3. The possessor triggers agreement on the possessee.
4. The possessor is definite and is likely to act as the clausal topic, while the possessee is indefinite and rarely has a topic function.
5. The possessor is what Biermann (1985:135) calls a fully specified noun phrase, while the possessee is not.

To summarize, the Hungarian have-construction has developed a form that has no immediate parallel elsewhere in the clausal syntax of the language. Even if some of its characteristics can also be observed in other parts of the language, the construction as a whole is "*sui generis,*" as Biermann (1985:83) calls it.

Processes of shift, as in this Hungarian example, appear to be most dramatic in the case of have-constructions derived from the Goal Schema. Hebrew offers another example of such a case: Its major have-construction is a canonical instance of the Goal Schema, as illustrated in (30). There are two varieties of modern Hebrew, however: Colloquial Israeli Hebrew (henceforth: colloquial Hebrew) and Normative Literary Hebrew (henceforth: literary Hebrew), and the process has affected only colloquial Hebrew.

(30) Literary Hebrew (Ziv 1976:130)
      haya   lemoshe shaon   shveycari.
      was.3.M to. Moshe watch:M Swiss:M
      'Moshe had a Swiss watch.'

The possessee (*shaon shveycari* 'Swiss watch') is the formal subject, while the possessor (*lemoshe* 'to Moshe') is an oblique participant. In colloquial Hebrew, the possessee has lost most subject properties, while the possessor appears to be gaining in subject properties. This process is reflected in the following developments observed by Ziv (1976):

1. As (30) shows, the possessor normally precedes the possessee. Note that this applies to both literary and colloquial Hebrew.
2. Whereas in literary Hebrew a definite nominal possessee occurs in the subject case—that is, the nominative—it is assigned the definite accusative case marker *et* in colloquial Hebrew.

3. In literary Hebrew, the possessee controls verb agreement; in colloquial Hebrew, however, the definite nominal possessee loses control of verb agreement.
4. In literary Hebrew, the nominal possessee can undergo subject raising to subject position; the definite possessee of colloquial Hebrew, however, does not normally undergo subject raising.
5. In some cases, the nominal possessor is now emerging in subject position—that is, before the verb *haya* (Ziv 1976:144).

To summarize, the definite possessee of colloquial Hebrew has been reanalyzed as a nonsubject, if not as a direct object, while the possessor has acquired subject properties. Note, however, that this process is largely confined to definite possessees; it has not (yet) affected indefinite possessees. The result is a hybrid have-construction in colloquial Hebrew, a construction that has neither a clear subject nor a clear object.

Similar observations have been made by Hagège (1993). On the one hand, his concern is with the transition from possession to tense, aspect, and modality. On the other hand, he is concerned with what he calls the reanalysis of "be structures" as "have structures." With regard to the latter process, Hagège presents, in particular, the following examples:

1. Nineteenth-century Manchu, an Altaic language, developed its Goal Schema ('*Y* exists for/to *X*') into a have-construction whereby the possessor loses the dative case marking and is reanalyzed as the subject of the clause.
2. Classical Arabic has grammaticalized the Goal Schema to a have-construction. Maltese has gone one step further. In this closely related Semitic language, the dative-marked possessor phrase has acquired a number of subject properties: The nominal possessor phrase has assumed the role of a sentence-initial subject and topic, showing agreement with the predicate verbal *kon* 'be'. (1993:66ff.)

The final stage of this general evolution is reached when a transitive have-verb emerges, as appears to have happened in Cornish (Stassen 1995).

These few examples may suffice to illustrate what happens, or may happen, when a nonpossessive source gives rise to a possessive schema. Different effects can be observed when source schemas other than the one looked at here (the Goal Schema) are involved. With the use of the Topic Schema, for example, a clause structure having two subjects is likely to evolve (Heine 1997). What all this seems to imply is that people do not care much about what morphological or syntactic complexities and irregularities they create by choosing a certain schema; there must be other motivations that are of greater concern to them.

5.4   Explaining possessive constructions

On the basis of the observations made in the preceding sections, we are now in a position to answer the questions raised in section 5.1.

1. The question of why expressions for predicative possession frequently resemble expressions for location, existence, or description can be answered in the following way: The majority of schemas employed for the grammaticalization of predicative possession involve predicates whose original meaning has to do with location, existence, and the like.

2. This also answers the question of why so many languages employ "nonverbal" expressions for predicative possession, or why have-constructions frequently involve verbs with a "marginal status" that exhibit, for instance, systematic paradigmatic gaps. First, one can appeal to the nature of the verbs figuring in the source schemas of have-constructions: Structures such as the Location, the Companion, and other schemas frequently involve copula-like items as predicates, and such items typically exhibit reduced verbal behavior. Second, one may invoke the effects of grammaticalization. Even if the source schema involves a full-fledged verb, as is always the case when the Action Schema is recruited, that verb tends to lose in verbal properties once it becomes a marker of predicative possession. Such properties include the ability to take the whole range of morphological trappings characteristic of full verbs, or to be associated with distinctions of tense, aspect, negation, person, and number.

3. We also asked why predicative possession exhibits such a large variety of different encodings in the languages of the world. That the possessor in have-constructions is encoded either as a subject, an object, a locative, a comitative, or a genitival constituent—that is, that it may be associated with virtually any of the existing case markings—is due to the fact that such constructions can be traced to a small pool of contrasting conceptual schemas and that each schema provides a specific template for the morphosyntax of the resulting possessive construction. Thus, as can be seen in table 5-3, the possessor will be encoded as the sentence subject in languages that have recruited the Action or the Companion Schema, while the possessor can be predicted to be encoded as a locative complement in languages that have made use of Location, or as a dative (that is, an allative, benefactive, or dative) adjunct in languages using the Goal Schema.

4. A number of authors have pointed out that the situation found in European languages is typologically somewhat exotic. There is an obvious reason for this: The linguistic structure of have-constructions in the Romance and the Germanic languages (though much less so in the Slavic, Celtic, or Finno-Ugric languages) is determined primarily by the effects of one particular schema—that is, the Action Schema (even if this is no longer synchronically recoverable in most of the cases concerned). This fact accounts for a pattern of encoding of verbal possession that is relatively uniform on the one hand and "exotic" on the other: uniform, in that the possessor is typically encoded as the sentence subject, and the possessee as the object, and

"exotic" because the Action Schema is not among the most frequently employed source structures in the languages of the world.

5. Another issue concerns the question of why quite a number of languages employ locative morphology for have-constructions. Here the answer has two parts. First, the Location Schema is one of the predominant sources for have-constructions in the languages of the world. Second, it is not infrequent that verbs of existence, which form the predicate nucleus of a number of different source schemas (see table 5-1), are historically derived from locative predicates. Thus, even in cases where the Location Schema is not immediately involved, we should not be surprised to find have-constructions that are etymologically related to locatives.

6. This brings us to perhaps the most widely discussed issue in this general debate—namely, the question of how such notions as existence, identification, and location are related to the notion of possession. Are they all the same? Are they different, while belonging to the same general ontological category? Or are the structural similarities to be observed between them in many languages accidental? As we have tried to establish in the preceding discussion, all these questions have to be answered in the negative. There is no reason to doubt that these notions are conceptually distinct. Nevertheless, they are in a relation of conceptual and diachronic derivation, in that expressions for predicative possession are derived from expressions for action, location, and the like. Thus, perhaps the most meaningful way to account for these structural similarities is by referring to the cognitive transfer patterns involved.

7. The question of why the syntax of possessive constructions is frequently peculiar, in that it cannot be reconciled with rules operative elsewhere in the language concerned, has been dealt with chiefly in section 5.3. For example, as we saw there, locative complements tend to acquire subject properties, and subjects acquire object properties, when the Goal Schema ('*Y* exists to/for *X*') is grammaticalized to a have-construction.

The preceding answers all relate to the structure of have-constructions. But in section 5.1 we also raised a couple of questions regarding attributive possession. We wondered, for example, why markers of attributive possession frequently resemble markers of clausal case relations, such as locative, dative/benefactive, or ablative case relations. The answer to this question is by now obvious: These are the kind of markers that figure in the source structures concerned. Thus, languages that have made use of the Location Schema are likely to have genitive markers that resemble or are identical with locative morphemes, while in languages that have drawn on the Source Schema, like English (*of*) or Spanish (*de*), we are likely to find genitive markers that resemble ablative case morphemes, be they adpositions or inflectional items.

We were also concerned with why possessive markers precede the possessor in languages like English (*of*) and Spanish (*de*), but follow the possessor in others. There is a straightforward answer: Predictably, prepositional languages like English and Spanish have the genitive/possessive marker *before* the possessor because in the development from source to target schema we are dealing with the reinterpretation of a prepositional structure like (31a) as (31b). Conversely, we will predict that in postpositional languages using the Source, Goal, or Location Schema, the opposite order can be expected to obtain—that is, the genitive/possessive marker will follow the possessor, since we are dealing with a reinterpretation of (32a) as (32b), as illustrated by our Kxoé example (28b) (note that instead of a postposition, there may be, for instance, a case suffix in [32a]).

(31) a. preposition   + noun phrase   >
      b. genitive marker   + possessor

(32) a. noun phrase   + postposition   >
      b. possessor   + genitive marker

In conclusion, after having looked at a wide range of languages worldwide, one may raise the following question: Why is it that the English have-construction has transitive syntax? And why is the possessor encoded as the subject and the possessee as the direct object, considering the fact that such a structure is not extremely common in the languages of the world? The answer has been provided essentially in the preceding remarks: the English have-construction (like that of other Germanic or Romance languages) is derived from the Action Schema involving an Indo-European verb meaning 'seize, take' as the predicate nucleus. And although that meaning has disappeared, the English construction has retained the main syntactic properties associated with this schema—namely, a transitive clause structure where the possessor is encoded as the subject and the possessee is encoded as the direct object (see table 5-3). This leaves us with the question of why English *have* is a transitive verb but at the same time lacks essential properties associated with transitive verbs, such as the ability to passivize (ignoring rare examples like 'A good time was had by everyone'; Orin Gensler, personal communication). The answer has to do with cross-linguistic regularities in the evolution of grammatical categories: This evolution entails decategorialization. With reference to the Action Schema, this means that the verb loses in properties characteristic of its category; in the case of action verbs, the ability to passivize is one of the earliest casualties to be observed in such decategorialization (see Heine 1993).

Thus, although the English have-construction has come a long way since the time it arose, its morphosyntax can be understood meaningfully only with reference to the way it evolved. In short, we need to know how this, or any other, construction is motivated in order to explain why it has the properties it has, and why it differs so drastically from corresponding have-constructions, say, in Turkish or Swahili.

5.5 Summary

Discussions of possession and/or ownership have occasionally focused on issues that concern the relationship between language structure and extralinguistic human behavior.

One such issue centers around the question of whether linguistics might not shed light on the evolution of mankind—for example, whether earlier generations of mankind might not have conceptualized possession differently from the way modern societies do. According to a widespread thesis expounded by Indo-Europeanists and others, "primitive societies" lacked grammaticalized expressions for possession, or at least had a different understanding of it. For Isačenko, for example, possession proper "is a legal notion appearing in societies after they have reached a certain stage of development" (1974:64), and he is therefore not surprised that he fails to reconstruct a have-verb for Proto-Indo-European. Another, related, claim has it that the spread of the Action Schema in the languages of Western societies has had to do with the development of "active" modes of social and economic interaction—more particularly, with the rise of capitalism. Finally, according to a third thesis, the development from concrete possession ('He has two cars') to abstract possession ('He has two problems') is characteristic of Western societies and is indicative of the "alienation" that these societies have experienced (Fromm 1976).

We have found no empirical substantiation for any of these theses. The grammaticalization of the Action Schema is not confined to the Western world; it is also found in other parts of the world where quite different social, economic, and technological conditions obtain. Also, abstract possession is in no way characteristic solely of languages like English and German but may be found in much the same way in other languages.

These, as well as many other generalizations that have been proposed on extralinguistic correlates of possessive constructions, suffer from what one might call the "literal-meaning fallacy." A given linguistic expression, it is argued, has a basic or literal meaning; if that expression is found to have additional meanings, this fact is taken as evidence for speculations on the mental, cultural, social, and other attributes presumed to be characteristic of the people using that expression. Two things are ignored in this kind of research. First, in many languages worldwide, abstract concepts like possession are expressed by exploiting a small pool of concrete source structures. Once the Location or Companion Schema has given rise to a have-construction, the new meaning of possession is likely to gradually replace the old one, with the effect that, in the end, there is a possessive construction characterized by a locative or comitative morphology even if a locative or comitative meaning is no longer discernible. Second, the transfer from source structures to the target structures of possession leads to the emergence of chainlike linguistic structures: Possessive constructions are only part of more extensive grammaticalization chains. A simplified form of these chains is sketched in (33), where P_1, P_2, and so on stand for the various possessive notions distinguished above, and X, Y are nonpossessive:

(33) $X > P_1 > P_2 \ldots > P_n > Y$

The grammaticalization chain associated with a given linguistic form may cover any subrange of the concepts figuring in (33). If, in addition to one or more of the possessive notions, it also includes either X or Y, as is frequently the case, then the form concerned is "polysemous" to the extent that it has both possessive and nonpossessive uses. The English have-construction expresses a number of different possessive notions, like the one exemplified in (34a), but it has also expanded beyond P_n into the Y region, in that it has entered new domains of grammatical meaning such as aspect, as in (34b), or modality, as in (34c).

(34)   a. Jane has a cough.
      b. She has left.
      c. Ron has to leave too.

Thus, the fact that expressions for possession are also used to convey other meanings can be accounted for in a principled way by reference to the cognitive forces that gave rise to them; it need not be due to culture-specific mental, social, or other conditions.

A question that may arise in this connection is whether possession belongs to, or should be treated within, the domain of the lexicon or those of grammar. Closely related to this issue is the following question: Are verbs meaning 'have' less meaningful than other verbs? Is English *have* meaningless, as Bach (1967:476–7) and others have claimed, or are its semantics not really different from those of other verbs, as others argue (see Brugman 1988:41ff.)? An answer to this question depends crucially on the theoretical framework one adopts. On the basis of the present framework, one may say that possession is located along a conceptual chain that is lexical at one end (X in [33]) and grammatical at the other (Y). As we just noted, the English have-construction covers a wide spectrum of uses along the chain in (33). In utterances like (34a) its use is located somewhere in the center of the chain where one might still find grounds for relating *have* to the lexicon. In utterances like (34b) and (34c), however, it no longer makes much sense to treat *have* as a lexical item.

To summarize, grammaticalization chains like the one represented by the various uses of English *have* do not stop at boundaries such as the one between a lexical and a grammatical domain. More often than not they ignore such boundaries: Possessive constructions are likely to include uses that may be said to be primarily lexical, while others are more strongly suggestive of grammatical behavior. Thus the opposition of lexicon versus grammar is a false dichotomy.

A number of detailed treatments have become available on the subject matter discussed here (see especially Locker 1954; Benveniste 1960; Ultan 1978a; Clark 1978; Seiler 1983; Wilson 1983; Hengeveld 1992). In most of these studies, the relationship between be- and have-constructions has been an issue of major concern. With few exceptions, such as Locker (1954) and Claudi (1986), however, no attempt was made in these studies to account for this relationship in terms of conceptual transfer patterns—in short, with reference to grammaticalization. These patterns are diachronic in nature, but, since diachronic processes tend to be retained in the synchronic state of a given language in the form of contextually defined variation, they are in much the same way an issue for synchronic description, too.

OUR MAIN CONCERN in this chapter has been with crosslinguistic generalizations relating to a fairly complex subject area. It goes without saying that a number of questions could not be addressed, such as the following. What makes schema X, rather than schema Y, eligible for a specific grammatical concept? Are there any correlations between a given source schema and a specific kind of possessive concept? For example, how does the distinction between alienable and inalienable possession relate to the distinction of source schemas? Why are source schemas grammaticalized exactly the way they are? For example, why does the use of the Location Schema inevitably lead to the development from 'Y is located at X' to 'Possessee is located where the possessor is', rather than to 'Possessor is located where the possessee is'? Some possible answers may be proposed, but a more comprehensive understanding of such patterns of grammaticalization is obviously needed.

The observations made here explain why any attempt at setting up one single universal structure of possession, which would account for all the morphosyntactic variation to be found in all the languages of the world, is doomed to failure. Such attempts have been made time and again in the history of linguistics, most recently by Freeze (1992). Obviously, there can be no one universally uniform linguistic pattern for have-constructions, since schemas like Action and Location require drastically different patterns of linguistic encoding. The observations made also show why a number of other generalizations proposed for have-constructions can easily be falsified. For example, in his worldwide survey of have-constructions, Ultan (1978a:37) concludes that a subject-marked possessor implies a comitative-marked possessee; translated into our terminology, this means that the Companion Schema would be the only source for possessors encoded as subjects. This claim can easily be falsified since, as we saw, there is a second schema that gives rise to possessors marked as sentence-subjects—namely, the Action Schema. Predictably, therefore, European languages like English, German, French, and Spanish, whose major source schema for have-constructions is the Action Schema, have subject-marked possessors but not comitative-marked possessive expressions.

We have confined ourselves in this chapter to just one domain of grammar—possession. But many of the generalizations made also hold true for other kinds of categories. For example, most of the auxiliaries used for the expression of tense and aspect in the languages of the world can be traced back to ten basic event schemas (Heine 1993). What is perhaps even more noteworthy is that the same concrete source schemas are always recruited as structural templates for the expression of more abstract meanings. Thus, schemas like Action (what one does), Location (where one is located), Motion (where one moves from/to), or Companion (who one is accompanied by or associated with) can be expected to provide the most convenient and the most frequently employed templates—not only for the expression of possession but also for expressions of grammatical categories like perfect/anterior, progressive, and comparative. Moreover, the same linguistic process—grammaticalization—is always triggered. One characteristic of this process is that it involves an overlap stage, where the expression concerned can be interpreted simultaneously with reference to both the source meaning and the target meaning—that is, where there is ambiguity between the two meanings. Thus, rather than being unusual or abnormal, ambiguity constitutes a predictable component in the development and uses of possessive constructions.

As in the preceding chapters, the main goal here was to illustrate that grammar is an embodiment and a reflection of the way we both conceptualize the world around us and use the knowledge acquired to communicate with others of our species. In this respect, the present observations are in agreement with those made by others working in the field of cognitive linguistics, for instance (especially Lakoff 1987; Langacker 1987; Wierzbicka 1988). I differ from these authors in that I argue that embodiment does not take place overnight and out of context; for a locative construction to turn into a have-construction, it takes time and requires an appropriate communicative environment.

6

COMPARISON

The domain of comparison in general, and the term "comparative construction" in particular, refer to a number of different conceptual and linguistic forms. The main kinds of comparative notions that are commonly distinguished are listed in table 6-1. One may wonder whether (a) is an instance of a comparative construction at all, since it never receives any formal marking in the languages of the world (Ultan 1972:121). Like (f) and (g), (a) does not specify the standard of comparison. Types (b), (c), and (d), on the other hand, have a formal expression of comparison. Type (e) is somewhat complicated. It is formally implicit, yet it implies more than two compared items; one major characteristic of superlatives is precisely that they entail comparisons between at least three different comparees or items compared (cf. Andersen 1983:100).

Table 6-1   Types of comparative notions (cf. Ultan 1972; Andersen 1983:100; Stolz & Stolz 1994)

Notion	Example
a Positive	David is smart.
b Equative	David is as smart as Bob.
c Superior comparative	David is smarter than Bob.
d Inferior comparative	David is less smart than Bob.
e Superlative	David is the smartest.
f Elative	David is very smart.
g Excessive	David is too smart.

My interest here is exclusively with (c)—that is, with superior comparatives, which are considered by some to represent the most prototypical of all comparative constructions. Accordingly, I will confine myself to predications of the kind illustrated in (1).

(1)   David is smart-er than Bob.
       X   *Y*   *D M*   *Z*

Such constructions are based on propositions involving the following five elements:

(2)   *X* = comparee
       Y = predicate
       D = degree marker
       M = marker of standard
       Z = standard

In example (1), *David* would be the comparee *X*, that is, the item compared; *is smart*, the predicate *Y*; and *Bob*, the standard *Z*. The degree marker *D* is encoded as -*er*, and the marker of standard *M* as *than*.

In many languages, *M* (the marker of standard) constitutes the only formal expression of comparison—that is, there is no degree marker *D*. Such languages include, among others, Telugu, Japanese, Eskimo, Gujarati, Aramaic, Worora, Swahili, and Ewe. In other languages again, such as Yurok, Malagasy, Kui, Coptic, and Eastern Cheremis, the use of a degree marker is optional. Finally, in languages including English, German, French, Russian, Hungarian, Samoan, and Kanuri, there is an obligatory degree marker. Our concern here is with *M*, the marker of standard, irrespective of whether it also denotes the degree.

The way the concepts distinguished in (2) are linguistically encoded differs from one language to another, but also from one construction to another within the same language. For example, the degree marker may be an affix like English -*er* or an independent word or particle like *more*, and the marker of standard may be encoded as an adposition, a clitic, or a case inflection; it may even lack any formal expression whatsoever. What is essential for a comparative construction to exist is that a distinction between the comparee *X* and the standard *Z*, involving the predicate *Y* and the marker of standard *M*, should be conveyed to the hearer in some way or other, irrespective of how these concepts are encoded in a given case.

There is some confusion surrounding the terminology of comparative constructions, as can be seen in the list of labels compiled in (3). This list contains terms that have been used as alternatives for those proposed in (2).

(3)   Alternative names for comparative notions
       X = topic, pivot (Friedrich 1975:27); link (Andersen 1983:116)
       Y = comment, adjective (Greenberg 1963a:69–70)
       D = marker (Lehmann 1972:179; Andersen 1983:116–7); comparative concept ("more";
             Heine 1994a:56–7); grade (Stolz & Stolz 1994)
       M = pivot (Lehmann 1972:179); marker (Greenberg 1963a:69; Friedrich 1975:27;
             Andersen 1983:116–7); relator (Stolz & Stolz 1994)

The confusion concerns in particular the fact that one and the same term—"pivot" or "marker"—is sometimes used for entirely different concepts.

The notion of a crosslinguistic comparative construction is not easy to establish, especially since in all languages we are familiar with there are a host of differing constructions that can be subsumed under this label, and not all of them are entirely functionally equivalent. According to Stassen (1985:24), a comparative construction is present if the relevant construction "has the semantic function of assigning a graded (i.e. non-identical) position on a predicative scale to two (possibly complex) objects." We will adopt this definition wherever possible, although Stassen's interpretation differs in some ways from the one presented here. More specifically, we will use the term "comparative construction" (or, for short, "comparative") whenever comparisons

- involve the two entities X and Z and a quality or property (Y)
- express inequality between X and Z
- are explicit (as in [c] in table 6-1) rather than implicit (e.g., 'David is smarter')
- involve a result rather than the process of comparison (cf. Andersen 1983:99)

The situation to be found for English in table 6-1 is perhaps not typical of what one might expect in the majority of the languages of the world: Frequently, there is no separate form for the degree marker D; rather, comparisons are marked exclusively by means of M, the marker of standard, or else by an item that combines the meaning of D and M, as can be seen in the following example:

(4) Swahili (Bantu, Niger-Congo)
     Hamisi mfupi kushinda Juma.
     Hamisi short than   Juma
     'Hamisi is shorter than Juma.'

The item *kushinda* in (4), whose literal meaning is 'to defeat', is the only marker that signals comparison.

6.1 Event schemas

The main claim made in this chapter is that, like other grammatical expressions, comparative markers tend to be derived from other, more concrete, entities. In particular, I argue that most comparative constructions in the languages of the world are derived from a limited number of conceptual source structures, which are referred to as event schemas (see section 5.2). The majority of language data presented here is taken from Stassen's (1985) seminal work *Comparison and Universal Grammar*.

A large variety of morphological and syntactic structures are employed in the languages of the world to express comparatives. To describe and explain these structures, a knowledge of the source schemas from which comparatives are derived seems indispensable. The main schemas that have been found to be employed in the languages of the world are summarized in table 6-2. Note that the structures listed are not all of the same importance (see the following discussion).

That there exists a limited pool of event schemas that can be held responsible for structuring certain domains of experience and for expressing abstract concepts has been illustrated in the previous chapter, where we were concerned with possession. Similarly, it has been shown that the primary way of developing tense and aspect categories in the languages of the world is the grammaticalization of a small number of basic event schemas which are either identical or similar to the ones listed in table 6-2 (Heine 1993).

As the following discussion shows, the frequency of occurrence of the schemas listed in table 6-2 differs greatly across languages. While the first five schemas (Action, Location, Source, Goal, and Polarity) are relatively common, the remainder are virtually negligible as sources for comparatives.

Neither the taxonomy nor the terminology proposed in table 6-2 is exactly the same in all the works devoted to the present subject. The classification used by other authors differs in a number of ways from that proposed here. Approximate correspondences between the schemas proposed here and the construction types distinguished elsewhere are laid out in table 6-3. We will now look at each of the various source schemas in turn.

6.1.1   The Action Schema

When the Action Schema is employed, the comparee is portrayed as a kind of agent. The concept *surpasses* in the formula 'X is Y surpasses Z' stands for verbal notions such as 'defeat', 'win over', 'exceed', and the like (see the following discussion), not all of which, however, are necessarily verbs of action. The Action Schema may be illustrated in English with examples such as 'He surpasses all of them in cleverness.'

There are a number of different variants of the Action Schema (cf. Stassen 1985:43ff.). Perhaps the most common variant consists of a sequence of two clauses or predications where the comparee (X) is presented first and the standard (Z) thereafter, as in (5a). The others consist, first, of a variant where there is only a single predication, with a nonfinite verb occurring instead of a second predication, roughly

Table 6-2   The main source schemas for comparative constructions (cf. Heine 1994a:58ff.; the target schema means in all cases 'X is Y-er than Z')

Source schema	Label of schema
X is Y surpasses Z	Action
X is Y at Z	Location
X is Y from Z	Source
X is Y to Z	Goal
X is Y, Z is not Y	Polarity
X is Y, then Z	Sequence
X is Y (like) Z	Similarity
X and Z, X is Y	Topic

Table 6-3 Alternative terms for source schemas of comparative constructions [C.]

Heine	Andersen (1983:118)	Stassen (1985)
Action	Verbal C.	Exceed C.
Location	Adpositional, Case C.	Locative C.
Source	—	Separative C.
Goal	—	Allative C.
Polarity	Juxtaposition C.	Conjoined C.
Sequence	—	—

as sketched in (5b); or one where the standard (Z) is presented first, followed by the comparee (X), as in (5c); or, finally, one where the comparee (X) appears as the subject and the standard (Z) as the object and the predicate as a locative or other adjunct, as sketched in (5d). Patterns (5a–d) are illustrated in (6a–d), respectively.

(5) Variants of the Action Schema
a. *X* is *Y* surpasses *Z*.
b. *X* is *Y* to surpass *Z*.
c. *Z* is *Y* (but) *X* exceeds.
d. *X* surpasses *Z* (at) *Y*-ness.

(6) a. Yoruba (Kwa, Niger-Congo; Stassen 1985:43)
O tobi ju   u.
he big exceed him·
'He is bigger than him.'

b. Swahili (Bantu, Niger-Congo)
Yeye mrefu ku- shinda mimi.
s/he tall   to- defeat me
'He is taller than I.'

c. Tamazight (Berber, Afro-Asiatic; Stassen 1985:49)
Aiis ennek ioularen, oua hin ioufi.
horse your is. good   that my exceeds
'My horse is better than your horse.'

d. Hausa (Chadic, Afro-Asiatic; Kraft & Kirk-Greene 1973:132)
Bellò yā fi   Mūsā girmā.
Bello he surpass Musa tallness
'Bello is bigger than Musa.'

Note that the variant presented under (5d) may receive an alternative interpretation, in that it can also be analyzed as a "blend" of two different schemas; we will return to this issue in the following discussion.

Stassen (1985:43) points out that distinctions such as those illustrated in (5) are conceptually not of major importance; rather, what matters is the presence of what he calls "a transitive exceed-verb which takes the standard NP as its direct object"— that is, a verb expressing the notion 'defeat', 'exceed', 'surpass', and the like, which has the standard of comparison as its sentence object. This is a fundamental point that is also essential to our analysis.

The verb figuring in the Action Schema may have a variety of literal meanings such as 'defeat', 'win over', 'exceed', 'be more than', 'be better than', or 'surpass'; we use the cover label "Surpass" instead of Stassen's "Exceed," since the former appears to be semantically closer to the ultimate source of comparative markers. A cursory survey of African languages suggests that the verb expressing the comparative notion in this schema tends to be derived from action verbs meaning either 'pass' or 'defeat, conquer', which appear to take on the more abstract meaning 'surpass', 'exceed', 'be more than', and the like (cf. Zimzik 1992). There are a number of other verbs, in addition, that may figure as a predicate nucleus in instances of the Action Schema. In Ewe, for example, there is a canonical Action construction using the verb *wú* 'defeat, surpass, exceed'; in the case of comparisons involving nonphysical attributes, however, the complex verb *po ta ´* 'beat someone's head' is more likely to be used, as in the following example:

(7)   Ewe (Kwa, Niger-Congo; Westermann 1907:102)
      é- po mía ta´ le veviedodo me.
      he- beat our head at industry   in
      'He is more industrious than we.'

The Action Schema appears to be a popular source for comparatives in pidgin and creole languages, as is apparent in the following remark by Romaine:

> A number of creoles have a primary or secondary option of forming a comparative construction, whose main characteristic is that the noun which serves as the standard of comparison is the direct object of a transitive verb whose meaning is 'surpass or exceed'. For example, in Cameroon Pidgin English, the following comparative constructions are found: pas mi fo big—'he is bigger than I'; i big pas Bill—'He is bigger than Bill'. Reflexes of English pass are used in Jamaican Creole, Krio, Gullah and Sranan. (1988:56–7)

6.1.2   The Location Schema

In the formula '*X* is *Y* at *Z*' the notion "at" stands for a variety of static locative functions such as 'at', 'on', 'above', 'in', 'by', and the like. The formula can be described as conveying roughly the meaning '*X* has property *Y*, and if *Z* is placed in the same location as *X*, *X* has more of *Y* than *Z* does.' Examples of this schema are presented in (8).

(8)   a. Naga (Tibeto-Burman, Sino-Tibetan; Stassen 1985:147)
         Themma hau lu ki vi- we.
         man   this that on good- is
         'This man is better than that man.'

      b. Hungarian (Ultan 1972:133)
         János nagyobb József- nál.
         John bigger   Joseph- at
         'John is bigger than Joseph.'

An example of a more complex instance of the Location Schema, reported by Zigmond, Booth, and Munro (1990), is reproduced in (9), which literally means 'My house is good beside the other side of your house.'

(9)   Kawaiisu (Southern Numic, Uto-Aztecan; Zigmond, Booth, & Munro 1990:62)
    nɨga- ya   kahni= ni hɨ?ɨ- tɨ   kwiiya- gapi- ṣu=   ika kahni- a=   mi.
    me-   ACC house= my good- NOMIN other : side- beside- EMPH= its house- ACC= your
    '*My* house is better than yours.'

In some studies, the Location Schema has been used as a cover term for three main variants or subschemas—namely, what is called here the Source, the Goal, and the Location Schemas, since they treat the standard (Z) as a source ('from'), a goal ('to'), or a static locative concept ('at', 'on', etc.). What the three have in common is that they conceptualize the standard (Z) in terms of relations that are essentially spatial in nature (irrespective of whether these relations are encoded by means of adpositions, case inflections, or verbal affixes). The main reason for keeping them apart is that they also behave differently when used as source schemas for other grammatical notions such as possession, as we saw in the preceding chapter (see also the following discussion).

Stassen (1985:42) observed a striking word order behavior characterizing constructions based on this schema: Among the twenty languages of his sample that have Location as either a major or a minor schema, none has a verb-medial (SVO) basic word order—that is, he found this schema to be used only in verb-initial (VSO or VOS) and verb-final (SOV) languages. There are a number of exceptions if one looks at a broader sample; for example, quite a number of SVO Niger-Congo languages (including Swahili) have Location as a major or minor schema. Still, this correlation is remarkable and is in need of explanation.

6.1.3   The Source Schema

In instances of this schema, the comparee can have essentially any grammatical function, while the standard is normally encoded as an ablative adverbial phrase. Instances of the schema are found in (10).

(10) a. Mundari (Munda; Stassen 1985:39)
        Sadom- ete hati   mananga- i.
        horse-   from elephant big-   PRES. 3. SG
        'The elephant is bigger than the horse.'

      b. Turkish (Turkic, Altaic; Ultan 1972:131)
        Türkiye Lübnan'dan büyüktür.
        Turkey Lebanon.from is. big
        'Turkey is bigger than Lebanon.'

Worldwide, the Source Schema is one of the most widespread sources for comparatives, if not the most widespread; it appears in close to half the languages of Ultan's (1972:130–1) sample and in almost one-third of the languages in Stassen's (1985) sample.

Ultan (1972:131, 134) observes that in Eskimo, Finnish, Georgian, classical and modern Greek, Lapp, and Russian, genitives figure as markers of standard. He speculates that these cases can also be linked with "the notion of separation"—that is, with the Source Schema.

In a manner similar to what was observed with reference to Location, the Source Schema shows a strong correlation with word order. Eight out of Stassen's (1985:40) ten sample languages that have Source as their major schema are verb-final (SOV).

6.1.4   The Goal Schema

Stassen (1985:40) regards this schema as the mirror image of the Source Schema. What characterizes it is that it has the standard (Z) encoded as a directional participant, be it an allative, benefactive, or dative. An example is presented in (11).

(11)   Susu (Mande, Niger-Congo; Friedländer 1974:62)
     Afriki fura   foretaa be.
     Africa be. hot Europe for
     'Africa is hotter than Europe.'

The Goal Schema may also be said to be present in an English construction of the type 'X is superior/inferior to Y', where a directional/dative case marker is employed to present the standard.

Of the three schemas that have a locative conceptual base, Source appears to be by far the most common in the languages of the world (thirty-two languages in Stassen's 109-language sample), followed by Location (twelve languages), while the Goal Schema is least frequent (seven languages).

6.1.5   The Polarity Schema

The Polarity Schema involves an antithetic juxtaposition of two antonymical qualities (Andersen 1983:108). Its linguistic structure is described by Stassen in the following way:

> In this type, NP-comparison is typically effected by means of the adversative coordination of two clauses; one of these clauses contains the comparee NP, and the other clause contains the standard NP. Furthermore, there is a structural parallelism between the two clauses, to the effect that the grammatical function which the comparee NP fulfils in its clause is matched by the grammatical function of the standard NP in its clause. As a result, this type of comparative involves two grammatically independent clauses, which are connected in such a way that a gradation between the two objects can be inferred. (1985:44)

Propositions involving polarity have the structure of what Stassen calls adversative coordination: "its literal interpretation is something along the lines of 'A is p, but B is q'" (1985:38).

There are two basic subschemas of Polarity, one involving antonymy and the other positive-negative polarity. The conceptual structures of these two subschemas are sketched in (12), and examples are provided in (13) and (14).

(12)　Antonymy:　　　　　　　　'X has property *p* while Z has the opposite property *q*.'
　　　Negative-positive polarity:　'X has property *p* while Z lacks *p*.'

(13)　Antonymy subschema: Cayapo (Ge; Stassen 1985:184)
　　　Gan ga prik, bubanne ba i pri.
　　　you you big but　　I I small
　　　'You are bigger than me.'

(14)　Negative-positive polarity subschema: Hixkaryana (Carib, Stassen 1985:185)
　　　Kaw- ohra naha Waraka, kaw naha Kaywerye.
　　　tall-　not　he.is Waraka　tall　he.is Kaywerye
　　　'Kaywerye is taller than Waraka.'

As the characterization in (12) suggests, polarity is a discrete notion: Comparison is described in terms of either presence or absence of a property *p*. Occasionally, however, relative notions of polarity also appear to provide templates for expressing comparatives of inequality. The following construction, for example, seems to be based on a graded scheme of comparison, and, accordingly, is clearly compatible neither with canonical antonymy nor with negative-positive polarity:

(15)　Cherokee (Iroquoian, Keresiouan; Ultan 1972:130)
　　　utli　nikatv, eska ayv.
　　　more he.is.big less　I
　　　'He is bigger than I.'

6.1.6　The Sequence Schema

The Sequence Schema consists of two consecutive predications, where the second follows the first in time and is connected with the first by means of a marker of consecutive events ('and', 'and then', or 'thereafter'). This schema can be paraphrased roughly thus: 'X has property Y, and only then Z follows (i.e., Z has less of Y than X has).' The schema is rarely found, and the little evidence available is not sufficient to allow for an adequate description of it.

Whereas the Location Schema places the comparee (X) and the standard (Z) in a spatial relation, the Sequence Schema establishes a temporal relation between the two; this schema has therefore been referred to by Heine (1994a:58) as the "Temporal Schema." The inference underlying this schema appears to be something like 'What comes earlier has more of quality Y than what comes later.' Examples of this schema can be found in Stassen (1985:59ff.); we may cite the following examples from Javanese and Dutch, involving, respectively, the particles *karo* and *dan*, which serve both as markers of standard (*M*) and as consecutive conjunctions. Examples (16a) and (17a) are instances of this schema in its grammaticalized form, while (16b) and (17b) illustrate the literal use of the consecutive conjunctions.

(16)   Javanese (Austronesian; Stassen 1985:60)
    a. Enak   daging karo iwak.
       is. good meat   than fish
       'Meat is better than fish.'

    b. Bapaq menjang ing- desa karo simboq menjang ing- desa uga.
       father go   to- field and mother go   to- field too
       'Father went to the field and mother went to the field too.'

(17)   Dutch (Stassen 1985:61)
    a. Jan is groter dan Piet.
       Jan is taller   than Piet
       'Jan is taller than Piet.'

    b. Eerst ga ik, dan gaat Jan.
       first go I   then goes Jan
       'First I will go, then Jan will go.'

The major comparative pattern of English has also sometimes been interpreted as an instance of the Sequence Schema: According to Andersen (1983:130), for example, the construction 'X is Y-er than Z' can be traced back to something like 'X is Y-er, then Z is Y', where *than* is interpreted historically as a variant of *then*.

    Note that some of the examples that Stassen discusses under his "particle comparative" (see the following discussion) might more profitably be regarded as instances of Sequence, like example (18) from Toba Batak involving the marker *asa* 'then, and after that':

(18)   Toba Batak (Austronesian; Stassen 1985:60)
    Dumejak utang- na asa torop di obuk.
    more-many debt- his than crowd of hair
    'He has more debts than hairs on his head.'

6.1.7   The Similarity Schema

In the Similarity Schema, a relationship of similarity or equation is asserted between the comparee (*X*) and the standard (*Z*). Its basic structure is given in (19a) and can be paraphrased as in (19b).

(19)   a. [X is Y (like) Z]
    b. [X is Y-er compared to Z]

As the examples of the Similarity Schema in (20) show, the formal exponent of the schema is an adposition meaning 'like' or 'as'.

(20)   a. Finnish (Andersen 1983:117)
      pitempi kuin sinä
      bigger   as   you
      'bigger than you'

b. Colloquial German
   Klaus ist größ- er wie ich.
   Klaus is tall- er like I
   'Klaus is taller than I.'

c. Sranan (English-based creole; Stassen 1985:191)
   Hugo can lon moro betre liki   Rudi.
   Hugo can run more better "like" Rudi
   'Hugo can run better than Rudi.'

In works on the comparative, Latin is usually quoted as having two contrasting comparative constructions, exemplified, respectively, by *te maior* (you.ABL bigger) and *maior quam tu* (bigger how/like you), both meaning 'bigger than you'. (The two differ, however, in their presuppositional significance; see Andersen 1983:119.) The former construction has the standard (Z) encoded as an ablative participant and hence is an instance of the Source Schema 'X is Y from Z', while the latter is suggestive of the Similarity Schema.

Like Sequence, Similarity is seldom found as a source for comparatives of inequality. Other languages that have constructions suggestive of Similarity are Malagasy, Hungarian, Latvian (cf. Stassen 1985:192–5), and the Romance languages.

However, although it is relatively uncommon as a source for comparatives, Similarity appears to provide the main conceptual template for equatives (or comparatives of equality), as in English 'Rob is as smart as his father'. The occurrence of this schema with two different kinds of comparative notions is probably not coincidental; rather, it would seem that, wherever both the equative and the comparative can be traced back to the Similarity Schema in a given language, the former provided the conceptual template for the latter—that is, propositional schemas like (21b) are likely to be cognitively modeled on something like (21a). This is suggested by the fact that languages using the Similarity Schema for the comparative are likely to also use this schema for the equative. Thus, examples (20a) and (20b) have corresponding equative constructions in (22a) and (22b).

(21) a. 'X is as Y as Z.'
      b. 'X is Y-er as (> than) Z.'

(22) a. Finnish (Andersen 1983:117)
         yhtä pitkä kuin sinä
         as big as you
         'as big as you'

      b. German
         Klaus ist so groß wie ich.
         Klaus is so big like I
         'Klaus is as big as I.'

Note that the Similarity Schema differs from other schemas in that it appears to be strongly associated with the use of degree markers ('more'; see (2) above).

6.1.8   The Topic Schema

In this schema, the comparee (*X*) and the standard (*Z*)—that is, the two items compared—are copresented as the propositional theme in the form of a conjunct of two noun phrases, and the subsequent clause makes a predication on one of them, roughly in the following way: 'As regards David and Bob, David is tall(er).' The format assumed by this schema is sketched in (23). So far, only one example has been found, which is presented in (24).

(23)   '*X* and *Z*, *X* is *Y* > *X* is *Y*-er than *Z*.'

(24)   Nyanja (Bantu, Niger-Congo; Jensen 1934:117)
        madzi ni   čakudia komo čakudia.
        water   and food   good   food
        'Food is better than water.'

6.1.9   "Particle comparatives"

In a number of languages the marker of standard (*than*) is etymologically non-transparent, or *opaque* (see section 2.4)—that is, the marker cannot be related to existing adpositions, case inflections, or other words or affixes to be found in the language concerned. Such markers are called "particles," and the constructions concerned are called "particle constructions" (Andersen 1983:118ff.; Stassen 1985:39). The English *than*-comparative, the French *que*-comparative, and the Latin *quam*-comparative have been treated as examples of this type. Stassen refers to the type as "only a minor class, if a class at all"; at least it "is not a homogeneous category" (Stassen 1985:55).

Particle comparatives differ from the comparative constructions discussed previously in that they have been grammaticalized to such an extent that the cognitive schema underlying them is not readily reconstructible, or in any event has not yet been reconstructed. Note, however, that a number of the particle constructions discussed by Andersen and Stassen do not actually qualify as such, since their conceptual source is in fact not opaque: They can be traced back to various of the source schemas mentioned above, chiefly to the Sequence and Similarity Schemas.

WHILE THE SCHEMAS presented in the previous discussion account for the majority of comparatives of inequality in the languages of the world, there are a number of additional patterns. First, there is a wide range of less common schemas that are of regional significance. Second, there are what we may call schema blends—that is, combinations of two different schemas. Not infrequently, schemas occur in a mixed form—that is, the comparative construction in a given language may combine the properties of two different schemas. In example (25) from Aztec, for example, parts of both the Action and the Polarity Schemas are combined.

(25)   Aztec (Uto-Aztecan; Thomas Stolz, personal communication)
        tla-panahuɨa ɨc ni̵-   cuztɨc ɨn   a̵mo tehua : tl
        surpass. 3. SG   with 1.SG- yellow DET NEG PRON. 2. SG
        'My skin is more red than yours.' (Lit.: 'It surpasses with I am yellow, you not so.')

In a number of cases it remains unclear whether we are dealing with an instance of a single schema or with a schema blend. Take the following example from Motu:

(26) Motu (New Guinean; Stassen 1985:48)
      Una na namo, ina herea-ia.
      that is good   this exceeds
      'This is better than that.'

For Stassen, such examples are suggestive of mixed cases, in that we are dealing both with an adversative predication of the type '*X* is good (but) *Y* is better', which is suggestive of the Polarity Schema, and with the Action Schema involving a verb meaning 'surpass, exceed'. We do not wish to decide whether examples like (26) are suggestive of schema blend or whether they can be interpreted as special instances of the Action Schema. What is beyond reasonable doubt is that schema blend does exist and is far from uncommon.

As has been noted by most authors dealing with the present topic, any given language tends strongly to have one dominant comparative schema. This, however, does not mean that in that language there can only be one schema employed; on the contrary, often there are a number of different schemas that are likely to be in use in one and the same language. German, for example, has a strongly grammaticalized comparative expressed by *-er als* 'more than', whose conceptual source is opaque. While this construction provides the primary option available to speakers of German, other less-used constructions do occur. Thus, the constructions exemplified in (27) may express the notion of a comparative of inequality, given the right context; here the participant encoding can have the properties of four different schemas.

(27) German
      a. Sie ist ihm   überlegen.   Goal Schema
         she is to.him superior
         'She is superior to him.'

      b. Sie ist die klügere   von ihnen.   Source Schema
         she is the more.clever from them
         'Between them, she is more clever.'

      c. Neben Paul wirkt Ernst klein.   Location Schema
         next.to Paul appears Ernst small
         'Compared to Paul, Ernst appears to be short.'

      d. Sie übertrifft ihn an Klugheit.   Action Schema
         she surpasses him at cleverness
         'She surpasses him in cleverness.'

In a survey of twenty West African languages carried out by Zimzik (1992), five of these languages have two major schemas, which in all cases concerned are the Action and the Location Schemas.

Furthermore, one and the same schema may have various linguistic encodings—not only across languages but also within one and the same language. For example, in the Angas language of northern Nigeria, the Action Schema, involving the verb *del* 'to surpass', may have four different structures. The respective meanings of these structures are illustrated by Foulkes (1915:61) by means of the following English glosses (the exact meaning of item 1 is not entirely clear):

1. This woman is pretty, but that one surpasses beauty her.
2. This woman is pretty, but the beauty of that one surpasses her.
3. This woman is pretty, but that one surpasses her beauty.
4. This woman is pretty, but that one surpasses her with beauty.

A number of attempts have been made to understand the multiplicity of comparative constructions to be found in the languages of the world. In one of the pioneering studies of the subject matter discussed here, Jensen (1934) proposed a psychologically motivated sequence of comparative constructions. Translated into the present framework, Jensen's evolutionary scenario can be presented by means of a scale of constructions, roughly as sketched in table 6-4. Irrespective of whether this scale is interpreted as reflecting a diachronic development or an achronic cognitive relationship pattern, Jensen's sequence may serve to draw attention to one important factor in our understanding of comparative constructions: While there is only a limited range of conceptual sources, the variety of ways the notion of a comparative of inequality can be linguistically encoded is enormous.

In most previous works, comparative constructions have been described purely with reference to linguistic parameters. Such works yielded a number of valuable insights, and this applies most of all to the monograph by Stassen (1985). The main thesis of the present work, however, is that underlying these constructions is a small number of basic cognitive patterns that account for the particular linguistic structure of the given construction. In the present section, the relation between these cognitive patterns and the resulting linguistic constructions is examined.

What is crucial for the linguistic encoding of the above schemas is the fact that they involve at least four formal elements: the comparee, the standard, the predicate, and the marker of standard. This number exceeds the scope of a basic proposition, which normally does not have more than three basic elements (as in a prototypical Action Schema of the form 'X does Y', where in addition to the participants X and Y there is the predicate 'does'). This means that comparative constructions require for

Table 6-4 An evolutionary scenario of comparative constructions according to Jensen (1934)

Stage	Schematic example	Schema
I	X is Y, Z is -Y	Antonymy
II	X is Y, Z is not Y	Negative-positive polarity
III	X and Z, X is Y	Topic
IV	X is Y at Z	Location
V	X is Y from Z	Source
VI	X surpasses Z in Y-ness	Action
VII	X is Y-er than Z	Opaque constructions

their expression a structure that is more complex than a basic proposition. "More complex" means that in addition to a basic proposition, comparative constructions involve another constituent which almost invariably is either an adjunct, typically encoded as an adverbial phrase or oblique case role, or else an additional proposition. Accordingly, the structures used for the expression of comparatives are usually of either of the following types:

(28) The main construction types of comparatives
    a. Proposition 1 + Proposition 2
    b. Proposition + Adjunct

With reference to the psychologically motivated sequence proposed by Jensen (1934), sketched in table 6-4, it is noteworthy that that sequence involves a transition from (28a) structures to (28b) structures—more specifically, from comparative expressions characterized by two coordinated clauses to monoclausal expressions.

There is, in fact, a strong association between event schemas and propositional structures: The Location, Source, and Goal Schemas are strongly associated with (28b), while the Polarity Schema is associated with construction type (28a).

But the situation is more complicated than the above examples might suggest: Correlations between event schema and syntactic construction type are limited. First, there are many instances of different event schemas that share one and the same construction type. The following near-synonymous sentences taken from Swahili, for example, are suggestive of the Location (29a) and the Action Schemas (29b) yet are constructed essentially in the same way.

(29) Swahili (Bantu, Niger-Congo)
    a. Juma ni   m-   refu ku - li- ko   Ali.
       Juma COP Cl.1- long LOC- be- LOC Ali
       'Juma is taller than Ali.'

    b. Juma ni   m-   refu ku- shinda Ali.
       'Juma is Cl.1- long INF- defeat Ali
       'Juma is taller than Ali.'

Second, one and the same schema may be encoded by means of contrasting construction types. This applies most of all to the Action Schema, as we saw earlier when dealing with this schema. That this schema may also be associated with entirely different construction types within one and the same language can be shown with the following examples from Duala (30):

(30) Duala (Bantu, Niger-Congo; Stassen 1985:181)
    a. Bono bo kolo   buka ndabo.
       boat it big. PRES exceed house
       'The boat is bigger than the house.'

    b. Modi a buki   Edimo bwala.
       Modi he exceed Edimo laziness
       'Modi is lazier than Edimo.'

6.2   A note on the superlative

We have been concerned thus far with just one kind of comparative construction—that is, with the explicit superior comparative, which we have referred to for short as "the comparative." What has been said about this construction applies to some extent also to other comparative constructions. Ultan (1972) found that comparatives differ considerably from equatives (e.g., 'David is as smart as Bob') but resemble superlatives ('David is the smartest') in a number of ways. Among the 30 languages for which he had sufficient data, 18 (or 60%) shared the same markers for the comparative and the superlative.

In fact, much of what has been said about comparatives also applies to superlatives. First, the two are likely to involve the same construction, in that the superlative is often built on the model of the comparative. Second, the conceptual sources are, at least to some extent, the same. For example, the Source Schema appears to be the most frequently employed conceptual template for both (cf. Ultan 1972:134). Perhaps the predominant pattern for forming superlatives is that of replacing an individual standard of comparison (Z) by the entire class of possible individuals, which means typically that the standard is modified by the quantifier 'all' and the like. Thus, a schematic formula for the comparative, as in (31a), is replaced by one like (31b) to express the notion of a superlative.

(31)   a. *X* is *Y*-er than Z.
        b. *X* is *Y*-er than all others.

The following examples illustrate this pattern: (32) is an instance of the Action, (33) of the Source, (34) of the Location, and (35) of the Goal Schemas.

(32)   a. Swahili (Bantu, Niger-Congo)
           Ali m-   fupi ku- shinda w-   ote.
           Ali Cl.1- short to- defeat Cl.2- all
           'Ali is the shortest.' (Lit.: 'Ali is short to surpass all others.')

        b. Nandi (Southern Nilotic, Nilo-Saharan; Creider & Creider 1989:150)
           nyúmnyûm ko- si : r kìy   ake   túkûl.
           easy   3- pass thing other all
           'It is the easiest of all.'

(33)   Amharic (Semitic, Afro-Asiatic; Ultan 1972:134)
        kə-   hullu yamral.
        from- all   he.is.handsome
        'He is the handsomest of all.'

(34)   a. Tamil (Dravidian; Ultan 1972:134)
           ēlla malaikalilum   inta malai   uyaramānatu.
           all   mountains. LOC. too this mountain is. high
           'This mountain is the highest of all.'

        b. Latin (Jensen 1934:120)
           super omnes   beatus
           above all. ACC. M. PL happy. M. SG
           'happier than all (others)'

(35) Sinhalese (Indo-Iranian, Indo-European; Ultan 1972:135)
mē lámayā hama lámayiṇṭa ma   váḍā hoñda y.
this boy   all   boys. DAT EMPH more good   is
'This boy is the best of all.'

Third, the above observations suggest that superlatives may be derived from comparatives but not the converse, and Ultan (1972:141) in fact concludes that the superlative is a marked category vis-à-vis the comparative. In Tswana, this markedness is expressed by reduplicating the comparative degree marker:

(36) Tswana (Bantu, Niger-Congo; Ultan 1972:140)
tlôu   ethata bogolo- bogolo môdiphôlôgôlông.
elephant strong more-   more   LOC.animals
'The elephant is the strongest of the animals.'

At the same time, there are also a number of differences in the structure of comparatives and superlatives. First, while both use essentially the same conceptual templates, the relative frequency of use differs. For example, genitive markers are occasionally found to give rise to markers of standard (*M*) in comparative constructions. The same applies to superlative constructions, the difference being that genitive markers are much more common in the case of the latter (Ultan 1972:134). An example is provided in (37).

(37) Russian (Ultan 1972:134)
on vs'ex   stárše.
he all. GEN older
'He is the oldest of them all.'

Second, the Goal Schema occurs as a means of expressing comparatives but appears to be rarely used for superlatives, and the same applies to the Polarity Schema (Ultan 1972:138). Third, although superlatives are described by Ultan (1972) as marked categories vis-à-vis comparatives, there are also unmarked superlatives, and these are rather widespread. Ultan (1972:141) cites the following as an example of an unmarked superlative, which appears to be a straightforward instance of the Location Schema:

(38) Kannada (South Dravidian; Ultan 1972:141; no exact alignment provided by the author)
i : mənd ae : ga awa sa : ṇae.
these-people-LOC   he   is-wise
'He is the wisest among these people.'

Fourth, certain forms of expression are used for superlatives but never for comparatives. This applies, for example, to constructions where the superlative concept is expressed by means of intensifiers like 'very' or 'too', as in the following examples involving 'very':

(39) a. Kanuri (Nilo-Saharan; Norbert Cyffer, personal communication)
mâi- wá Bòrnó- bè   zâu- rò   nòwátà- dɔ́ fál- nzá.
king- PL Borno- GEN very- ADV known-   DET one- their
'He is one of the best-known kings of Bornu.'

b. Nandi (Southern Nilotic, Nilo-Saharan; Creider & Creider 1989:151)

nyúmnyûm misí : ng.

easy   very

'It is the easiest.'

Fifth, Ultan (1972:124, 142) observes that while comparatives are likely to be associated with indefinite marking, superlatives tend to be definite. He cites in this connection the examples of Danish, where the comparative is always indefinite and the superlative definite, and French, where the superlative is formed by adding the definite article to the comparative. Thus, the superlative example in (40b) differs from the comparative one in (40a) only in that the former has the (feminine) definite article *la* in it.

(40)   French

a. Marie est plus sage.

Mary is   more wise

'Mary is wiser.'

b. Marie est la plus sage.

Mary is the more wise

'Mary is the wisest.'

Note that items presented as superlatives tend to be encoded as having unique reference: If I say 'He is the biggest', then I am claiming, rightly or wrongly, that there is no other person on earth that fits this description.

In fact, Jensen (1934:111) cites a number of languages where definiteness appears to be the only means of marking superlatives—that is, where an expression of the form 'X is the big one' has been grammaticalized to a superlative construction (= 'X is the biggest').

Finally, there are some languages where (emphatic) reflexive pronouns may be employed for the expression of a superlative notion, as in Latvian *pats labais* 'the best' (lit.: 'the good one itself'), or Russian *sámaja čístaja vodá* 'the purest water' (lit.: 'the pure water itself') (Jensen 1934:111).

The purpose of this section has been to relate and contrast the comparative with a closely related grammatical notion. What our observations have shown is that a typological analysis of the superlative is an important desideratum. Such an analysis should not ignore the structure of comparatives where relevant; nevertheless, it should focus on superlatives in their own right.

6.3   Areal forces

It is a commonplace in linguistics that when languages are in contact, borrowing is likely to arise, and that borrowing will be most pronounced in the lexicon while grammar will be much less affected. The fact that grammar belongs to those parts of language that are most resistant to borrowing has been observed independently by quite a number of authors. Yet it does not seem to apply equally to all areas of grammar.

Clause conjunctions and interjections, for example, are easily borrowed, and comparative particles are also likely candidates for borrowing. Stolz & Stolz (1994) provide a wealth of information on the way Spanish comparative markers like *más* 'more' and/or *que* 'than, like' have intruded into the languages of Central America. The way this happens can be illustrated with the following examples from Mopan. Example (41a) illustrates the original native pattern. This pattern involves the comparative marker *tuwich* 'in the face of, in front of' as a marker of standard corresponding to English *than*: the locative marker *tuwich* suggests that we are dealing with an instance of the Location Schema. In (41b), this traditional pattern has been enriched by the Spanish marker *más* 'more', whose use remains optional. Finally in (41c), *más* appears twice, although both uses are essentially redundant; the sentence-initial *más* is in free variation with the indigenous marker *top* 'very' (cf. [41b]).

(41)   Mopan (Mayan; Stolz & Stolz 1994:8–9)
   a. ki'   a   ximbaL- a   tuwich ka   tin- lak- en.
      good ART run-   PRT in. front CONJ sit- SUBJ- 1. SG. ABSO
      'It is better for me to run than to sit here and wait for the bus.'

   b. top kich'pan bin   kuchi más tuwich   a   prinseesah- a.
      very pretty   QUOT but   more in. front ART princess-   PRT
      'But she is said to have been much prettier than the princess.'

   c. más sasil u wich u na'   más tuwich ti   kuxa'an ti   yok'olkab- a.
      more clear 3 eye   3 mother more in. front LOC alive   LOC earth-   PRT
      'The eye of his mother was brighter than that of all other living beings on earth.'

The study carried out by Stassen (1985) contains a wealth of data that can be exploited for an analysis of the geographical distribution of comparative constructions. We will now try to determine to what extent the distribution of comparative constructions relates to areal factors.

The linguistic classification I propose to use deviates from Stassen's in that I will confine myself essentially to geographical, rather than genetic, criteria. For example, in Stassen's (1985:352–5) classification, English and Japanese belong to the same class (Eurasia), while Japanese and Korean belong to different classes (Eurasia and Asia, respectively). In my classification, both Japanese and Korean are treated as "Asian" languages, and so are Indo-European languages such as Hindi, Kashmiri, and Tajik. Finally, if a language is found to have two equivalent sources for comparatives, then only the one that is described by Stassen as the "primary option" is considered in the statistical breakdown of table 6-5. Assuming that the figures provided in table 6-5 are truly representative of their respective areas, there appear to be some significant correlations between construction type and areal distribution—in particular, the following:

1. Particle comparatives are most widespread in Europe. Some 93% of all European languages have them as their primary option, while they are rarely found elsewhere in the world. Of all instances of particle comparatives occurring in Stassen's sample, 72% are located in Europe.

2. At least 66% of all Asian languages use the Source Schema.
3. Languages of Africa and the Middle East are associated primarily with the Action Schema. Almost two-thirds (65%) of all languages with this schema are African, and the Action Schema is found in every other language of this general region. A survey of twenty West African languages (Zimzik 1992) shows in fact that the only schemas occurring are Action and Location: Fourteen of these languages use exclusively the Action Schema, another five have the Location Schema in addition, and one language (Senufo) makes exclusive use of the Location Schema.
4. The Polarity Schema is not found in Africa; it is confined to the Americas and the Indian and Pacific Oceans area. However, whereas only 36% of all American languages have this kind of comparative, more than half (56%) of the languages around the Indian and Pacific Oceans have it.
5. Comparatives having some locative base—that is, Location, Source, and Goal—while being the most numerous worldwide are statistically insignificant in Europe and the Indian and Pacific Oceans area.

On the basis of such quantitative data, it is possible to formulate some probabilistic predictions, such as the following:

1. If there is a language that uses primarily particle constructions, then this is likely to be a European language and unlikely to be an African or Asian language.
2. If there is a language that has the Polarity Schema as its primary option, then this is likely to be an American language or one from the Indian/Pacific Oceans area, but unlikely to be a European, Asian, or African language.
3. Given some random Asian language, chances are highest that it uses the Source Schema as its primary option.

Table 6-5   Sources for comparative constructions in 109 languages according to areal distribution (based on Stassen 1985; only major schemas are considered)

	No. of languages in					
Source schema	Europe	Asia	Africa / Middle East	The Americas	Indian / Pacific Ocean	Total
Action	0	4	13	1	2	20
Location	0	4	3	4	1	12
Source	0	16	6	9	1	32
Goal	1	0	3	3	0	7
Polarity	0	0	0	10	10	20
Particle C.	13	0	0	1	4	18
Total	14	24	25	28	18	109

4. Given some random language of the Indian/Pacific Oceans area, chances are highest that it makes use of the Polarity Schema for comparative constructions.
5. Similarly, a given random African language is most likely to make use of the Action Schema.

That it is in fact areal distribution, rather than genetic relationship, that is crucial in determining the choice of event schemas is suggested in particular by the following example. Stassen's (1985) sample contains altogether thirteen Indo-European languages, of which three are spoken in Asia and ten in Europe. All three Asian languages (Hindi, Kashmiri, and Tajik) are characterized by use of the Source Schema, while none of the ten European languages makes use of this schema; rather, nine out of the ten European languages (Greek, Latin, Latvian, Russian, French, Dutch, English, Gaelic, and Albanian) have particle comparatives, and one (Breton) a Goal comparative.

Similarly, among the nine Ural-Altaic languages found in Stassen's sample, two are spoken in Europe and seven in Asia. Both European languages (Finnish and Hungarian) have particle comparatives, while all seven Asian languages (Jurak, Lamutic, Manchu, Turkish, Khalka, Japanese, and Korean) make use of the Source Schema. To summarize, the use of the various schemas cuts across genetic boundaries but becomes almost predictable once we define it in geographical terms.

6.4   Summary

We saw in chapter 5 that possession is a derived concept in that it requires other concepts for its expression. The same applies to comparison. As the present chapter suggests, there are additional correspondences between possession and comparison, most of all the following: Both are derived from the same general pool of source concepts, concepts which have to do with predications on actions, location, motion, and the like.

Another important message of the preceding sections is phrased by Andersen in the following way:

> To sum up, for the purposes of word order we must investigate all of the morpho-syntactic constructions in the particular language of the same underlying type and set up different (implicational) word order universals accordingly. In other words, we should replace Greenberg's one universal (#22) and all subsequent implicational universals concerning comparative constructions by a number of other universals. (1983:125)

While the universals Andersen has in mind are not exactly the ones I am proposing here, the message is the same: In order to understand the grammar of comparative constructions, not much is gained by looking for one uniform universal structure; rather, what is required is that the entire pool of possible conceptual sources be considered.

I have noted that the many constructions serving the expression of comparatives in the languages of the world can be reduced to a small set of cognitive patterns, referred to as event schemas. These schemas have to do with what one does, where one is located, where one moves from or to, and the like. They determine the particular linguistic shape a given comparative construction is going to take. Similar positions have been maintained by other authors—for instance, by Jensen (1934) from a psychological perspective and by Andersen (1983) from a linguistic perspective.

I have ignored a number of problems associated with the structure and the reconstruction of comparatives. One might mention, for example, that it is not always possible to unambiguously identify the source schema concerned, either because the construction is so old that its genesis is no longer fully recoverable or because the morphology employed for its expression is ambiguous and allows for a reconstruction to more than one possible source schema (cf. Stassen 1985:34–7). I have also not been concerned with word order. Stassen (1985) observes that there are strong crosslinguistic correlations between types of comparative constructions and basic word order (see section 6.1).

Perhaps the main observation made in this chapter is that some significant correlations exist between the source schemas of comparative constructions and their areal distribution (section 6.3). While the cognitive patterns that underlie comparative constructions are limited to essentially a handful of schemas, the choice between these schemas appears to be determined primarily by areal factors. Thus, it is possible to predict within limits which particular schema can be expected to be found in a given Oceanic language, as opposed to some Asian or African language.

7

BEYOND GRAMMAR

Most of what was discussed in the preceding chapters relates to processes that in some way or other have to do with grammar; it falls within the scope of grammaticalization theory. For example, I looked at a number of instances where words belonging to open classes, like nouns or verbs, develop into closed-class items like numerals, adverbs, adpositions, articles, and the like. The main goal of this chapter is to demonstrate that essentially the same principles are at work within the lexicon— that is, when lexical items acquire new meanings.

One of the most complex and most controversial issues in linguistics concerns the structure and development of meaning. In spite of all the research that has been devoted to semantics (see, e.g., Paul [1880] 1975; Stern 1931; Ullmann 1962), not much headway has been made in our knowledge of semantic change: Everything seems possible, and Anttila concludes that "there are no exact rules for handling semantic change; the final factor here is necessarily the common sense and the experience of the individual scholar" (Anttila 1989:229). Nevertheless, recent work on conceptual transfer suggests that a few generalizations may allow us to handle semantic change more successfully than previously, and this chapter summarizes some of the findings that have been made in this area. This chapter also demonstrates that the patterns of evolution observed in preceding chapters are not confined to grammatical meaning but extend far beyond the confines of grammar.

The primary source domain in the preceding chapters was the human body. For the sake of continuity, this domain is also used here. In section 7.1 we see that body-parts can be traced back to other concepts. In section 7.2 the evolution from one body-part term to another is examined. In section 7.3 I look into the question of how body-part terms are employed to create terms for other concepts. Finally, in section 7.4, a more general issue is addressed—namely, the mechanism underlying the kind of conceptual shift discussed in this book.

7.1   From object to body-part

Terms for body-parts belong to the most conservative domains of the lexicon. In the historical reconstruction of earlier language states, items like 'eye', 'head', or 'back' are likely to prove more resistant to language change than many other words. Still, even body-parts tend to be derived from other domains of conceptualization; French *tête* 'head', which is derived from Late Latin *testa* 'pot', or English *vagina*, which goes back to a Latin word for 'sheath', are not uncommon examples. A few more examples may illustrate the nature of the process. The data are taken overwhelmingly from Brown and Witkowski (1981) and Wilkins (1993, 1996). On the basis of a survey of body-part nomenclature in 118 languages of worldwide distribution, these authors observe certain regularities in the transfer from object to body-part terms, including the ones summarized here:

- Terms for 'pupil (of the eye)' are most likely to be derived from nouns denoting a small human like a baby, or a child, or a diminutive humanlike object like a doll. It is not always diminutive size that matters; in some languages, 'pupil' is expressed as 'person of the eye' or 'angel of the eye' (Quechua), or even the 'hailstone of the eye' (Maori), the 'candle of the eye' (Welsh), or the 'beetle of the eye' (Hungarian).
- There are contrasting transfer patterns for thumbs and big toes on the one hand and the remaining digits on the other: Whereas the former are likely to be built on kin-terms of an older, ascending generation (e.g., 'mother of the hand/foot'), the remaining fingers and toes tend to be derived from expressions involving terms for offspring or other younger relatives (e.g., 'child of the hand/foot').
- The notion 'muscle' is expressed predominantly by using small mammals as structural templates. As in the case of English *muscle* (which is ultimately derived from Latin *musculus* 'little mouse'), terms for 'mouse' or 'rat' appear to provide the most common source for 'muscle' or 'muscular part of the body', where the latter may refer to such notions as 'thigh', 'calf of the leg', or 'biceps'. Other animals, such as lizards, rabbits, toads, or calves, are used less frequently than mice and rats.
- For the concept 'testicle', by far the most widespread source is provided by terms for 'egg', alternative options being 'stone', 'pebble', 'seed', and 'fruit' (Brown & Witkowski 1981; Wilkins 1993:12; see section 7.5).

It is probably premature to generalize on the basis of the few data that have become available so far. Nevertheless, certain preferred source domains for body-parts appear to emerge. Perhaps the most salient one is that of basic human role-relations like father, mother, and child. Animals appear to provide another domain, and finally there is also a range of inanimate items that provide an additional domain. Probably the most frequently employed parameters for selecting objects are similarity in shape and function, where the source item provides a conspicuous, eye-catching model for naming a less conspicuous body-part. The middle ear contains three important bones; still they are less eye-catching than the items that we have chosen to refer to them: the 'hammer' (Latin *malleus*), the anvil (*incūs*), and the stirrup (*stapes*). The Gnau people in Papua New Guinea call the Achilles tendon *wangen* 'the bowstring', and the fontanelle (the soft part on an infant's skull) *basyilape* 'grasshopper, cricket', probably because of the jumping pulse of the fontanelle's membrane when the infant coughs or sneezes (Lewis 1974:53–4; Matisoff 1978:175, 190).

7.2 From one part of the body to another

The study of body-parts has been a popular subject in the past decades. It is associated with the rise of folk taxonomy as a field of research. But human anatomy—more precisely, the study of parts of the human body and their classification in terms of folk biology—is only remotely related to folk taxonomy. Body-parts are not in a kind-of relationship with their whole: Fingernails are parts of fingers, fingers are parts of hands, hands are parts of arms, but fingernails are not normally called parts of arms.

While this section is concerned with the relationship between different parts of the human body, neither taxonomy nor partonomy (or meronomy or meronymy) will play any major role. Rather, we will be concerned with conceptual transfer patterns between different body-parts. Nevertheless, we cannot avoid issues of partonomy in cases where they have an immediate bearing on naming strategies. For example, the human body contains a number of parts whose status within the partonomic hierarchy is unclear, for which we therefore might expect different societies to come up with different ways of partonomic conceptualization. 'Shoulder blade' is one such part. The English term suggests that this part shares a partonomic relationship with the 'shoulder'. But this is only one of several possible partonomic relationships. Consider the examples in (1), taken from Kenyan languages: Rather than the shoulder, it may be the breast or the neck that 'shoulder blade' is associated with. The different labeling patterns in (1) suggest that there are also differences between the societies concerned in the way they divide up the human body in partonomies.

(1) Terms for 'shoulder blade' in Kenyan languages (Schladt 1997:63)
  a. Rendille (East Cushitic, Afro-Asiatic)
   láf ti gárab
   bone of shoulder (= 'bone of shoulder')

  b. Kamba (Bantu, Niger-Congo)
   ĩvĩndĩ ĩnene ya ĩĩthũĩ
   bone   big   of breast (= 'big bone of breast')

c. Pokot (Eastern Nilotic, Nilo-Saharan)
kɔwɔ káat
bone neck (= 'bone of neck')

On the basis of the conceptual transfer patterns they are associated with, body-parts may be divided into basic and less basic ones. Basic parts are likely to exhibit the following properties:

1. They are expressed linguistically by means of short, morphologically simple, unanalyzable terms.
2. They are likely to be named first when informants are requested to name examples of body-parts.
3. They may serve as structural templates to denote other body-parts, as well as other items not connected with the human body—that is, concepts which are perceived to be related to the former with reference to shape, location, and/or function (Schladt 1997:69ff.).
4. With few exceptions, basic body-parts are exterior ones—that is, they are visible and tangible.

Basic body-parts typically include blood, ear, eye, hand/arm, head, heart, leg/foot, mouth, stomach, tongue, tooth (cf. Andersen 1978:353). Less basic body-parts, which include all remaining parts, are characterized by a lack of most, or all, of the properties just listed. The boundary between the two, however, is fuzzy, and no attempt is made here to define it.

My interest here is, above all, with property (3): There are certain parts of the body that tend to be employed for the expression of other body-parts, while other parts hardly ever are. What I wish to argue here is that the unidirectionality principle observed, for instance, in the development from body-part to numeral or locative marker is also at work when a given body-part serves as a model to also refer to other body-parts. The discussion will be confined to two basic principles of transfer that appear to regulate transfer strategies within the domain of the human body. These principles are: the top-down strategy, and the part-to-whole strategy. Certainly these are not the only strategies that would need to be considered; still, they account for the larger part of transfers between body-parts.

7.2.1. Top-down strategy

According to the top-down strategy, transfer proceeds from upper to lower parts of the human body—that is, the lower half of the body tends to be conceptualized in terms of the upper half. This strategy appears to be based on an asymmetric conceptualization of the human body according to which the upper half is perceptually more differentiated and more salient for perceptual and communicative purposes. The main transfers that characterize this strategy are summarized in table 7-1.

The top-down strategy is unidirectional—that is, we may expect that in a given language toes will be referred to as 'fingers of the foot' but never that fingers will be called the 'toes of the hand'. Similarly, the anklebone is referred to in many East and Southeast Asian languages as 'foot-eye', while eyes are not called 'anklebones of the head' (Matisoff 1978:198). Note, however, that the transfer pattern is not of

Table 7-1   Conceptual transfer patterns based
on the top-down strategy (cf. Andersen 1978)

Source		Target
'Face'	>	'shin'
'Finger'	>	'toe'
'Fingernail'	>	'toenail'
'Head'	>	'buttocks'
'Neck'	>	'ankle'
"Nose"	>	'finger, toe'
'Wrist'	>	'ankle'

unlimited applicability. For example, while there is a transfer pattern from 'finger' to 'toe', no corresponding one from 'hand' to 'foot' has been observed so far.

There are hardly any exceptions to the top-down strategy, and if there are, they can be accounted for with reference to alternative factors. For example, there are terms like German *Handschuh* ('hand shoe') 'glove', which seemingly constitutes an exception to the top-down principle; yet it probably is not, for two interrelated reasons. First, this term concerns not a body-part but a manufactured product worn on a certain body-part. Accordingly, we will not be surprised if the principles of conceptual transfer are not exactly the same as those applying to body-parts. Second, covering one's feet for protection is cross-culturally much more common than covering one's hands. It is therefore more likely that terms for footwear are recruited as models to refer to "hand-wear" than the other way round.

There are also a few examples where parts of the lower half of the body figure in terms for body-parts located in the upper half. Andersen (1978:356) observes, for example, that 'elbow' is rendered in Hausa as 'knee of arm' (*gwiwàr hannu*); here, a part of the lower half of the body ('knee') is transferred to the upper half. But in this case there is an alternative principle at work: Parts of the back side of the body ('elbow') are not seldom conceptualized in terms of front body-parts ('knee').

In fact, a second directionality exists in addition to the top-down strategy—let us call it the front-to-back strategy. According to this strategy, parts located at the front of the human body are likely to also refer to parts located at the back side, while the opposite direction of transfer appears to be rare. There would seem to be an obvious reason for this fact: The reference points 'up' and 'front', as opposed to 'down' and 'back', are where all organs associated with perception and communication are located. Thus, Andersen remarks:

> Similarly, the natural directions 'upward', or 'above', and 'forward', or 'in front', which are optimally perceptible, appear to be conceptually unmarked directions in categorizing and labeling body-parts, and serve as the basis for deriving terms whose referents are in the lower or back portions of the body. (1978:364)

The top-down strategy is among the most common means of conceptual transfer within the domain of body-parts. In Schladt's (1997) data from East African languages, fifteen out of eighteen languages—that is, 83%—were found to have derived their term for 'toe' from 'finger', the former being expressed as 'finger of the foot/leg'. This strategy might also be held responsible to some extent for a number of what Andersen

(1978:351–2) calls universals of categorization, such as the following (see also Brown 1976):

1. If in a given language there is a separate term for 'leg' (as opposed to 'foot'), then there is also a term for 'arm' (as opposed to 'hand').
2. If there is a separate term for 'foot', then there is also one for 'hand', but not vice versa.
3. In all languages known so far there appear to be labels for 'toe' and 'finger'. But if there are terms for individual toes, then there are also terms for individual fingers, though not vice versa.

Further examples of the top-down strategy in transfers within the human body can be found in many languages. In Tzeltal (Levinson 1994:804), for example, the term for 'nipple' is rendered as 'nose of breast', and 'knee' is 'head of leg'.

7.2.2   Part-to-whole strategy

While the top-down strategy appears to be based on similarity in shape or function, the part-to-whole strategy has to do with physical contiguity: Not infrequently, a body-part receives its name from an immediately adjacent body-part. In most cases, this process involves unidirectional transfers from a part to its whole. A number of instances of this strategy have been identified by Wilkins (1996), who refers to them as "intrafield metonymic changes." The kinds of unidirectional evolution proposed by Wilkins are summarized in table 7-2 (where the formula "$X > Y$" stands for "terms for X may develop historically into Y").

Wilkins's reconstructions are supported by Witkowski and Brown (1985:203), who observe that the hand/arm polysemy, which they found in 50 out of 109 languages worldwide, typically develops by expansion of 'hand' to encompass 'arm'. Similarly, the foot/leg polysemy, found in 42 out of 109 languages, develops by the expansion of 'foot' to include 'leg'. They conclude that expansion in the opposite direction is not common. These authors consider 'hand' and 'foot' to be "high salience referents" and 'arm' and 'leg' to be relatively "low salience referents."

There are a few counterexamples to the unidirectionality principle, however. Examples of bidirectional development appear to include the following: Words for 'skull' may be derived from words for 'head', and vice versa; and the same bidirec-

Table 7-2   Conceptual transfer patterns based on the part-to-whole strategy (according to Wilkins 1996)

Source		Target
'Nail', 'sole', 'heel'	>	'foot'
'Foot', 'thigh', 'shin/calf'	>	'leg'
'Nail'	>	'finger'
'Finger', 'palm'	>	'hand'
'Navel'	>	'belly'
'Belly', 'trunk', 'skin'	>	'body'
'Body'	>	'person'
'Eyebrow', 'mouth', 'lip', 'eye'	>	'face'
'Face', 'hair', 'ear'	>	'head'

Table 7-3 Some common transfer patterns from body-part to abstract schema

Source		Target
'Head'	>	'top end', 'tip'
'Buttocks', 'foot'	>	'bottom end'
'Mouth'	>	'opening', 'edge'
'Neck', 'wrist'	>	'narrow section'

tional pattern exists between 'bone' and 'leg', and between 'stomach' and 'belly' (Wilkins 1996; Schladt 1997).

7.3 From body-part to inanimate object

In addition to the kind of transfer discussed in the preceding section, there is another involving the generalizing potential associated with the conceptualization of body-parts. In some cases, terms for certain body-parts receive a more general meaning, referring to more abstract schematic notions. A few canonical examples are found in table 7-3. 'Top end', 'opening', and other target meanings resulting from this kind of transfer are not confined to the domain of body-parts; they relate primarily to the domain of inanimate objects. Body-parts do in fact also serve as templates to describe items that have no association whatsoever with the human body. In this way, terms for body-parts can give rise to terms for what we called *object-deictic orientation* in section 1.2.3.

The extent to which parts of the human body (and occasionally the animal body) serve as structural templates for object-deictic orientation is limited: Not all body-parts may be used for this purpose, nor can all inanimate items be described with reference to the body-part model. But there is at least one society which has created a framework to allow virtually any physical item to be described in terms of body-parts. This is Tzeltal society; here objects such as knives, pots, leaves, feathers, and planks have conceptual properties that are almost entirely derived from the human body. The main transfer patterns are illustrated in the following discussion. (I will confine myself to a few examples and to terms that still exist as body-part lexemes; items such as *y-olil* 'middle' and *y-util* 'inside' are therefore not included. Further, a few examples in which the exact nature of the transfer pattern is not clear are omitted. The shape of Tzeltal terms is that used in possessed forms.) On the basis of the data presented by Levinson (1994), three main kinds of transfer can be distinguished. These are:

1. From body-part to object part where *shape* properties are transferred. The following appear to be examples of this transfer:

(2) a. *s-ni'* 'nose' > (a) pointed extremity or extremity having a sharp convexity;
(b) protrusion of three-dimensional depth

  b. *s-ti'* 'mouth' > (a) edge or outline of a two-dimensional plane;
(b) three-dimensional ring or band (cf. lips);
(c) orifice, or closure or 'stopper' of orifice

c. *snuk'* 'neck'	>	narrow section, e.g., of a container
d. *x-chikin* 'ear'	>	flattened protrusion
e. *s-jol* 'head'	>	protrusion with more gently curved, circular outline and only minor concavities on either side of the outline
f. *y-akan* 'lower leg, foot'	>	relatively large protrusion

2. From body-part to object part where, in addition to *shape* properties, *space* properties are transferred:

(3)

a. *y-it* 'buttocks'	>	bottom end, the reverse end of *s-jol*
b. *s-pat* 'back'	>	the reverse end of surface of *y-elaw* and *x-ch'ujt*
c. *y-akan* 'lower leg, foot'	>	multiple projections near the base
d. *y-elaw* 'face'	>	(a) the head ends in a wide flattened rectangular or oval surface; (b) the opposite end of *s-pat*
e. *x-ch'ujt* 'belly'	>	the opposite end of *s-pat*
f. *s-k'ab* 'hand/arm'	>	multiple projections near the head

Within this group, shape properties appear to be secondary to *space* properties (where 'space' refers more precisely to relative location). This is suggested at least by observations like the following: A Tzeltal knife has a *y-it* 'buttocks' at the end of the handle, opposite the point, regardless of the shape of the handle (Levinson 1994:819). The fact that space is a distinctive property can be illustrated with the following example: Due to their different relative locations (near the head, not near the base), the branches of a tree are referred to as *s-k'ab* 'hand/arm', but the legs of a chair are referred to as *y-akan* 'lower leg, foot' (Levinson 1994:830–1).

3. Items that can be described exclusively with reference to *space* properties. There is probably only one body-part item that could be said to belong here—namely, *s-jol* 'head': At least in certain contexts, this item appears to have lost its shape component and is "extensionally equivalent" to the relational item *s-ba* 'top surface, edge, on top of, above' (Levinson 1994:803). Whenever type 3 obtains, then, we are dealing with a separate domain of conceptualization, namely, that of spatial orientation; we have dealt with this domain in detail in chapter 3.

Note that a given body-part can be associated with more than one kind of transfer. Thus, *y-akan* 'lower leg, foot' appears both in types 1 and 2, and *s-jol* 'head' appears in types 1 and 3.

It is shape and space (i.e., the location of a body-part vis-à-vis other body-parts) that provide the primary means for structuring the transfer pattern from body-part to object part in Tzeltal. But there is at least one more parameter in addition, which is size. Size is crucial for distinguishing items that are identical with reference to the other two parameters. For example, to designate relatively small protrusions on objects, the body-part *s-ni'* 'nose' is used, while for relatively large and unique protrusions the Tzeltal make use of *y-akan* 'foot, lower leg'. Perhaps more importantly, however, size is crucial for distinguishing the main axes of the human body: Rather than gravity, the Tzeltal have appealed to size to distinguish the vertical and the horizontal axes of the human body. The top-bottom axis is the one that, as Levinson (1994:814) puts it, "generates the generalized cone with the greatest volume"—that is, it is normally the longest axis available. The front-back axis is obviously shorter.

There appear to be two main kinds of models determining these transfers. On the one hand, there is a relational model that has, for instance, the head and the buttocks as extreme ends. Here the head appears to be conceptualized typically as a protrusion or sharp convexity, or as located opposite the flattest, most "squashed" end, and the buttocks are defined as constituting the spatial opposite to the head. On the other hand, there are individual body-part models based on shape properties of a given body-part. Thus, certain parts of inanimate items appear to be conceptualized as resembling a human nose or mouth and hence trigger the nose-model or the mouth-model, respectively. The nose-model, for example, applies to items having "a pointed protrusion at the head of the main axis of an object," where *s-ni'* 'nose' is largely stripped of its bodily associations (Levinson 1994:821).

I do not know of any other language that has exploited what may be called the body-part metaphor to such an extent to describe shape, space, and size properties of inanimate objects. Still, the principles underlying this metaphor appear to be the same across cultures, accounting for the fact that transfers like the ones listed in table 7-3 can be observed in a large variety of genetically and areally diverse languages.

7.4 Discussion

The transfers that we are dealing with in this chapter are in fact commonly described as involving *metaphor*. But in spite of the many treatments that have been devoted to the study of metaphor, most of them do not agree on the way metaphor should be defined. One may therefore not be surprised to come across a certain transfer that is called a metaphor by one author but not by others. We will be satisfied to assume that a metaphor is involved whenever the following criteria are met:

1. The source and the target concept are different referents.
2. The transfer involves two different domains of experience.
3. The transfer is not formally expressed.
4. The predication expressed by the metaphor is, if taken literally, false.

For example, if I call Peter a pig, then the two are not the same referent (Criterion [1]). One of them belongs to the domain of human beings and the other to that of domestic animals (Criterion [2]). There is no formal expression such as would exist in the case of a simile like 'Peter behaves like a pig', where *like* establishes a comparison between source and target (Criterion [3]). And the predication is literally false, since

I know that my friend Peter is not an animal (Criterion [4]). These criteria probably cover most canonical instances of metaphor, even if we will find many controversial cases.

If one is to trust the views expressed in most of the relevant literature, one is led to assume that there can hardly be any doubt that the processes described in the preceding sections have a metaphorical base.

An account in terms of metaphor handles many of the characteristics commonly associated with the transfer patterns described here (see Heine, Claudi, & Hünnemeyer 1991; Svorou 1994; Stolz 1994b); still, there are alternative views on this matter. First, metaphor takes care of only one aspect of the process concerned; what is required in addition is an analysis of how meanings are manipulated in discourse—in particular, of context-induced reinterpretation (Heine, Claudi, & Hünnemeyer 1991, chapter 3); I have alluded to this point in section 4.5. Second, at least one position questions the relevance of metaphor altogether, at least in cases like the ones discussed in the preceding section. On the basis of a detailed analysis of Tzeltal data, Levinson (1994) comes to the conclusion that, rather than metaphor, it is "internal geometry" that accounts for the terminological identity between body-parts and inanimate objects. He adduces a number of arguments to substantiate this claim.

One argument against an analysis in terms of metaphor concerns the fact that the mapping between body-part and inanimate object is not complete. Humans have only two hands/arms (s-k'ab) and two feet/lower legs (y-akan). Yet in Tzeltal, the s-k'ab 'branches' of a tree or the y-akan 'legs' of a chair are more numerous—that is, there is no one-to-one correspondence between source concept and target concept. It would seem that this argument is based on a strange understanding of metaphor, since "mismatches" of this kind not only are not unusual but indeed are to be expected in metaphorical transfers. An English hill has only one foot, while an Irish potato may have one eye or many eyes, and certainly not necessarily two; still, we may call the foot of a hill a metaphorical foot and the eye of an Irish potato a metaphorical eye. Typically it is only one salient part of the source concept that is highlighted for a metaphorical mapping, the other parts being backgrounded, or even ignored entirely.

Another argument adduced by Levinson goes like this: It may be difficult to establish whether in a given case the transfer involved is anthropomorphic (that is, leading from the human body to an inanimate object), zoomorphic (having the body of an animal as its source), or based on some other model. Hence it is hard to falsify the metaphorical approach, since someone using such an approach can easily choose between a number of alternative source schemas and "even invent others," as Levinson (1994:834) adds.

We do not think that this is a relevant argument, either. Comparative data that have become available in the course of the last decades suggest that Levinson's description of the relative contribution of the various kinds of source models has to be reconsidered (see especially Heine, Claudi, & Hünnemeyer 1991; Bowden 1991; Svorou 1994). To be sure, there are clear cases of zoomorphic transfer: It is common that the location of part of an object is described as the 'tail' of that object, and in such cases there is every reason to claim that a zoomorphic model has been at work (see section 3.1). On the whole, however, such cases are exceptional. It is almost invariably the human body—hence the anthropomorphic model—that provides the basis for conceptual transfers of the kind discussed by Levinson (1994); for example, in Tzeltal, transfers from 'mouth' to the 'mouth of a house' (= 'door'), or from 'nose' to the 'nose of the breast' (= 'nipple'). It is reasonable, therefore, to assume that it is the human body, rather than that of an animal or a plant, that was involved in a given instance of this kind of transfer, and to have recourse to alternative models only in cases where the anthropomorphic model fails to apply.

But there is a far more important observation: To decide which of the conceivable models was actually involved is a matter not of descriptive convenience or logical plausibility but of *historical truth*. Even if the linguist or anthropologist has problems deciding whether the Tzeltal term for 'nipple' owes its existence to a concept belonging to the human body or to some animal body, those Tzeltal people who were the first to introduce the transfer pattern must have known which source model they were opting for, and it is the task of the linguist or anthropologist to reconstruct what those Tzeltal people thought and did. Thus, the question of why a Tzeltal nipple is called the way it is—or, more generally, why people across languages and cultures regularly describe body-parts in terms of other body-parts, and inanimate objects in terms of body-parts—must be answered primarily not with reference to certain methodological parameters but with reference to whether or not the hypothesis considered is in accordance with historical reality.

Levinson (1994:834) argues, further, that he would have predicted that all body-part terms should be exploitable if metaphorical transfer had truly been involved, yet he finds that fewer than twenty actually are. Once more, such an argument is suggestive of a strange conception of metaphor. Obviously, certain body-parts are highly likely to serve as templates on account of their shape, size, and/or spatial characteristics, while other body-parts are less likely, or even unlikely, to do so. For example, the head is a body-part that naturally offers itself for transfers having to do, for instance, with spatial orientation or intellectual ability. A body-part like the liver, on the other hand, is less likely to be recruited for such transfers, or indeed for most other kinds of transfers. Accordingly, while in principle all body-parts can be exploited metaphorically, it is usually only a small portion that actually are.

Levinson also sees problems with the metaphor approach in accounting for what he calls "the generative application of body-part terms without hesitation to the parts of novel objects or to objects of indefinitely varying shape" (1994:835). But this is exactly what metaphor does, and in the case of Tzeltal we seem to be dealing with an instance of extraordinary metaphorical creativity. Some of these metaphorical creations will be conventionalized and end up as "dead metaphors," but this is unlikely to affect the overall creativity underlying the use of metaphor.

Finally, Levinson argues that it is more advantageous and simpler to analyze his Tzeltal data in terms of an "intrinsic geometry" than in terms of metaphor because the latter "is a mysterious and complex process" (Levinson 1994:834, 835). Apart from the fact that I do not see why metaphor should be mysterious or complex, this argument does not seem to be in accordance with the nature of the problem at hand: Which of the two hypotheses—metaphor or geometry—is correct is not a matter of which of the analyses proposed is more "advantageous," simpler, or more elegant, but is rather a matter of historical reality. The fact that the Tzeltal refer to both the branch of a tree and the human hand as a 'hand' (Levinson (1994:834) is the result of a historical process and has to be accounted for with reference to the historical facts that can be held responsible for this situation.

That in our discussion of a transfer from body-part to inanimate object we are in fact dealing with a metaphorical transfer from the human body in its upright position to inanimate objects is suggested by the following observations:

1. The process is entirely in accordance with our proposed definition of metaphor:
   a. The source and the target concept are different referents—that is, they are, respectively, a body-part and an inanimate object.
   b. The transfer involves two different domains of experience— namely, that of the human body and that of inanimate items.
   c. The transfer is not formally expressed.
   d. The metaphor consists of a predication that, if taken literally, is false: The 'hand of a tree' is not really a 'hand'.

2. The terminology employed to describe the shape, size, and spatial contours of inanimate items is taken from the human body.

3. The shape of an object part resembles that of the body-part with which it shares the name. Thus, small protrusions on objects are referred to as *s-ni'* 'nose' and larger ones as *y-akan* 'foot'. As this last example suggests, in addition to shape it may also be the relative size that is mapped from the source domain of body-parts to that of inanimate objects.

4. Similarly, the spatial axes used to describe properties of inanimate items are exactly as one would expect them to be, on the basis of one's knowledge of the human body: In Tzeltal, the end points of the vertical axis are conceptualized in terms of the body-parts 'head' (> 'up') and 'buttocks' (> 'down'). Similarly, the horizontal axis has the 'back' (> 'back') and either the 'belly' or the 'face' (> 'front') as its end points; similar situations are found in many other languages (see, e.g., Svorou 1994).

5. Another observation has to do with markedness. If we assume a metaphorical transfer from body-part to inanimate object, then we may not be surprised to find cases where the term concerned continues to be more basically associated with the original body-part domain than with the derived domain. This means, for instance, that the object part would be distinguished from the body-part by adding the name of the object. There are indeed such examples. Thus, the Tzeltal refer to the 'nipple' as *s-ni' chu'il*, the 'nose of the breast', while the human nose is simply referred to as 'nose' (rather than as 'nose of the head'; cf. Levinson 1994:808).

6. Finally, and most important, evidence from genetically and areally diverse languages suggests that if there exists a word in a given language that denotes both a body-part and a part of an inanimate item, then almost invariably the former meaning is historically

earlier—that is, the inanimate item-meaning is historically derived
from the body-part meaning. While we are not aware of any historical
records on Tzeltal, we do not expect this language to behave any
differently from other languages for which appropriate evidence does
exist. Thus, English items like 'foot', 'mouth', 'tongue', 'neck', and
'eye' probably served to denote parts of the human body before their
use was extended to inanimate items like mountains, rivers, shoes,
bottles, and potatoes.

To summarize, we are led to conclude that metaphor, while certainly not in every respect ideal for understanding processes of the kind discussed in this chapter, is
the only tool that takes care of the main features that characterize the transfer from
object to body-part (e.g., from 'mouse' to 'muscle'), from one body-part to another
(e.g., from 'finger' to 'toe'), or from body-part to inanimate part (e.g., from 'eye' to
the 'eye of a potato').

That the Tzeltal linguistically conceptualize objects as having internal coordi-
nate systems might seem exotic; in actual fact, however, it is not. What differs, for
instance, from the standard average European linguistic conceptualization is perhaps most of all the scope and rigidity with which the metaphorical mappings are
executed. In European cultures we do find individual mappings, but there are no
patterns of transfer that are nearly as regular and pervasive as those described by
Levinson (1994) for Tzeltal.

What these observations also seem to suggest is that there are tremendous cultural differences as to where the boundary between intrinsically described objects is
to be traced. Nevertheless, the ability to use the human body as a structural template
to understand and describe other objects can be assumed to be universal; hence, we
may expect this to be reflected in all languages.

One major concern in this chapter has been with defining conceptual shift as a
unidirectional process leading from source concepts—that is, items that are concrete, clearly delineated, and/or close to our cognitive apparatus—to more abstract,
less clearly delineated, and/or more remote target concepts. In order to determine
the directionality, we have appealed to a number of parameters, in particular the
following:

Diachrony. Terms for target concepts are historically derived from terms
    for source concepts—that is, the former are younger than the latter.
    Thus, the term 'leg' in the English expression 'table-leg' can be
    expected to be younger than its conceptual source, an animate 'leg'.

Markedness. The use of the term in its source meaning is likely to
    represent the unmarked one (e.g., 'leg'). This means, for example,
    that when the term is used without any further contextual clues, it is
    the source meaning that is implied. In order to make it clear that the
    target meaning is intended instead, one usually adds some modifier
    (e.g., 'of the table'). In a similar fashion, the Romanian term *deget*
    means both 'finger' and 'toe' (i.e., 'digit'), but in neutral contexts,

when there is no further contextual information, it denotes the digits of the upper half of the body—that is, the fingers (Andersen 1978:356). In more general terms, there are languages where the concepts 'finger' and 'toe' are referred to by one and the same label. In such languages one may expect that if one wants to distinguish between the two concepts one is likely to refer to 'toe' as 'finger of the foot(/leg)', while it is probably hard to find a language where 'toe' is the unmarked concept—that is, where one would refer to a finger as 'the toe of the hand'. Again, all historical evidence that is available suggests that whenever there is a word in a given language that denotes both 'finger' and 'toe', then the former meaning must have preceded the latter one.

Description. As opposed to the unmarked source item, there may be some descriptive phrase that is added to designate a derived concept. Description tends to relate to shape (e.g., German *Augapfel* 'eye apple', English *eyeball*, Finnish *silmä muna* 'eye-egg'); location (Czech *zá pesti* 'behind fist' or 'wrist'); or function (Finnish *käsi varsi* 'hand handle' or 'arm').

Context. It may happen that marking no longer offers any clues for determining directionality. In such cases it is likely that the source meaning can be inferred with reference to the larger range of contexts in which the item concerned occurs. For example, a number of languages have an 'eye/face' polysemy (where 'eye' and 'face' are expressed by one and the same term). The term *hual* in Huastec exemplifies such a situation. That the 'eye'-meaning is basic and the 'face'-meaning the derived one is suggested by the fact that when *hual* is used in compounded forms designating diseases, the form usually refers to conditions of the eye rather than conditions of the face—for example, *ya' ul-hual* 'eye irritation' (Andersen 1978:356). This interpretation is in agreement with the historical evidence that has become available so far: Wherever there is such evidence, it suggests that 'eye' is the source and 'face' the target meaning; that is, in the history of the term, there was a phase where it had the meaning 'eye' but not yet 'face' (see table 7-2).

7.5   Summary

Work on grammaticalization has shown that the evolution of grammatical categories is unidirectional—that is, it proceeds from lexical to grammatical forms, from open-class to closed-class categories, from concrete to abstract meanings, and so on (see, for instance, Traugott & Heine 1991a, 1991b; Heine, Claudi, & Hünnemeyer 1991; Bybee, Perkins, & Pagliuca 1994).

The main purpose of the present chapter was to demonstrate that the unidirectionality principle is not confined to the evolution of grammar but rather applies as well to lexical domains like the one looked at here. Other examples of unidirectional semantic evolution within the lexicon are not hard to come by (cf., e.g., Williams's 1976 work on synaesthetic adjectives, or Viberg's 1984 study of perception verbs). In all cases concerned there are likely to be exceptions (see, e.g., section 7.2). But exceptions are rare and frequently are not really to be viewed as "exceptions" as much as instances that are suggestive of some alternative principle.

It would seem that in the preceding sections we were faced with such an exception: In section 7.1 our interest was with transfers from objects to body-parts, while in section 7.3 we were looking at what appears to be suggestive of a reverse directionality: from body-part to inanimate object. Upon closer examination, however, it turns out that the object items discussed in section 7.1 are not exactly the ones looked at in 7.3. In the former we were dealing with items like German *Ohrmuschel* 'external ear (auricle)', which means literally 'ear-shell', or the fact that the eyeball is an 'eye-egg' in Finnish but an 'eye-apple' in German. What most of the items that serve as sources for body-parts appear to have in common is that they are *not a part of some whole* but rather independent entities. Things like shells, balls, eggs, or apples are not normally relational items whose occurrence implies a part-whole relationship, nor is their use restricted to possessor-possessee phrases.

Our concern in section 7.3, on the other hand, was with items like 'mouth of a river', 'legs of a table', or 'neck of a bottle'—that is, with relational concepts that form part of some whole. Still, one may argue, the examples discussed in section 7.1 also include relational items as sources—that is, human role relations such as 'mother', 'father', or 'son'. This fact does not seem to pose a problem for the analysis proposed here, either. It would seem that kinship terms and body-parts are relational items of two different orders: The latter, but not the former, are instances of a part-whole relation. Whereas 'Regina's nose' suggests a part-whole relation, 'Regina's father-in-law' does not, unless used in some transferred sense.

This means that we are faced with an evolution that leads from names for animate or inanimate items to body-parts—that is, to animate part-whole relations—and from body-parts to inanimate part-whole relations. The overall development dealt with in this chapter would then seem to be largely as sketched in (4).

(4)   Animate or inanimate item → animate part of a whole → inanimate part of a whole

This evolution suggests two separate kinds of development: one from whole to part, and one from animate to inanimate item. This evolution is unidirectional, even if exceptions are found occasionally (like Finnish *käsi varsi* 'arm', which literally means "hand handle"; see the preceding discussion), or if no convincing hypothesis can be postulated (as, e.g., in the case of Tzeltal *y-akan*, which has equal reference to the handles of implements and to the legs of animals; Levinson 1994:808).

I have been concerned here with only a limited spectrum of semantic evolution. For example, terms for body-parts are not only derived from other body-parts or objects; they may also be derived from terms for activities relating to the functions of the body-parts concerned. Thus, the German word *Gesicht* 'face' is related to *sehen* 'see', and the English word 'ear' may perhaps ultimately be related to the word 'hear' (see, e.g., Buck 1949 for more details). This chapter has emphasized that lexical items belonging to specific semantic domains are exploited time and again to designate other items, and that this development is unidirectional. In the preceding chapters, by contrast, I was concerned with the emergence of new word and morpheme types— more specifically, with the evolution from open-class words like nouns and verbs to closed-class items like adverbs, adpositions, articles, and the like. The overall pattern of transfer, however, appears to be essentially the same.

That this is in fact so can be illustrated with an example already touched upon briefly in section 7.1. To express the notion 'testicle', certain options offer themselves and, in fact, appear to be drawn upon over and over across cultures. These options, Wilkins argues, are shaped by the fact that testicles are perceived as small-ish, roundish, and naturally occurring (rather than man-made). Items that come close to fitting this characterization are 'egg', 'seed', 'fruit', and 'stone', and it is exactly these items that provide the most common options crosslinguistically for words meaning 'testicle' (Brown & Witkowski 1981:603–4; Wilkins 1996). As we saw (section 7.1), one can predict with a certain degree of probability that 'testicles' will be called 'eggs' or 'nuts' or 'potatoes' in a given society; still, it is hard to predict which of these options will be chosen.

Exactly the same principles govern the evolution of grammatical categories, as we have seen in the preceding chapters. Usually only a small pool of source concepts offer themselves for grammaticalization. Which of these concepts is recruited is a matter of culture-specific choice, and even if one of them is conventionalized as a grammatical category, this does not exclude the possibility that the other options, or some of them, may also be made use of for specific purposes. In the same way as a word for 'egg' will lose a number of its properties in contexts where it acquires the secondary meaning 'testicle', so a verb meaning 'want' or 'go to', when conventionalized as a future tense marker, will lose a number of the properties it had when used as a lexical item.

In order to understand and account for language structure, then, we must combine a universalist and a relativist perspective. The former enables us to define the narrow range of options that are normally drawn upon for the expression of a given concept; the latter may help us understand why in a given part of the world it is Option X, rather than Y or Z, that is made use of, or why the pool of options normally employed cross-culturally is ignored altogether by a given speech community.

8

OUTLOOK

Suppose you have a daughter and you want to give her a name that is not biased in any way—that is, a name that has no meaning. You might decide to call her "X." A possible or even likely reaction that your decision will trigger is that people will wonder: Why is she called X? There must be a special meaning to it. Naming, we argue, is not arbitrary; it is inherently motivated, irrespective of whether it involves the naming of persons, objects, or activities, and irrespective of whether the name is chosen from the language concerned or from some other language. Essentially the same applies to the "naming of grammatical meanings"—that is, to the strategies used to find linguistic forms for the expression of grammatical functions.

Accordingly, if we fail to reconstruct the motivation that can be held responsible for a given name, as is frequently the case, then we must assume that this is due to our ignorance. A conclusion like "I cannot see any motivation, hence, there is no motivation" runs the risk of turning ignorance into a scientific dogma.

No attempt is made here to determine the exact nature of the motivating force that underlies naming. Nevertheless, until further evidence becomes available, I assume, as has also been done in other works on grammaticalization (Heine, Claudi, & Hünnemeyer 1991:29ff.; Hopper & Traugott 1993:67), that the processes described in this book have to do with the psychological notion of problem solving. The problem or problems to be solved are extralinguistic: They relate to our desire to interact as well as possible with others of our species and, more specifically, to communicate successfully. It is the latter goal in particular that accounts for "the very systematic nature of the mental and communicative processes that govern language use" (Bybee, Perkins, & Pagliuca 1994:298).

But our concern here has not been primarily with communication. Successful speaker-hearer interaction presupposes conceptualization processes on which communication is built. Thus, in addition to dealing with speaker-hearer interaction, the study of the motivation underlying the development of grammar must be concerned with the strategies used for understanding the world around us. And most of what has been said in this book relates to the latter goal (see the following discussion).

LANGUAGE STRUCTURE, it has been argued, is an immediate reflection of thought, of the way the mind works. Language tells us how and what people think. While I wish to underscore this assertion, especially since it constitutes one of the cornerstones of my methodology, one has to bear in mind that it is essentially false, and I have therefore referred to this assertion as the "literal-meaning fallacy" (section 5.5). It is false for a number of reasons. First, we do not always say what we think, even if we think we do. Second, and more important, language is a historical product, and almost everything that is part of it came into being before we were born. In order to understand and account for the forms that constitute our language, therefore, it is not enough to analyze modern habits of language use; rather, we must understand what purpose these forms served at the time they were created. Thus, as was pointed out in section 1.1 (Assumption D), linguistic explanations are of necessity incomplete unless they are supported by appropriate historical reconstructions. In the course of this book, I discussed a number of examples to illustrate this observation. In chapter 4, for example, I pointed out that indefinite articles are in most cases derived from the cardinal numeral 'one'. In order to understand the meaning, the morphosyntax, and even the phonetic properties of indefinite articles, therefore, we must consider their history as quantifiers; otherwise we will miss important insights into their behavior.

Further, chapter 5 illustrates that possessive constructions tend to retain uses of the source schemas from which they are derived, such as Location, Action, and the like. Drawing on the fact that in a number of languages the constructions used for expressing possession are also those that serve to express location, some linguists, as well as many nonlinguists, tend to believe that certain cultures lack the concept of possession or ownership. Such claims are usually unjustified, first, because there is evidence to suggest that possession is a universal concept that is distinguished both linguistically and conceptually in all societies known so far (see Heine 1997), and second, because crosslinguistically, expressions for possession (rather than the concept of possession itself) turn out to be derived from other domains of human experience, such as location and action. Such linguistic observations are corroborated by extralinguistic considerations—for instance, by the fact that concepts like 'to rob' and 'to steal' tend to be part of the legal system of most societies worldwide, hence theft is likely to result in legal actions. The findings made in the preceding chapters not only allow us to explain why grammatical categories are structured the way they are but also enable us to predict within limits what is going to happen (Stolz 1994b; Heine 1995). As the preceding chapters have shown, the range of concepts from which a linguistic form can be derived is severely constrained. In a number of cases, there is essentially only one source concept, as, for instance, in the case of terms for some cardinal directions (chapter 3) or for indefinite articles (chapter 4).

In such cases it is possible to propose probabilistic predictions, like the following (1) through (3).

1. If new terms for the cardinal directions 'east' and 'west' are acquired, then most likely these terms are derived from expressions relating, respectively, to the rising and the setting sun.
2. If in a given language a definite article arises, then most likely this article is derived from a demonstrative attribute.
3. If in a given language an indefinite article develops, then this article is almost invariably derived from the cardinal numeral 'one'.

In other cases it may be more difficult to propose meaningful predictions. But even if there is a larger number of possible source concepts, as appears to be the case with spatial orientation (chapter 3), possession (chapter 5), or comparison (chapter 6), it is sometimes possible to formulate reasonable predictions. Adverbs or adpositions for the spatial orientation point 'front' ('in front (of)', 'before', etc.), for example, are likely to be derived from the noun 'face', though there are a number of alternative sources in addition, like 'eye', 'head', 'breast', and the like (see chapter 3). What these sources have in common is that they all denote body-parts. We can therefore formulate a more general prediction of the kind proposed in (4):

4. If in a given language a new term for 'front' is introduced, then that term is almost invariably derived from a body-part noun.

But even if it is not possible to propose a universally defined prediction for a certain grammatical or other category, there are nevertheless other parameters that can be helpful for making predictions. Areal distribution is one of these parameters. As we saw in chapter 6, areal influence as a result of language contact is an important driving force for conceptualization processes. When languages are in contact, borrowing is likely to arise. It is widely held that borrowing is most pronounced in the lexicon and grammar will be much less affected, if at all; the fact that grammar belongs to those parts of language that are most resistant to borrowing has been observed independently by quite a number of authors. But this view may be in need of modification. While we would not expect a language that is in contact with English to borrow the comparative marker -er or the genitive marker of, it is much more likely that the cognitive pattern used for the expression of the notion of comparison or possession might indeed be transferred from one language to another. One example to illustrate this point was presented in section 6.3: Whether the comparison of inequality 'X is Y-er than Z' is expressed by means of the Location Schema, the Polarity Schema, or any other particular source structure is determined to some extent by areal forces, and a number of probabilistic predictions based on areal distribution were presented in that section.

The explanatory potential of structural linguistics, be it of the Bloomfieldian or the Chomskyan brand, is modest, essentially because the phenomena deemed worthy of scholarly attention are severely limited in a number of ways. This is due most of all to the fact that linguistic explanation within that paradigm is largely internal and, furthermore, is limited to the synchronic state of language or languages. Accordingly, many of the explanatory accounts of structuralists are suggestive of epiphenomenal observations. Explaining the syntax of possessive constructions in terms of synchronic syntax, for example, as has been done in a number of structuralist works (e.g., Freeze 1992), tends to reduce explanation to a structural mechanism that one might hesitate to call an explanation (see Heine 1997). It fails to account, for instance, for the fact that have-constructions can have a large variety of different morphosyntactic forms, and that the structure of these forms is predictable on the basis of the conceptual templates from which these forms are derived. Such templates have to do with more concrete experiences relating to such notions as action, location, and accompaniment. As we saw in chapter 5, these templates account for all the main structural properties of have-constructions—for example, why the possessor is encoded as the subject of the clause in some languages, but as an object, a goal, a genitive, a comitative, or some other clausal participant in other languages.

In accordance with Assumption C of the introductory chapter (section 1.1), the first priority in this book has been to look for external explanations for language structure. Grammar, I argued, is the result of an interaction between conceptualization strategies and communication strategies. Conceptualization strategies are employed, for example, to understand nonspatial relations, such as temporal ones, in terms of spatial relations, or spatial relations in terms of physical objects. This strategy may then be recruited for communication purposes—more specifically, for structuring discourse. Both spatial and temporal relations are further exploited to mark what is sometimes referred to as "logical relations" in discourse. This means that erstwhile expressions for spatial and temporal concepts turn into markers for discourse functions such as anaphora or cataphora, or into markers for conditional, causal, purposive, adversative, concessive, and other relations, and this again may also have the effect that adverbs and adpositions originally used for locative or temporal concepts tend to end up as elements whose main function it is to express clausal subordination (see, e.g., Frajzyngier 1991; Heine et al. 1993).

To conclude, what I have tried to demonstrate in the preceding chapters is that language is a product of our interaction with the world around us. The way we build discourses and develop linguistic categories can be derived from the way we experience our environment and use that experience to communicate with others of our species. Furthermore, some of the dynamics that underlie the use of linguistic forms have been highlighted. These dynamics are also reflected in the structure of linguistic categories. Describing these forms as discrete categories by means of a fixed set of criteria based on necessary and sufficient conditions may be useful, or even indispensable, depending on the purpose that the description is meant to serve. But if the purpose is to explain language structure, then such a description is not necessarily very helpful; it is more likely to be a straitjacket that constitutes an obstacle to understanding language structure. Such obstacles have been pointed out by many scholars working in the various functionalist traditions (see, e.g., Givón 1979, 1995; Lakoff 1987; Taylor 1989). With regard to the structures examined in this book, such characteristics are, for example:

1. Linguistic items tend to retain some of the properties of the items
   from which they are derived, a characteristic that has been called

persistence by Hopper (1991). This applies especially to the earlier stages in the development of grammatical categories. In their later stages, new properties can emerge that are suggestive of the rise of a new item. Accordingly, on the basis of the evolution sketched in (1), we may expect item B to include properties of its historical source A, even while it can already have acquired properties of C, which is a new form derived from B.

(1)   A > B > C

2. As the examples in the preceding chapters have hopefully shown, the transfer from A to B, or from B to C, starts with meaning before it spreads to the morphosyntax and phonology of the items concerned. Semantic change thus precedes all other changes (cf. Assumption A, section 1.1). This means that B can still overwhelmingly have the syntactic, morphological, and/or phonological trappings of A while its meaning may bear virtually no resemblance to A. Auxiliaries, for example, may still retain syntactic, morphological, and phonetic properties of a main verb while their meaning is already that of a grammatical item.

3. The evolution sketched in (1) is likely to be reflected in the patterns of contextual expansion, and it is therefore likely to be synchronically recoverable in the form of complementary contextual use. This means, for example, that even if the shift from A to B has already been concluded, A may still survive in restricted contexts. Similarly, although no shift from B to C is discernible as yet, B may have developed uses in certain contexts that are no longer compatible with other uses of B but rather suggest that B is reinterpreted in such contexts as something new—namely, as C. We may refer to the three characteristics just outlined as persistence, form-meaning asymmetry, and contextual expansion, respectively.

4. Finally, the dynamics that underlie the use of linguistic forms constitute a challenge to the claim that lexicon and grammar are discrete and separate entities. It may happen, for example, that A refers to the lexical use of a given linguistic item (e.g., a body-part noun), while B can be interpreted both lexically and grammatically (when that noun occurs in adpositional use), and C refers to the use of that item exclusively as a grammatical marker (e.g., as a locative adposition). In such cases, one and the same linguistic item is associated simultaneously with uses that are lexical, uses that are neither clearly lexical nor clearly grammatical, and uses that are grammatical. The way this may happen is illustrated in figure 8-1 on the basis of data discussed in chapters 2, 3, and 4.

A number of other examples have become available in the preceding chapters. Indefinite articles, for example, are likely to have properties that link them with numerals (see chapter 4). Even if an indefinite article has been conventionalized to the

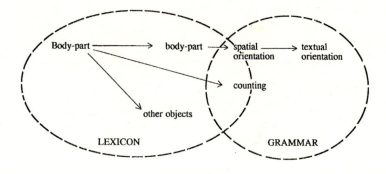

Figure 8-1   From lexicon to grammar: The contribution of body-parts.

extent that its erstwhile semantics as a numeral is bleached out entirely, much of its morphosyntax and/or phonological shape may still be that of the numeral 'one'. Furthermore, the use of the indefinite article (B) may have been generalized as an obligatory marker on nouns (C), even if the article is phonologically still identical with the numeral (A). Finally, the extent to which the indefinite article still retains properties of numerals is largely dependent on the contexts in which it is used (see chapter 4).

What these observations would seem to suggest is that linguistic categories are more appropriately described as chains, clines, continua, or linear family resemblance categories (Heine 1992; Hopper & Traugott 1993), rather than as sharply delineated, discrete structures.

The methodology used here is based on regularities in the structure of conceptual transfer, where transfer concerns the evolution of individual items and structures. What this methodology does not offer, however, is a principled way of relating different items and structures to one another. For example, in chapter 4 I proposed a few generalizations on indefinite articles, and I also drew attention to correlations between definite and indefinite articles. Languages that have grammaticalized indefinite articles, I observed there, are also likely to have definite articles, while the opposite is not necessarily the case. How such observations can be integrated within a more diversified framework of conceptual dynamics is an open question.

Another problem that has been associated with the present methodology concerns Assumption F (section 1.1)—namely, the unidirectionality principle. According to one of the main premises underlying this work, established in a number of previous works, grammaticalization is a unidirectional process (Lehmann 1982; Heine & Reh 1984; Heine, Claudi, & Hünnemeyer 1991; Hopper & Traugott 1993; Bybee, Perkins, & Pagliuca 1994). This is a strong claim, and a number of exceptions to the principle have been pointed out (cf. Campbell 1991; Greenberg 1991; Ramat 1992). The exact status of such exceptions remains to be investigated; for the time being, I will assume that certain specific forces can be held responsible for exceptions. Such forces will have to do, in particular, with the pragmatics of linguistic communication (cf. Forchheimer 1953:37ff.) and relate to psychological and sociological factors such as taboo strategies and euphemism, politeness, humbleness, paternalism, and the like (see Allen & Burridge 1991). To use a common example, spatial concepts tend to be expressed in terms of body-parts (chapter 3): What is behind/in front of us is likely to be expressed in terms of where our back/face is located. At the same time, however, certain body-parts, most of all private parts, can also be labeled by means of locative expressions. Sexual organs, for example, can be called 'the thing in front' or 'the bottom thing', and such euphemistic expressions may be conventionalized as the only word for the relevant item, as appears to have happened, for instance, in some Swahili dialects, where the expression *mbeleni* 'in front' came to become a regularly used term for 'genital organs'. In such cases, the unidirectionality principle, whereby body-parts serve as structural templates for spatial reference, is violated in that we observe a reversed directionality from spatial term to body-part term—but for a particular reason.

Yet, although it can be violated in the presence of alternative cognitive principles, the unidirectionality principle turns out to be statistically significant and can serve as a basis for generalizations on both linguistic evolution and language structure. But unidirectionality is also relevant in another way. For example, we observed in the preceding chapter that terms for certain body-parts serve as structural templates for other body-parts. Thus, the human hand or foot provides a convenient template for expressing 'finger' and 'toe', respectively, for example by adding a diminutive marker. Accordingly, there are a number of languages where 'finger' is expressed as something like 'child of the hand' or 'little hand'.

Conversely, one might expect that the reverse process is also possible—that is, that 'hand' is expressed by adding an augmentative marker to the lexeme for 'finger'. However, there appears to be no language in which, say, 'hand' is expressed as the 'big finger'. Expressions that literally mean 'big finger' have commonly served as a basis for conceptual transfer, almost invariably leading to new expressions for 'thumb' but not for 'hand'. In a similar fashion, combinations of words for 'toe' plus an augmentative marker are apparently a widespread source for words for 'big toe', but never for 'foot'. To conclude, unidirectionality is constrained in specific ways; fingers can be conceptualized as small hands, but hands are unlikely to be conceptualized as big fingers.

Lexical items or constructions lose their original meaning when pressed into service for grammatical functions, and they become etymologically opaque. But what is likely to survive are structural properties still reflecting the original use. These properties are suggestive of what I proposed in section 2.4 to call *pattern transparency*; they help us reconstruct earlier patterns of language use that are no longer etymologically accessible (see section 2.4).

The observations made throughout this book have illustrated the significance of the assumptions made in the introductory chapter (section 1.1). On the basis of these assumptions, I have proposed linguistic explanations that go beyond the scope of alternative grammatical models. I have been concerned, however, primarily with the initial phase in the evolution of new meanings and new forms. The further this evolution proceeds, the more it becomes affected by other forces whereby free and unconstrained patterns of language use turn into conventionalized grammatical constructions, and semantic phenomena increasingly give way to morphosyntactic and morphophonological ones. The way this process is structured has been described in some detail in the works on grammaticalization cited herein.

These observations also suggest a different perspective with regard to the role played by the speaker in linguistic interaction. In most schools of modern linguistics, both the speaker and the hearer are portrayed somehow as the victims of their grammar—as passive beings that have to cope with the language or languages acquired. This book emphasizes that there is an alternative view on this matter. According to this view, speakers and hearers are not only language consumers; they are, to use the wording proposed by Hagège (1993), just as much language builders.

REFERENCES

Abraham, Roy Clive. 1933. *The Tiv people*. Lagos: The Government Printer.

Agheyisi, Rebecca Nogieru. 1971. *West African Pidgin English: Simplification and simplicity*. (Ph.D. diss., Stanford University.) Ann Arbor, Michigan: University Microfilms.

Ahlqvist, Anders (ed.). 1982. *Papers from the 5th International Conference on Historical Linguistics*. (Amsterdam Studies in the Theory and History of Linguistic Science, 21.) Amsterdam: John Benjamins.

Allan, Keith, & Kate Burridge. 1991. *Euphemism and dysphemism: Language use as a shield and weapon*. New York: Oxford University Press.

Amborn, Hermann, Gunter Minker, & Hans-Jürgen Sasse. 1980. *Das Dullay: Materialien zu einer ostkuschitischen Sprachgruppe*. (Kölner Beiträge zur Afrikanistik, 6.) Berlin: Dietrich Reimer.

Ameka, Felix K. 1991. Ewe: Its grammatical constructions and illocutionary devices. Ph.D. diss., Australian National University, Canberra.

Andersen, Elaine S. 1978. Lexical universals of body-part terminology. In: Greenberg, *Universals*, Vol. 3, pp. 335–68.

Andersen, Paul Kent. 1980. On the reconstruction of the syntax of comparison in PIE. In: Ramat, *Linguistic reconstruction*, pp. 225–36.

———. 1983. *Word order typology and comparative constructions*. (Amsterdam Studies in the Theory and History of Linguistic Science, 25.) Amsterdam: John Benjamins.

Anderson, John M. 1971. *The grammar of case: Towards a localistic theory*. London: Cambridge University Press.

———. 1973. *An essay concerning aspect: Some considerations of a general character arising from the Abbé Darrigol's analysis of the Basque verb*. (Janua Linguarum, Series Minor, 167.) The Hague: Mouton.

155

————. 1979. Serialization, dependency, and the syntax of possessives in Moru. *Studia Linguistica* 33,1:1–25.

Anderson, Lloyd B. 1975. Grammar-meaning universals and proto-language reconstruction or, Proto-World NOW! *Chicago Linguistic Society* 11:15–36.

Anderson, R. C., R. J. Spiro, & W. E. Montague (eds.). 1977. *Schooling and the acquisition of knowledge.* Hillsdale, N.J.: Erlbaum.

Antal, L. 1964. The possessive form of the Hungarian noun. *Linguistics* 3:50–61.

Anttila, Raimo. 1989. *Historical and comparative linguistics.* (Current Issues in Linguistic Theory, 6.) 2nd rev. ed. Amsterdam: John Benjamins.

Austin, Peter. 1981. *A grammar of Diyari, South Australia.* (Cambridge Studies in Linguistics, 32.) Cambridge: Cambridge University Press.

Auwera, Johan van der (ed.). Forthcoming. *Adverbial constructions in the languages of Europe.* Berlin: Mouton de Gruyter.

Bach, Emmon. 1967. *Have* and *be* in English syntax. *Language* 43,2:462–85.

Bach, Emmon, & Robert T. Harms (eds.). 1968. *Universals in linguistic theory.* New York: Holt, Rinehart and Winston.

Bailard, Joelle. 1982. Le français de demain: VSO ou VOS. In: Ahlqvist, *Papers from the 5th International Congress,* pp. 20–28.

————. 1987. Il s'en va où le français, et pourquoi? In: Ramat, Carruba, & Bernini, *Papers from the Seventh International Conference,* pp. 35–55.

Bally, Charles. 1926. L'expression des idées de sphère personelle et de solidarité dans les langues indo-européennes. In: Fankhauser & Jud, *Festschrift Louis Gauchat,* pp. 68–78.

Bargery, G. P. 1934. *A Hausa-English dictionary and English-Hausa vocabulary.* Oxford: Oxford University Press.

Barr, L. I. 1965. *A course in Lugbara.* Nairobi: East African Literature Bureau.

Bartlett, Frederic C. 1932. *Remembering: A study in experimental and social psychology.* Cambridge: Cambridge University Press.

Bates, Elizabeth, & Brian MacWhinney. 1989. Functionalism and the competition model. In: MacWhinney & Bates, *Crosslinguistic study,* pp. 3–73.

Bavin, Edith. 1996. Body parts in Acholi: Alienable and inalienable distinctions, and extended uses. In: Chappell & McGregor, *Grammar of inalienability,* pp. 841–64.

Beckmann, Petr. 1972. *The structure of language: A new approach.* Boulder: Golem Press.

Beeler, M.S. 1961. Senary counting in California Penutian. *Anthropological Linguistics* 3,6:1–8.

Bendix, Edward Herman. 1966. *Componential analysis of general vocabulary: The semantic structure of a set of verbs in English, Hindi, and Japanese.* Bloomington: Indiana University Press.

Benveniste, Emile. 1960. "Etre" et "avoir" dans leurs fonctions linguistiques. *Bulletin de la Société de Linguistique* 55,1:113–34. Reprinted in *Problèmes de linguistique générale,* pp. 187–207. Paris, Gallimard, 1966.

Bhaskararao, Peri. 1972. On the syntax of Telugu existential and copulative predications. In: Verhaar, *Verb 'be',* Part 2, pp. 153–206.

Bhat, D.N.S. 1991. *Grammatical relations: The evidence against their necessity and universality.* London: Routledge.

Bickel, Balthasar. 1993. The possessive of experience in Belhare. Paper presented at the workshop "From Body to Emotion and Cognition," Cologne, 2–3 July.

————. 1994. *Spatial operations in deixis, cognition, and culture: Where to orient oneself in Belhare.* (Cognitive Anthropology Research Group, Working Paper 28.) Nijmegen: Max Planck Institute for Psycholinguistics.

Bickerton, Derek. 1977. Pidginization and creolization: Language acquisition and language universals. In: Valdman, *Pidgin and creole linguistics*, pp. 49–69.

——. 1981. *Roots of language*. Ann Arbor: Karoma Publishers.

——. 1990. *Language and species*. Chicago: University of Chicago Press.

Biermann, Anna. 1985. *Possession und Zuschreibung im Ungarischen*. (Continuum—Schriftenreihe zur Linguistik, 4.) Tübingen: Gunter Narr.

Bills, Garland D., Bernardo Vallejo C., & Rudolph C. Troike. 1969. *An introduction to spoken Bolivian Quechua*. Austin: University of Texas Press.

Bird, Charles S. 1972. The syntax and semantics of possession in Bambara. Paper presented at the Conference on Manding Studies, London.

Bisang, Walter. 1995. Areal typology and grammaticalization: Processes of grammaticalization based on nouns and verbs in East and mainland South East Asian languages. Paper presented at the Annual Meeting of the Societas Linguistica Europaea, University of Leiden, 31 August to 2 September.

Blake, Barry J. 1984. Problems of possessor ascension: Some Australian examples. *Linguistics* 22:437–53.

——. 1990. *Relational grammar*. London: Routledge.

——. 1994. *Case*. Cambridge: Cambridge University Press.

Boeder, Winfried. 1980. "Haben" in den Kartwelsprachen. In: Lehmann & Brettschneider, *Wege der Universalienforschung*, pp. 207–17.

Bowden, John. 1991. Behind the preposition: Grammaticalization of locatives in Oceanic languages. M.A. thesis, University of Auckland.

Bowers, J. S. 1975. Some adjectival nominalizations in English. *Lingua* 37:341–61.

Brainerd, C. J. (ed.). 1982. *Children's logical and mathematical cognition*. New York: Springer.

Brauner, Siegmund. 1993. *Einführung ins Schona*. (Afrikawissenschaftliche Lehrbücher, 5.) Cologne: Rüdiger Köppe.

Brinkmann, Hennig. 1959. Die "haben"-Perspektive im Deutschen. In: *Sprache—Schlüssel zur Welt: Festschrift für Leo Weisgerber*. Düsseldorf: Schwann, pp. 176–94.

Brown, Cecil H. 1976. General principles of human anatomical partonomy and speculations on the growth of partonomic nomenclature. *American Ethnologist* 3,3:400–24.

——. 1983. Where do cardinal direction terms come from? *Anthropological Linguistics* 25,2:121–61.

Brown, Cecil H., & Stanley R. Witkowski. 1981. Figurative language in a universalist perspective. *American Ethnologist* 8,3:596–615.

——. 1983. Polysemy, lexical change and cultural importance. *Man* (n.s.) 18:72–89.

Brown, Penelope, & Stephen C. Levinson. 1993a. *Linguistic and nonlinguistic coding of spatial arrays: Explorations in Mayan cognition*. (Cognitive Anthropology Research Group, Working Paper 24.) Nijmegen: Max Planck Institute for Psycholinguistics.

——. 1993b. 'Uphill' and 'downhill' in Tzeltal. *Journal of Linguistic Anthropology* 3,1:46–74.

Brugman, Claudia Marlea. 1981. The story of "over." M.A. thesis, University of California, Berkeley.

——. 1983. The use of body-part terms as locatives in Chalcatongo Mixtec. *Survey of Californian and Other Indian Languages* 4:235–90.

——. 1984. The *very* idea: A case study in polysemy and cross-lexical generalization. *Chicago Linguistic Society*, Parasession on Lexical Semantics, pp. 21–38.

——. 1988. The syntax and semantics of HAVE and its complements. Ph.D. diss., University of California, Berkeley.

Brugman, Claudia Marlea, & Monica Macaulay. 1986. Interacting semantic systems: Mixtec expressions of location. *Berkeley Linguistics Society* 12:315–27.

Buck, Carl Darling. 1949. *A dictionary of selected synonyms in the principal Indo-European languages: A contribution to the history of ideas.* Chicago: University of Chicago Press.

Bugenhagen, Robert D. 1986. Possession in Mangap-Mbula: Its syntax and semantics. *Oceanic Linguistics* 25,1/2:124–66.

Burgess, Don. 1984. Western Tarahumara. In: Langacker, *Studies in Uto-Aztecan grammar,* pp. 1–149.

Burridge, Kate. 1990. Sentence datives and the grammaticization of the dative possessive: Evidence from Germanic. *La Trobe University Working Papers in Linguistics* 3:29–47.

Butterworth, Brian, Bernard Comrie, & Östen Dahl (eds.). 1984. *Explanations for language universals.* Berlin: Mouton de Gruyter.

Byarushengo, E. R., A. Duranti, & Larry M. Hyman (eds.). 1977. *Haya grammatical structure.* (Southern California Occasional Papers in Linguistics, 6.) Los Angeles: Department of Linguistics, University of Southern California.

Bybee, Joan L. 1985. *Morphology: A study of the relation between meaning and form.* (Typological Studies in Language, 9.) Amsterdam: John Benjamins.

Bybee, Joan L., & Östen Dahl. 1989. The creation of tense and aspect systems in the languages of the world. *Studies in Language* 13,1:51–103.

Bybee, Joan L., & William Pagliuca. 1985. Cross linguistic comparison and the development of grammatical meaning. In: Fisiak, *Historical semantics,* pp. 59–83.

Bybee, Joan L., William Pagliuca, & Revere D. Perkins. 1991. Back to the future. In: Traugott & Heine, *Approaches to grammaticalization,* Vol. 2, pp. 17–58.

Bybee, Joan L., Revere D. Perkins, & William Pagliuca. 1994. *The evolution of grammar: Tense, aspect, and modality in the languages of the world.* Chicago: University of Chicago Press.

Byrne, Francis, & John Holm (eds.). 1993. *Atlantic meets Pacific: A global view of pidginization and creolization.* (Creole Language Library, 11.) Amsterdam: John Benjamins.

Campbell, Lyle. 1985. *The Pipil language of El Salvador.* (Mouton Grammar Library, 1.) Berlin: Mouton de Gruyter.

———. 1991. Some grammaticalization changes in Estonian and their implications. In: Traugott & Heine, *Approaches to grammaticalization,* Vol. 1, pp. 285–99.

Capell, A. 1949. The concept of ownership in the languages of Australia and the Pacific. *Southwestern Journal of Anthropology* 5,3:169–89.

Carlin, Eithne. 1993. *The So language.* (Afrikanistische Monographien, 2.) Cologne: Institut für Afrikanistik, University of Cologne.

Casagrande, J. B., & Kenneth L. Hale. 1967. Semantic relations in Papago folk definitions. In: Hymes & Bittle, *Studies in Southwestern ethnolinguistics,* pp. 165–96.

Chappell, Hilary, & William McGregor. 1989. Alienability, inalienability and nominal classification. *Berkeley Linguistics Society* 15:24–36.

———. (eds.) 1996. *The grammar of inalienability: A typological perspective on body part terms and the part-whole relation.* Berlin: Mouton de Gruyter.

Chomsky, Noam. 1965. *Aspects of the theory of syntax.* Cambridge, Mass.: MIT Press.

———. 1972. Remarks on nominalization. In: *Studies on semantics in generative grammar.* The Hague: Mouton, pp. 11–61.

———. 1986. *Knowledge of language: Its nature, origin, and use.* New York: Praeger.

Christie, J. 1970. Locative, possessive and existential in Swahili. *Foundations of Language* 6:166–77.

Clark, Eve V. 1970. Locativeness: A study of 'existential,' 'locative,' and 'possessive' sentences. *Stanford University Working Papers in Language Universals* 3:1–36.

———. 1978. Locationals: Existential, locative, and possessive constructions. In Greenberg, *Universals,* Vol. 4, pp. 85–126.

Clasen, Bernd. 1981. *Inhärenz und Etablierung.* (Arbeiten des Kölner Universalien-Projekts, 41.) Cologne: University of Cologne.

Claudi, Ulrike. 1986. To have or not to have: On the conceptual base of predicative possession in some African languages. Unpublished manuscript, University of Cologne.

———. 1993. *Die Stellung von Verb und Objekt in Niger-Kongo-Sprachen: Ein Beitrag zur Rekonstruktion historischer Syntax.* (Afrikanistische Monographien, 1.) Cologne: Institut für Afrikanistik, University of Cologne.

———. 1994. Word order change as category change: The Mande case. In: Pagliuca, *Perspectives on grammaticalization,* pp. 191–231.

Claudi, Ulrike, & Fritz Serzisko. 1985. Possession in Dizi: Inalienable or not? *Journal of African Languages and Linguistics* 7,2:131–54.

Claudi, Ulrike, & Bernd Heine. 1985. From metaphor to grammar: Some examples from Ewe. *AAP* (Afrikanistische Arbeitspapiere) 1:17–54.

———. 1986. On the metaphorical base of grammar. *Studies in Language* 10,2:297–335.

———. 1989. On the nominal morphology of "alienability" in some African languages. In: Newman & Botne, *Current approaches,* pp. 3–19.

Colby, Benjamin N., James W. Fernandez, & David B. Kronenfeld. 1981. Toward a convergence of cognitive and symbolic anthropology. *American Ethnologist* 8, 3:422–50.

Cole, Desmond T. 1955. *An introduction to Tswana grammar.* Cape Town: Longman Penguin South Africa.

Cole, Peter (ed.). 1976. *Studies in modern Hebrew syntax and semantics: The transformational generative approach.* Amsterdam: North-Holland.

Comrie, Bernard. 1981. *Language universals and linguistic typology.* Chicago: University of Chicago Press.

Condillac, Etienne Bonnot de. 1746. *Essai sur l'origine des connaissances humaines.* Paris.

———. 1749. *Traité des systèmes.* Paris.

Conrad, Rudi (ed.). 1988. *Lexikon sprachwissenschaftlicher Termini.* Leipzig: VEB Bibliographisches Institut.

Cooke, Joseph R. 1968. *Pronominal reference in Thai, Burmese, and Vietnamese.* (University of California Publications in Linguistics, 52.) Berkeley: University of California Press.

Corbett, Greville G. 1978a. Universals in the syntax of cardinal numerals. *Lingua* 46:355–68.

———. 1978b. Numerous squishes and squishy numerals in Slavonic. *International Review of Slavic Linguistics* 3:43–73.

———. 1983. *Hierarchies, targets and controllers: Agreement patterns in Slavic.* London: Croom Helm.

———. 1991. *Gender.* Cambridge: Cambridge University Press.

Crazzolara, J. P. 1933. *Outlines of a Nuer grammar.* (Linguistische Anthropos-Bibliothek, 13.) Vienna: Anthropos.

Creider, Chet A., & Jane Tapsubei Creider. 1989. *A grammar of Nandi.* (Nilo-Saharan, 4.) Hamburg: Buske Verlag.

Creissels, D. 1979. Le comitatif, la coordination et les constructions dites "possessives" dans quelques langues africaines. *Annales de l'Université d'Abidjan,* Série H. Linguistique, 12,1:125–44.

Croft, William. 1991. *Typology and universals.* Cambridge: Cambridge University Press.

Croft, William, Keith Denning, & Suzanne Kemmer (eds.). 1990. *Studies in typology and diachrony: Papers presented to Joseph H. Greenberg on his 75th birthday.* (Typological Studies in Language, 20.) Amsterdam: John Benjamins.

Crowley, Terry. 1996. Inalienable possession in Paamese grammar. In: Chappell & McGregor, *Grammar of inalienability,* pp. 383–432.

Cyffer, Norbert. 1991. *We learn Kanuri*. (Afrikawissenschaftliche Lehrbücher, 2.) Cologne: Rüdiger Köppe.

Dal, I. 1952. *Kurze deutsche Syntax*. Tübingen: Max Niemeyer.

Dantzig, T. 1940. *Number: The language of science*. London: George Allen and Unwin.

Dayley, Jon P. 1985. Why all languages aren't SOV or VOS, or how competing motivations lead to natural inconsistency. *Berkeley Linguistics Society* 11:52–64.

Demiraj, Shaban. 1985. About the origin of the possessive perfect in Albanian and some other languages. (Sprachwissenschaftliche Forschungen: Festschrift für Johannes Knobloch.) *Innsbrucker Beiträge zur Kulturwissenschaft* 23:81–85.

de Sivers, Fanny (ed.). 1981. *La main et les doigts dans l'expression linguistique*. (Lacito-Documents, Eurasie 6, II.) Paris: SELAF.

Devitt, Dan. 1990. The diachronic development of semantics in copulas. *Berkeley Linguistics Society* 16:102–15.

Diem, Werner. 1986. Alienable und inalienable Possession im Semitischen. *Zeitschrift der Deutschen Morgenländischen Gesellschaft* 136,2:227–91.

Dik, Simon C. 1979. *Functional grammar*. (Linguistic Series, 37.) Amsterdam: North-Holland.

———. 1989. *The theory of functional grammar*. Part I: *The structure of the clause*. (Functional Grammar Series, 9.) Dordrecht: Foris Publications.

Dimmendaal, Gerrit Jan. 1983. *The Turkana language*. Dordrecht: Foris Publications.

———. 1993. Conversational implicatures, metonymy, and attitude markers in Turkana speech acts. Unpublished manuscript, Leiden, The Netherlands.

Dixon, Robert M. W. 1980. *The languages of Australia*. Cambridge: Cambridge University Press.

———. 1988. *A grammar of Boumaa Fijian*. Chicago: University of Chicago Press.

Doke, Clement M. 1930. *Textbook of Zulu grammar*. Cape Town: Maskew Miller.

Downing, Pamela, & Michael Noonan (eds.). 1995. *Word order in discourse*. (Typological Studies in Language, 30.) Amsterdam: John Benjamins.

Dryer, Matthew S. 1989. Discourse-governed word order and word order typology. *Belgian Journal of Linguistics* 4:69–90.

———. 1995. Frequency and pragmatically unmarked word order. In: Downing & Noonan, *Word order in discourse*, pp. 105–35.

Duridanov, Ivan. 1956. *Kum problemata za razvoja na bulgarskija ezik ot sintetizum kum analitizum*. (Godišnik na Filologičeski fakultet, 51.) Sofia: Sofiskija Universitet.

Durie, Mark, & Malcolm Ross (eds.). 1996. *The comparative method reviewed*. New York: Oxford University Press.

Emanatian, Michele. 1992. Chagga 'come' and 'go': Metaphor and the development of tense-aspect. *Studies in Language* 16,1:1–33.

Fachner, Regine. *See* Koroma, Regine

Fankhauser, F., & Jakob Jud (eds.). 1926. *Festschrift Louis Gauchat*. Aarau: Verlag Sauerländer.

Farris, Glenn J. 1990. Vigesimal systems found in California Indian languages. *Journal of California and Great Basin Anthropology* 12,2:173–90.

Ferguson, Charles A. 1968. Language development. In: Fishman, Ferguson, & Das Gupta, *Language problems*, pp. 27–35.

———. 1978. Historical background of universals research. In: Greenberg, Ferguson, & Moravcsik, *Universals of human language*, pp. 7–31.

Fillmore, Charles J. 1968. The case for case. In: Bach & Harms, *Universals in linguistic theory*, pp. 1–88.

Fishman, Joshua A., Charles A. Ferguson, & Jyotirindra Das Gupta (eds.). 1968. *Language problems of developing nations*. New York: Wiley.

Fisiak, Jacek (ed.). 1985. *Historical semantics, historical word formation*. Berlin: Mouton de Gruyter.

Fleischman, Suzanne. 1982a. *The future in thought and language: Diachronic evidence from Romance*. (Cambridge Studies in Linguistics, 36.) Cambridge: Cambridge University Press.

———. 1982b. The past and the future: Are they coming or going? *Berkeley Linguistics Society* 8:322–34.

Flier, Michael S. (ed.). 1974. *Slavic Forum: Essays in linguistics and literature*. (Slavistic Printings and Reprintings, 277.) The Hague: Mouton.

Foley, William A. 1991. *The Yimas language of New Guinea*. Stanford, Calif.: Stanford University Press.

Forchheimer, Paul. 1953. *The category of person in language*. Berlin: Walter de Gruyter.

Fortescue, Michael. 1984. *West Greenlandic*. (Descriptive Grammars.) London: Croom Helm.

———. 1988. Eskimo orientation systems. *Man and Society* 11:3–30.

Fortune, G. 1968. Predication of 'being' in Shona. In: Verhaar, *Verb 'be'*, Part 3, pp. 110–125.

Foulkes, H. D. 1915. *Angass manual: Grammar and vocabulary*. London: Kegan Paul.

Fox, Barbara. 1981. Body part syntax: Towards a universal characterization. *Studies in Language* 5:323–42.

Frajzyngier, Zygmunt. 1983. Marking syntactic relations in Proto-Chadic. In: Wolff & Meyer-Bahlburg, *Chadic and Afroasiatic linguistics*, pp. 115–38.

———. 1987. Encoding locative in Chadic. *Journal of West African Languages* 17,1:81–97.

———. 1991. The *de dicto* domain in language. In: Traugott & Heine, *Approaches to grammaticalization*, Vol. 1, pp. 219–51.

———. 1993. *A grammar of Mupun*. (Sprache und Oralität in Afrika, 14.) Berlin: Dietrich Reimer.

Freeze, Ray. 1992. Existentials and other locatives. *Language* 68,3:553–95.

Friedländer, Marianne. 1974. *Lehrbuch des Susu*. Leipzig: VEB Verlag Enzyklopädie.

———. 1992. *Lehrbuch des Malinke*. Leipzig: Langenscheidt.

Friedrich, P. 1975. Proto-Indo-European syntax. (JIES Monograph, 1.) Butte, Mont.

Fritze, Marie-Elisabeth. 1976. Bezeichnungen für den Zugehörigkeits- und Herkunftsbereich beim substantivischen Attribut. In: Kettmann & Schildt, *Der Einfachsatz*, pp. 417–76.

Fromm, Erich. 1976. *To have or to be?* New York: Harper & Row.

Geeraerts, Dirk. 1992. Prototypicality effects in diachronic semantics: A round-up. In: Kellermann & Morrisey, *Diachrony within synchrony*, pp. 183–203.

Gentner, Derdre. 1975. Evidence for the psychological reality of semantic components: The verbs of possession. In: Norman & Rumelhart, *Explorations in Cognition*, pp. 211–46.

Gerhardt, Ludwig. 1987. Some remarks on the numeral systems of Plateau languages. *Afrika und Übersee* 70,1:19–29.

Ginneken, Jacques van. 1939. Avoir et être (du point de vue de la linguistique générale). In: *Mélanges de linguistique offerts à Charles Bally*. Geneva: Georg et Cie, pp. 83–92.

Givón, Talmy (Tom). 1971. Historical syntax and synchronic morphology: An archaeologist's field trip. *Chicago Linguistic Society* 7:394–415.

———. 1973. The time-axis phenomenon. *Language* 49:890–925.

———. 1979. *On understanding grammar*. New York: Academic Press.

———. 1981. On the development of the numeral 'one' as an indefinite marker. *Folia Linguistica Historica* 2,1:35–53.

———. 1990. *Syntax: A functional-typological introduction*. Vol. 2. Amsterdam: John Benjamins.

———. 1993. *English grammar: A function-based introduction*. 2 vols. Amsterdam: John Benjamins.

———. 1994. The grammaticalization of verbs to postpositions in Ute. Unpublished manuscript, Linguistics Department, University of Oregon, Eugene.

———. 1995. *Functionalism and grammar*. Amsterdam: John Benjamins.

Goldap, Christel. 1992. Morphology and semantics of Yucatec space relators. *Zeitschrift für Phonetik, Sprachwissenschaft und Kommunikationsforschung* 45,6:612–25.

Greenberg, Joseph H. (ed.) 1963a. *Universals of language*. Cambridge, Mass.: MIT Press.

————. 1963b. Some universals of language, with particular reference to the order of meaningful elements. In: Greenberg, *Universals of language*, pp. 73–113.

————. (ed.) 1978a. *Universals of human language*. Vol. 4: *Syntax*. Stanford, Calif.: Stanford University Press.

————. (ed.) 1978b. *Universals of human language*. Vol. 3: *Word structure*. Stanford, Calif.: Stanford University Press.

————. 1978c. Generalizations about numeral systems. In: Greenberg, *Universals*, Vol. 3, pp. 249–95.

————. 1991. The last stage of grammatical elements: Contractive and expansive desemanticization. In: Traugott & Heine, *Approaches to grammaticalization*, Vol. 1, pp. 301–14.

Greenberg, Joseph H., Charles A. Ferguson, & Edith Moravcsik (eds.). 1978. *Universals of human language*. Vol. 1. Stanford, Calif.: Stanford University Press.

Greene, D. 1962. The development of the construction *is liom*. *Éigse* 10,1:45–48.

————. 1976. The preposition *in-* as subject marker. *Celtica* 11:61–67.

Hagège, Claude. 1993. *The language builder: An essay on the human signature in linguistic morphogenesis*. (Amsterdam Studies in the Theory and History of Linguistic Science, 94.) Amsterdam: John Benjamins.

Haiman, John. 1985a. *Natural syntax: Iconicity and erosion*. Cambridge: Cambridge University Press.

————. 1985b. *Iconicity in syntax*. Amsterdam: John Benjamins.

Haiman, John (ed.). 1985. *Iconicity in syntax*. Amsterdam: John Benjamins.

Halim, Amran, Lois Carrington, & Stephen A. Wurm (eds.). 1982. *Papers from the Third International Conference on Austronesian Linguistics*. Vol. 1: *Currents in Oceanic*. Pacific Linguistics, C-74.

Halliday, Michael A. K. 1961. Categories of the theory of grammar. *Word* 17:241–92.

————. 1985. *An introduction to functional grammar*. London: Edward Arnold.

Harris, Martin B. 1982a. The 'past simple' and the 'present perfect' in Romance. In: Vincent & Harris, *Studies*, pp. 42–70.

————. 1982b. On explaining language change. In: Ahlqvist, *Papers from the 5th International Conference*, pp. 1–14.

————. 1983. On the causes of word order change. *Lingua* 63:175–204.

Harweg, R. 1968. Besitzanzeigende *haben*-Konstruktionen als Katalysator für die Doppeldeutigkeit der Gruppe 'Nomen + Possessivsuffix' im Türkischen. *Archiv Orientální* 36:407–28.

Haspelmath, Martin. 1993a. *A grammar of Lezgian*. (Mouton Grammar Library, 9.) Berlin: Mouton de Gruyter.

————. 1993b. A typological study of indefinite pronouns. Ph.D. diss., Freie Universität, Berlin.

Haspelmath, Martin, & Oda Buchholz. Forthcoming. Equative and similative constructions in the languages of Europe. In Auwera, *Adverbial constructions*.

Hawkins, John A. 1978. *Definiteness and indefiniteness: A study in reference and grammaticality prediction*. London: Croom Helm.

————. 1979. Implicational universals as predictors of word order change. *Language* 55:618–48.

————. 1983. *Word order universals*. New York: Academic Press.

————. 1988. *Explaining language universals*. Oxford: Basil Blackwell.

————. 1991. On (in)definite articles: Implicatures and (un)grammaticality prediction. *Journal of Linguistics* 27:405–42.

Hawkins, Roger. 1981. Towards an account of the possessive constructions: *NP's N* and *the N of NP*. *Journal of Linguistics* 17:247–69.

Hawkinson, Annie K. 1979. Homonymy versus unity of form: The particle *-a* in Swahili. *Studies in African Linguistics* 10,1:81–109.

Heim, Irene. 1988. *The semantics of definite and indefinite noun phrases.* New York: Garland.

Heine, Bernd. 1982. *The Nubi language of Kibera—an Arabic creole: Grammatial sketch and vocabulary.* (Language and Dialect Atlas of Kenya, 3.) Berlin: Dietrich Reimer.

——. 1983. The Ik language. Unpublished manuscript, Cologne.

——. 1989. Adpositions in African languages. *Linguistique Africaine* 2:77–127.

——. 1990. The dative in Ik and Kanuri. In: Croft, Denning, & Kemmer, *Studies in typology,* pp. 129–49.

——. 1991. The Hausa particle *naa.* In: Mendel & Claudi, *Ägypten,* pp. 157–70.

——. 1992. Grammaticalization chains. *Studies in Language* 16,2:335–68.

——. 1993. *Auxiliaries: Cognitive forces and grammaticalization.* New York: Oxford University Press.

——. 1994a. Areal influence on grammaticalization. In: Pütz, *Language contact,* pp. 55–68.

——. 1994b. Grammaticalization as an explanatory parameter. In: Pagliuca, *Perspectives on grammaticalization,* pp. 255–87.

——. 1995. Conceptual grammaticalization and prediction. In: Taylor & MacLaury, *Language and cognitive construal,* pp. 119–35.

——. 1997. *Possession: Cognitive sources, forces, and grammaticalization.* Cambridge: Cambridge University Press.

Heine, Bernd, & Mechthild Reh. 1984. *Grammaticalization and reanalysis in African languages.* Hamburg: Helmut Buske Verlag.

Heine, Bernd, Ulrike Claudi, & Friederike Hünnemeyer. 1991. *Grammaticalization: A conceptual framework.* Chicago: University of Chicago Press.

Heine, Bernd et al. 1993. Conceptual shift: A lexicon of grammaticalization processes in African Languages. *AAP* (Afrikanistische Arbeitspapiere) 34/35:1–322.

Heine, Bernd, Ulrike Claudi, Christa Kilian-Hatz, Tania Kuteva, & Mathias Schladt. 1995. On indefinite articles. Paper presented at the International Conference on Functionalism, University of New Mexico, Albuquerque, New Mexico, 24–28 July.

Hengeveld, Kees. 1992. *Non-verbal predication: Theory, typology, diachrony.* (Functional Grammar Series, 15.) Berlin: Mouton de Gruyter.

Henry, David, and Kay Henry. 1969. Koyukon locationals. *Anthropological Linguistics* 11,4:136–42.

Hester, Thomas R. 1976. A universal explanation for several syntactic shifts in Basque. *Papers from the Parasession on Diachronic Syntax, Chicago Linguistic Society,* pp. 105–17.

Hetzron, Robert. 1970. Nonverbal sentences and degrees of definiteness in Hungarian. *Language* 46,4:899–927.

——. 1977. *The Gunnän-Gurage languages.* (Ricerche, 12.) Naples: Istituto Orientale di Napoli.

Hill, Clifford A. 1974. Spatial perception and linguistic encoding: A case study in Hausa and English. *Studies in African Linguistics* 4:135–48.

——. 1982. Up/down, front/back, left/right: A contrastive analysis of Hausa and English. In: Weissenborn & Klein, *Here and there,* pp. 13–42.

——. forthcoming. Spatial orientation: Cognition, language, and myth in Hausa culture. *Semiotica.*

Hill, Deborah. 1994. *Spatial configurations and evidential propositions.* (Cognitive Anthropology Research Group, Working Paper 25.) Nijmegen: Max Planck Institute for Psycholinguistics.

Hinnebusch, Thomas J., & Robert S. Kirsner. 1980. On the interference on "inalienable possession" in Swahili. *Journal of African Languages and Linguistics* 2:1–16.

Hockett, Charles F. 1958. *A course in modern linguistics.* New York: Macmillan.

Hodge, Carleton T. 1947. *An outline of Hausa grammar.* (Language Dissertations, 41.) Baltimore: Linguistic Society of America.

———. 1963. Morpheme alternants and the noun phrase in Hausa. *Language* 21:87–91.

———. 1969. Hausa *naà*—: 'To be' or not 'to be'? *African Language Review* 8:156–62.

Holes, Clive. 1990. *Gulf Arabic.* (Croom Helm Descriptive Grammars Series.) London: Routledge.

Hopper, Paul J. 1972. Verbless stative sentences in Indonesian. In: Verhaar, *Verb 'be'*, Part 5, pp. 115–52.

———. 1986. Discourse function and word order shift: A typological study of the VS/SV alternation. In: W. Lehmann, *Language typology 1985*, pp. 123–40.

———. 1987. Emergent grammar. *Berkeley Linguistics Society* 13:139–57.

———. 1991. On some principles of grammaticization. In: Traugott & Heine, *Approaches to grammaticalization*, Vol. 1, pp. 17–35.

———. 1994. Phonogenesis. In: Pagliuca, *Perspectives on grammaticalization*, pp. 29–45.

Hopper, Paul J., & Janice Martin. 1987. Structuralism and diachrony: The development of the indefinite article in English. In: Ramat, Carruba, & Bernini, *Papers from the Seventh International Conference*, pp. 295–304.

Hopper, Paul J., & Sandra Thompson. 1984. The discourse basis for lexical categories in universal grammar. *Language* 60:703–52.

Hopper, Paul J., & Elizabeth C. Traugott. 1993. *Grammaticalization.* Cambridge: Cambridge University Press.

Horne Tooke, John. 1857. *Epea pteroenta or the diversions of Purley.* 2 vols. London.

Hoskison, J. T. 1983. A grammar of the Gude language. Ph.D. diss., Ohio State University.

Humboldt, Wilhelm von. 1825. Über das Entstehen der grammatischen Formen und ihren Einfluß auf die Ideenentwicklung: Gelesen in der Academie der Wissenschaften am 17. Januar 1822. *Abhandlungen der Königlichen Akademie der Wissenschaften zu Berlin*, 401–30.

Hurford, James R. 1975. *The linguistic theory of numerals.* Cambridge: Cambridge University Press.

———. 1987. *Language and number: The emergence of a cognitive system.* Oxford: Basil Blackwell.

Hutchison, John P. 1980. The Kanuri associative postposition: A case for subordination. *Studies in African Linguistics* 11,3:321–51.

Hyman, Larry M. 1977. The syntax of body parts. In: Byarushengo, Duranti, & Hyman, *Haya grammatical structure*, pp. 99–117.

Hyman, Larry M., Danny Keith Alford, & Elizabeth Akpati. 1970. Inalienable possession in Igbo. *Journal of West African Languages* 7,2:85–101.

Hymes, Dell, & W. E. Bittle (eds.). 1967. *Studies in southwestern ethnolinguistics.* The Hague: Mouton.

Ifrah, Georges. 1981/86. *Universalgeschichte der Zahlen.* Frankfurt: Campus Verlag.

Isačenko, Alexander V. 1974. On 'have' and 'be' languages: A typological sketch. In: Flier, *Slavic Forum*, pp. 43–77.

Ittmann, Johannes. 1939. *Grammatik des Duala (Kamerun).* (Beihefte zur Zeitschrift für Eingeborenen-Sprachen, 20.) Hamburg: Dietrich Reimer.

Jackendoff, Ray S. 1977. *X̄-syntax: A study of phrase structure.* Cambridge, Mass.: MIT Press.

Janssen, Theo A. J. M. 1976. Hebben-*konstrukties en indirekt-objektskonstrukties.* Utrecht: HES Publishers.

———. 1993. "Possession:" Expressed or culturally conceived? Paper presented at the Third International Cognitive Linguistics Conference, Leuven, Belgium, 18–23 July.

Jensen, Hans. 1934. Der steigernde Vergleich und sein sprachlicher Ausdruck. *Indogermanische Forschungen* 52:108–30.

Kachru, Yamuna. 1968. The copula in Hindi. In: Verhaar, *Verb 'be,'* Part 2, pp. 35–59.

Kahn, C. H. 1966. The Greek verb "to be" and the concept of being. *Foundations of Language* 2:245–65.

Kastenholz, Raimund. 1988. Note sur l'expression énonciative de la possession en bambara. *Mandekan* 14–15:193–201.

———. 1989. *Grundkurs Bambara (Manding) mit Texten.* (Afrikawissenschaftliche Lehrbücher, 1.) Cologne: Rüdiger Köppe.

Kellermann, Günter, & Michael D. Morrissey (eds.). 1992. *Diachrony within synchrony: Language history and cognition.* Frankfurt: Peter Lang.

Kettmann, Gerhard, & Joachim Schildt (eds.). 1976. *Zur Ausbildung der Norm der deutschen Literatursprache auf der syntaktischen Ebene (1470–1730). Der Einfachsatz.* (Bausteine zur Sprachgeschichte des Neuhochdeutschen, 56/I.) Berlin: Akademie Verlag.

Kiefer, Ferenc. 1968. A transformational approach to the verb *van* 'to be' in Hungarian. In: Verhaar, *Verb 'be'*, Part 3, pp. 53–85.

Kilian-Hatz, Christa. 1995. *Das Baka: Grundzüge einer Grammatik aus der Grammatikalisierungsperspektive.* (Afrikanistische Monographien, 6.) Cologne: Institut für Afrikanistik, University of Cologne.

Kilian-Hatz, Christa, & Thomas Stolz. 1992. Comitative, concomitance, and beyond: On the interdependence of grammaticalization and conceptualization. Paper presented at the Annual Conference of the Linguistic Society of Belgium, University of Antwerp, 26–28 November.

———. 1993. Grammatikalisierung und grammatische Kategorien: Ein Bericht aus der Pathologie. (Arbeitspapier 14.) *ProPrinS* 14. University of Essen.

Kimball, J. 1973. The grammar of existence. *Chicago Linguistic Society* 9:262–70.

Köhler, Oswin. 1973. Grundzüge der Grammatik der Kxoe-Sprache. Unpublished manuscript, University of Cologne.

Kölver, Ulrike. 1984. *Local prepositions and serial verb constructions in Thai.* (Arbeiten des Kölner Universalien-Projekts, 56.) Cologne: University of Cologne.

König, Ekkehard, & Bernd Kortmann. 1991. On the reanalysis of verbs as prepositions. In: Rauh, *Approaches to prepositions,* pp. 109–25.

Koroma, Regine [= Regine Fachner]. 1988. Das Nominalsyntagma im Gola. M.A. thesis, Institut für Sprachwissenschaft, University of Cologne.

———. 1994. *Die Morphosyntax des Gola.* (Afrikanistische Monographien, 4.) Cologne: Institut für Afrikanistik, University of Cologne.

Kraft, Charles H. 1963. *A study of Hausa syntax.* 3 vols. Hartford: Hartford Seminary Foundation.

———. 1964a. A new study of Hausa syntax. *Journal of African Languages* 3:66–74.

———. 1964b. The morpheme *naà* in relation to a broader classification of Hausa verbals. *Journal of African Languages* 3:231–40.

Kraft, Charles H., & Salisu Abubakar. 1965. *An introduction to spoken Hausa.* Preliminary edition. (African Language Monograph, 5.) East Lansing: Michigan State University, African Studies Center.

Kraft, Charles H., & A. H. M. Kirk-Greene. 1973. *Hausa.* (Teach Yourself Books.) London: St. Paul's House.

Kuno, S. 1971. The position of locatives in existential sentences. *Linguistic Inquiry* 2:333–78.

Kuryłowicz, Jerzy. [1965] 1975. The evolution of grammatical categories. *Esquisses linguistiques* II:38–54. Munich: Fink.

Lakoff, George. 1987. *Women, fire, and dangerous things: What categories reveal about the mind.* Chicago: University of Chicago Press.

Lakoff, George, & Mark Johnson. 1980. *Metaphors we live by.* Chicago: University of Chicago Press.

Lambrecht, Knud. 1987. On the status of SVO sentences in French discourse. In: Tomlin, *Coherence and grounding*, pp. 217–61.

Langacker, Ronald W. 1968. Observations on French possessives. *Language* 44,1:51–75.

———. 1972. Possessives in Classical Nahuatl. *International Journal of American Linguistics* 38:173–86.

———. 1978. The form and meaning of the English auxiliary. *Language* 54, 4:853–84.

———. 1984. *Studies in Uto-Aztecan grammar*. Vol. 4: *Southern Uto-Aztecan grammatical sketches*. Arlington: Summer Institute of Linguistics and University of Texas at Arlington.

———. 1987. *Foundations of cognitive grammar*. Vol. 1: *Theoretical perspectives*. Stanford, Calif.: Stanford University Press.

———. 1991. *Foundations of cognitive grammar*. Vol. 2. Stanford, Calif.: Stanford University Press.

———. 1993. Reference-point constructions. *Cognitive Linguistics* 4,1:1–38.

———. 1994. Culture, cognition, and grammar. In: Pütz, *Language contact*, pp. 25–53.

Lass, Roger. 1980. *On explaining language change*. Cambridge: Cambridge University Press.

Lébikaza, Kézié K. 1991. Les constructions possessives prédicatives et nominales en kabiye. *Journal of West African Languages* 21,1:91–103.

Lehiste, Ilse. 1969. 'Being' and 'having' in Estonian. *Foundations of Language* 5:324–41.

———. 1972. 'Being' and 'having' in Estonian. In: Verhaar, *Verb 'be'*, Part 5, pp. 207–24.

Lehmann, Christian. 1982. *Thoughts on grammaticalization: A programmatic sketch*. (Arbeiten des Kölner Universalien-Projekts, 48). Cologne: University of Cologne.

Lehmann, Christian, & Gunter Brettschneider (eds.). 1980. *Wege der Universalienforschung. Festschrift für Hansjakob Seiler zum 60. Geburtstag*. (Tübinger Beiträge zur Linguistik, 145.) Tübingen: Gunter Narr.

Lehmann, Thomas. 1989. *A grammar of modern Tamil*. Pandicherry: Pandicherry Institute of Linguistics and Culture.

Lehmann, Winfred P. 1972a. Proto-Germanic syntax. In: van Coetsem & Kufner, *Grammar of Proto-Germanic*, pp. 239–68.

———. 1972b. Contemporary linguistics and Indo-European studies. *Publications of the Modern Language Association* 87:976–93.

———. 1972c. The comparative method as applied to the syntactic component of language. *Canadian Journal of Linguistics* 17:167–74.

———. (ed.) 1986. *Language typology 1985: Papers from the Linguistic Typology Symposium, Moscow, 9–13 December, 1985*. (Current Issues in Linguistic Theory, 47.) Amsterdam: John Benjamins.

Lessau, Donald A. 1994. *A dictionary of grammaticalization*. 3 vols. (Bochum-Essener Beiträge zur Sprachwandelforschung, 21.) Bochum: N. Brockmeyer.

Levinson, Stephen C. 1992. *Language and cognition: The cognitive consequences of spatial description in Guugu Yimithirr*. (Working Paper 13, Cognitive Anthropology Research Group.) Nijmegen: Max Planck Institute for Psycholinguistics.

———. 1994. Vision, shape, and linguistic description: Tzeltal body-part terminology and object description. *Linguistics* 32:791–855.

Lévy-Bruhl, Lucien. 1914. L'expression de la possession dans les langues mélanésiennes. *Mémoires de la Société de Linguistique de Paris* 19,2:96–104.

Lewis, Gilbert. 1974. Gnau anatomy and vocabulary for illnesses. *Oceania* 45, 1:50–78.

Lichtenberk, Frantisek. 1983. Relational classifiers. *Lingua* 60:147–76.

———. 1985. Possessive constructions in Oceanic languages and in Proto-Oceanic. In: Pawley & Carrington, *Austronesian linguistics*, pp. 93–140.

———. 1991. Language change and heterosemy in grammaticalization. *Language* 67,3:475–509.

Locker, Ernst. 1954. Etre et avoir: Leurs expressions dans les langues. *Anthropos* 49:481–510.

Lockwood, W. B. 1968. *Historical German syntax*. Oxford: Clarendon Press.

Löfstedt, Bengt. 1963. Zum lateinischen possessiven Dativ. *Zeitschrift für vergleichende Sprachforschung auf dem Gebiete der Indogermanischen Sprachen* 78:64–83.

Lukas, Johannes. 1970. *Studien zur Sprache der Gisiga (Nordkamerun)*. (Afrikanistische Forschungen, 4.) Glückstadt: J.J. Augustin.

Lynch, John. 1969. On Fijian possession. Unpublished manuscript.

———. 1971. Melanesian 'possession' and abstract verbs. Paper delivered to the Fifth Annual Congress of the Linguistic Society of Papua New Guinea.

———. 1973. Verbal aspects of possession in Melanesian languages. *Working Papers in Linguistics* (Honolulu) 5,9:1–29. Also published in *Oceanic Linguistics* 12,1/2 (1973):69–102.

———. 1982. Towards a theory of the origin of the Oceanic possessive constructions. In: Halim, Carrington, & Wurm, *Papers from the Third International Conference*, pp. 243–68.

———. forthcoming. Possessive structures in Lenakel. *Linguistic Communications*. Melbourne: Monash University.

Lyons, John. 1967. A note on possessive, existential and locative sentences. *Foundations of Language* 3:390–96.

———. 1968a. *Introduction to theoretical linguistics*. London: Cambridge University Press.

———. 1968b. Existence, location, possession and transitivity. In: van Rootselaar & Staal, *Logic, methodology, and philosophy*, pp. 495–509.

———. 1977. *Semantics*. 2 vols. Cambridge: Cambridge Univesity Press.

MacLaury, Robert E. 1989. Zapotec body-part locatives: Prototypes and metaphoric extensions. *International Journal of American Linguistics* 55,2:119–54.

MacWhinney, Brian, and Elizabeth Bates (eds.). 1989. *The crosslinguistic study of sentence processing*. Cambridge: Cambridge University Press.

Majewicz, Alfred F. 1981. Le rôle du doigt et de la main et leurs désignations dans la formation des systèmes particuliers de numération et de noms de nombres dans certaines langues. In: de Sivers, *La main et les doigts*, pp. 193–212.

Makino, Seiichi. 1968. Japanese 'be'. In: Verhaar, *Verb 'be'*, Part 3, pp. 1–19.

Malandra, Alfred. 1955. *A new Acholi grammar*. Nairobi: Eagle Press.

Mallinson, Graham, & Barry Blake. 1981. *Language typology*. Amsterdam: North-Holland.

Mann, Charles C. 1993. Polysemic functionality in pidgins and creoles: The case of *fò* in Anglo-Nigerian Pidgin. In: Byrne & Holm, *Atlantic meets Pacific*, pp. 57–67.

Marcel, Gabriel. 1935. *Etre et avoir*. Paris: F. Aubier, Editions Montaigne.

Marr, David. 1982. *Vision*. New York: Freeman.

Matisoff, James A. 1978. *Variational semantics in Tibeto-Burman: The "organic" approach to linguistic comparison*. (Occasional Papers of the Wolfenden Society on Tibeto-Burman Linguistics, 6.) Philadelphia: Institute for the Study of Human Issues.

Matlin, Margaret W. 1989. *Cognition*. 2nd ed. New York: Holt, Rinehart and Winston.

Matthews, Peter H. 1981. *Do languages obey general laws?* Inaugural Lecture of the University of Cambridge. Cambridge: Cambridge University Press.

McKay, Graham. 1996. Body parts, possession marking and nominal classes in Ndjébbana. In: Chappell & McGregor, *Grammar of inalienability*, pp. 293–326.

McMahon, April M. S. 1994. *Understanding language change*. Cambridge: Cambridge University Press.

Mead, Margaret. 1956. *New lives for old: Cultural transformation—Manus, 1928–1953*. London: Victor Gollancz.

Meillet, Antoine. 1912. L'évolution des formes grammaticales. *Scientia* 12. (Reprinted in A. Meillet, *Linguistique historique et linguistique générale*, 1:130–48. Paris: Edouard Champion, 1948.)

———. 1923. Le développement du verbe "avoir." *Festschrift, Jacob Wackernagel zur Vollendung des 70. Lebensjahres*. Göttingen: Vandenhoeck & Ruprecht, pp. 9–13.

———. [1926] 1948. *Linguistique historique et linguistique générale*. Paris: Champion.

Meinhof, Carl. 1948. *Grundzüge einer vergleichenden Grammatik der Bantusprachen.* 2nd ed. Hamburg: Dietrich Reimer.

Mendel, Daniela, & Ulrike Claudi (eds.). 1991. *Ägypten im afro-orientalischen Kontext: Aufsätze zur Archäologie, Geschichte und Sprache eines unbegrenzten Raumes, Gedenkschrift Peter Behrens.* (Afrikanistische Arbeitspapiere, Special Issue.) Cologne: Institut für Afrikanistik, University of Cologne.

Miller, George A., & Philip N. Johnson-Laird. 1976. *Language and perception.* Cambridge: Harvard University Press.

Moravcsik, Edith A. 1969. Determination. *Working Papers on Language Universals* (Stanford) 1:64–98.

Morrissey, Michael D., & Günter. Kellermann (eds.). 1992. *Diachrony within synchrony: Language, history and cognition.* Bern: Peter Lang Verlag.

Mosel, Ulrike. 1983. *Adnominal and predicative possessive constructions in Melanesian languages.* (Arbeiten des Kölner Universalien-Projekts, 50.) Cologne: University of Cologne.

Needham, Rodney (ed.). 1973. *Right and left: Essays on dual symbolic classification.* Chicago: University of Chicago Press.

Newman, Paul, & Robert D. Botne (eds.). 1989. *Current approaches to African linguistics.* Vol. 5. Dordrecht: Foris.

Newman, Paul, & Russell G. Schuh. 1974. The Hausa aspect system. *Afroasiatic Linguistics* 1,1:1–39.

Nichols, Johanna. 1988. On alienable and inalienable possession. In: Shipley, *In honor of Mary Haas,* pp. 557–609.

———. 1992. *Linguistic diversity in space and time.* Chicago: University of Chicago Press.

Nikiforidou, Vassiliki. 1991. The meaning of the genitive: A case study in semantic structure and semantic change. *Cognitive Linguistics* 2,2:149–205.

Noonan, Michael. 1992. *A grammar of Lango.* (Mouton Grammar Library, 7.) Berlin: Mouton de Gruyter.

Norman, Donald A., & David E. Rumelhart (eds.). 1975. *Explorations in cognition.* San Francisco: Freeman.

Norvig, Peter, & George Lakoff. 1987. Taking: A study in lexical network theory. *Berkeley Linguistics Society* 13:195–206.

Orr, Robert. 1984. An embryonic ergative construction in Irish? *General Linguistics* 24,1:38–45.

———. 1991. More on embryonic ergativity. *General Linguistics* 31:163–75.

———. 1992. Slavo-Celtica. *Canadian Slavonic Papers (Revue canadienne des slavistes)* 34,3:245–68.

Otten, Dirk. 1992. Strategien prädikativer Possession in afrikanischen Sprachen. Unpublished manuscript, Institut für Afrikanistik, University of Cologne.

Pagliuca, William (ed.). 1994. *Perspectives on grammaticalization.* (Current Issues in Linguistic Theory, 109.) Amsterdam: John Benjamins.

Pagliuca, William, & Richard Mowrey. 1987. Articulatory evolution. In: Ramat, Carruba, & Bernini, *Papers from the Seventh International Conference,* pp. 459–72.

Palmer, Frank R. 1965. Bilin "to be" and "to have". *African Language Studies* 6:101–11.

Park, Insun. 1994. Grammaticalization of verbs in three Tibeto-Burman languages. Ph.D. diss., Department of Linguistics, University of Oregon, Eugene.

Parsons, F. W. 1960. The verbal system in Hausa. *Afrika und Übersee* 44,1:1–36.

Pasch, Helma. 1985. Possession and possessive classifiers in 'Dongo-ko. *Afrika und Übersee* 68,1:69–85.

Paul, Hermann. [1880] 1975. *Prinzipien der Sprachgeschichte.* 9th ed. Tübingen: Niemeyer.

Pawley, Andrew. 1973. Some problems in Proto-Oceanic grammar. *Oceanic Linguistics* 12, 1/2:103–88.

Pawley, Andrew, & Lois Carrington (eds.). 1985. *Austronesian linguistics at the 15th Pacific Science Congress*. Pacific Linguistics, C-88.

Pei, Mario A., & Frank Gaynor. 1954. *Dictionary of linguistics*. New York: Wisdom Library.

Perlmutter, D. M. 1968. *On the article in English*. ERIC/PEGS 29.

Peschke, Andreas. 1995. Metaphorik in afrikanischen Rätseln. Paper presented at the *Forschungskolloquium* of the Institut für Afrikanistik, University of Cologne, 31 May.

Pit'ha, Petr. 1973. On some meanings of the verb *to have* (on material from the Czech language). *Folia Linguistica* 6:301–4.

Plank, Frans (ed.). 1979. *Ergativity: Towards a theory of grammatical relations*. New York: Academic Press.

Pott, Friedrich August. 1868. *Die Sprachverschiedenheit in Europa, an den Zahlwörtern nachgewiesen, sowie die quinäre und vigesimale Zählmethode*. Halle: Verlag der Buchhandlung des Waisenhauses.

Poulos, George. 1990. *A linguistic analysis of Venda*. Pretoria: Via Afrika.

Pountain, Christopher J. 1985. Copulas, verbs of possession and auxiliaries in Old Spanish: The evidence for structurally interdependent changes. *Bulletin of the Hispanic Society* 62:337–55.

Pütz, Martin (ed.). 1994. *Language contact and language conflict*. Amsterdam: John Benjamins.

Quirk, Randolph, Sidney Greenbaum, Geoffrey Leech, & Jan Svartvik. 1985. *A comprehensive grammar of the English language*. London: Longman.

Qvonje, Jørn Ivar. 1980. Die Grammatikalisierung der Präposition *na* im Bulgarischen. *Folia Linguistica Historica* I,2:317–51.

Ramat, Anna Giacalone, O. Carruba, & G. Bernini (eds.). 1987. *Papers from the Seventh International Conference on Historical Linguistics*. (Amsterdam Studies in the Theory and History of Linguistic Science, Current Issues in Linguistic Theory, 48.) Amsterdam: John Benjamins.

Ramat, Paolo (ed.). 1980. *Linguistic reconstruction and Indo-European syntax*. Proceedings of the Colloquium of the Indogermanische Gesellschaft. Amsterdam: John Benjamins.

———. 1992. Thoughts on degrammaticalization. *Linguistics* 30:549–60.

Ramos, Teresita V., & Resty M. Ceña. 1980. Existential, locative and possessive in Tagalog. *Philippine Journal of Linguistics* 11,2:15–26.

Rauh, Gisa (ed.). 1991. *Approaches to prepositions*. (Tübinger Beiträge zur Linguistik, 358.) Tübingen: Gunter Narr.

Raum, J. [1909] 1964. *Versuch einer Grammatik der Dschaggasprache (Moschi-Dialekt)*. Berlin. Reprint, Ridgewood, N.J.: Gregg Press.

Ray, Sidney H. 1919. The Melanesian possessives and a study in method. *American Anthropologist* 21:347–60.

Redfield, Robert. 1930. *Tepoztlan, a Mexican village: A study of folk life*. Chicago: University of Chicago Press.

Reh, Mechthild. 1983. Krongo: A VSO language with postpositions. *Journal of African Languages and Linguistics* 5,1:45–55.

———. 1985. *Die Krongo-Sprache (nìino mó-dì). Beschreibung, Texte, Wörterverzeichnis*. (Kölner Beiträge zur Afrikanistik, 12.) Berlin: Dietrich Reimer.

———. 1994. Anywa language: Description and internal reconstructions. Habilitationsschrift. Unpublished manuscript. University of Bayreuth.

Renzi, L. 1989–91. *Grande grammatica italiana di consultazione*. 2 vols. Bologna: Il Mulino.

Robins, Robert H. 1985. Numerals as underlying verbs: The case of Yurok. In: Pieper, Ursula, & Gerhard Stickel (eds.), *Studia linguistica diachronica et synchronica*. Berlin: Mouton de Gruyter, pp. 723–33.

Romaine, Suzanne. 1988. *Pidgin and creole languages*. London: Longman.

Ross, Malcolm. 1995. Proto Oceanic terms for meteorological phenomena. Unpublished manuscript, Canberra, Australian National University.

Sanford, Anthony J. 1985. *Cognition and cognitive psychology*. New York: Basic Books.

Santandrea, Stefano. 1965. *Languages of the Banda and Zande groups: A contribution to a comparative study*. Naples: Istituto Universitario Orientale.

Sapir, Edward. 1921. *Language: An introduction to the study of speech*. San Diego: Harcourt Brace Jovanovich.

———. 1949. *Selected writings in language, culture and personality,* edited by D. G. Mandelbaum. Berkeley: University of California Press.

Sasse, Hans-Jürgen. 1982. *An etymological dictionary of Burji*. (Cushitic Language Studies, 1.) Hamburg: Buske.

Saussure, Ferdinand de. 1922. *Cours de linguistique générale*. Paris: Payot.

Saxe, Geoffrey B. 1981. Body parts as numerals: A developmental analysis of numeration among remote Oksapmin in Papua New Guinea. *Child Development* 52:306–16.

———. 1982. Culture and the development of numerical cognition: Studies among the Oksapmin of Papua New Guinea. In: Brainerd, *Children's cognition*, pp. 157–76.

Schladt, Mathias. 1997. *Kognitive Strukturen von Körperteilvokabularien in kenianischen Sprachen*. (Afrikanistische Monographien, 8.) Cologne: Institut für Afrikanistik, University of Cologne.

Schlegel, August Wilhelm von. 1818. *Observations sur la langue et la littérature provençales*. Paris: Librairie Grecque-Latine-Allemande.

Schmidt, P. W. 1926. *Die Sprachfamilien und Sprachkreise der Erde*. (Kulturgeschichtliche Bibliothek, 5.) Heidelberg: Carl Winter's Universitätsbuchhandlung.

Schneider, Gilbert Donald. 1966. West African Pidgin English: A descriptive linguistic analysis with texts and glossary from the Cameroon area. Ph.D. diss., Athens, Ohio.

Schuh, Russell G. 1976. The Chadic verbal system and its Afroasiatic nature. *Afroasiatic Linguistics* 3,1:1–14.

Sebeok, Thomas A. 1943. The equational sentence in Hungarian. *Language* 19:320–27.

Seiler, Hansjakob. 1973. Zum Problem der sprachlichen Possessivität. *Folia Linguistica* 6,3/4:231–50.

———. 1977a. *Sprache und Sprachen: Gesammelte Aufsätze*. (Struktura: Schriftenreihe zur Linguistik, 11.) Munich: Wilhelm Fink.

———. 1977b. On the semanto-syntactic configuration 'Possessor of an Act'. In: Seiler, *Sprache und Sprachen*, pp. 169–86.

———. 1977c. Universals of language. In: Seiler, *Sprache und Sprachen*, pp. 207–29.

———. 1983. *Possession as an operational dimension of language*. (Language Universals Series, 2.) Tübingen: Gunter Narr.

———. 1988. *Die universalen Dimensionen der Sprache: Eine vorläufige Bilanz*. (Arbeiten des Kölner Universalien-Projekts, 75.) Cologne: University of Cologne.

———. 1989. *A dimensional view on numeral systems*. (Arbeiten des Kölner Universalien-Projekts, 79.) Cologne: University of Cologne.

Serzisko, Fritz. 1984. *Der Ausdruck der Possessivität im Somali*. (Continuum—Schriftenreihe zur Linguistik, 1.) Tübingen: Gunter Narr.

Shibatani, Masayoshi. 1996. Applicatives and benefactives: A cognitive account. In: Shibatani & Thompson, *Grammatical constructions*, pp. 157–94.

Shibatani, Masayoshi, & Sandra Thompson (eds.). 1996. *Grammatical constructions: Their form and meaning*. Oxford: Oxford University Press.

Shipley, William (ed.). 1988. *In honor of Mary Haas: From the Haas Festival Conference on Native American Linguistics*. Berlin: Mouton de Gruyter.

Spradley, James P. 1979. *The ethnographic interview.* New York: Holt, Rinehart and Winston.

Stafford, R. L. 1967. *An elementary Luo grammar. With vocabularies.* Nairobi: Oxford University Press.

Stampe, David. 1976. Cardinal numeral systems. *Chicago Linguistic Society* 12:594–609.

Stassen, Leon. 1985. *Comparison and universal grammar.* Oxford: Basil Blackwell.

———. 1995. The typology of predicative possession. Paper presented at the Annual Meeting of the Societas Linguistica Europaea, 31 August to 2 September, 1995, University of Leiden.

Steere, E. 1933. *Swahili exercises* (revised by Canon Hellier). London: Sheldon Press.

Stern, Gustaf. 1931. *Meaning and change of meaning. With special reference to the English language.* Bloomington: Indiana University Press.

Stolz, Christel, & Thomas Stolz. 1994. Spanisch-amerindischer Sprachkontakt (Hispanoindiana I): Die 'Hispanisierung' mesoamerikanischer Komparationsstrukturen. Unpublished manuscript, University of Essen.

Stolz, Thomas. 1991. *Von der Grammatikalisierbarkeit des Körpers.* Part I: *Vorbereitung.* (Prinzipien des Sprachwandels, 2.) Essen: University of Essen.

———. 1993. Wege zu einer Typologie des Komitativs. Paper presented at the Philosophische Fakultät, University of Potsdam, 3 December.

———. 1994a. Über Komitative: Natürlichkeit und Grammatikalisierung, Prädiktabilität von struktureller Organisation und Dynamik. Unpublished manuscript, University of Bochum.

———. 1994b. *Sprachdynamik: Auf dem Weg zu einer Typologie sprachlichen Wandels.* Vol. 2: *Grammatikalisierung und Metaphorisierung.* Bochum: Brockmeyer.

Svorou, Soteria. 1986. On the evolutionary paths of locative expressions. *Berkeley Linguistics Society* 12:515–27.

———. 1987. The semantics of spatial extension terms in Modern Greek. *Buffalo Working Papers in Linguistics* (University of Buffalo) 87,1:56–122.

———. 1988. The experiential basis of the grammar of space: Evidence from the languages of the world. Ph.D. diss., State University of New York at Buffalo.

———. 1994. *The grammar of space.* (Typological Studies in Language, 25.) Amsterdam: John Benjamins.

Swadesh, Morris. 1971. *The origin and diversification of language.* Edited by Joel Sherzer. Chicago: Aldine, Atherton.

Sweetser, Eve E. 1990. *From etymology to pragmatics: Metaphorical and cultural aspects of semantic structure.* (Cambridge Studies in Linguistics, 54.) Cambridge: Cambridge University Press.

Takizala, Alexis. 1974. On the similarity between nominal adjectives and possessive forms in Kihungan. *Studies in African Linguistics* (Supplement 5) (Los Angeles: University of California): 291–305.

Tannen, Deborah. 1993. *Framing in discourse.* New York: Oxford University Press.

Taylor, F. W. 1923. *A practical Hausa grammar.* Oxford: Oxford University Press.

———. 1959. *A practical Hausa grammar.* 2nd ed. Oxford: Oxford University Press.

Taylor, John R. 1989. *Linguistic categorization: Prototypes in linguistic theory.* Oxford: Clarendon Press.

Taylor, John R., & Robert E. MacLaury (eds.). 1995. *Language and the cognitive construal of the world.* Berlin: Mouton de Gruyter.

Tomlin, Russell S. (ed.). 1987. *Coherence and grounding in discourse.* (Typological Studies in Language, 11.) Amsterdam: John Benjamins.

Trask, R. L. 1979. On the origins of ergativity. In: Plank, *Ergativity,* pp. 385–404.

Traugott, Elizabeth C. 1980. Meaning-change in the development of grammatical markers. *Language Science* 2:44–61.

————. 1986. From polysemy to internal semantic reconstruction. *Berkeley Linguistics Society* 12:539–50.

Traugott, Elizabeth C., & Bernd Heine (eds.). 1991a. *Approaches to grammaticalization*. Vol. 1. Amsterdam: John Benjamins.

————(eds.). 1991b. *Approaches to grammaticalization*. Vol. 2. Amsterdam: John Benjamins.

Traugott, Elizabeth C., & Ekkehard König. 1991. The semantics-pragmatics of grammaticalization revisited. In: Traugott & Heine, *Approaches to grammaticalization*, Vol. 1, pp. 189–218.

Tsunoda, Tasaku. 1996. The possession cline in Japanese and other languages. In: Chappell & McGregor, *Grammar of inalienability*, pp. 565–630.

Tuan, Yi-Fu. 1974. *Topophilia: A study of environmental perception, attitudes, and values*. Englewood Cliffs, N.J.: Prentice Hall.

Tucker, A. N., & J. Tompo ole Mpaayei. 1955. *A Maasai grammar with vocabulary*. (Publications of the African Institute, Leyden, 2.) London: Longmans, Green.

Turner, Katherine. 1988. Salinan numerals. In: Shipley, *In honor of Mary Haas*, pp. 795–804.

Ullmann, Stephen. 1962. *Semantics: An introduction to the science of meaning*. Oxford: Basil Blackwell.

Ultan, Russell. 1972. Some features of basic comparative constructions. *Working Papers on Language Universals* (Stanford) 9:117–62.

————. 1978a. Toward a typology of substantival possession. In: Greenberg, *Universals*, Vol. 4, pp. 11–49.

————. 1978b. Some general characteristics of interrogative systems. In: Greenberg, *Universals*, Vol. 4, pp. 211–48.

Unseth, Pete. 1986. Word order shift in negative sentences of Surma languages. *AAP* (Afrikanistische Arbeitspapiere) 5:135–43.

Valdman, Albert (ed.). 1977. *Pidgin and creole linguistics*. Bloomington: Indiana University Press.

van Coetsem, Frans, & Herbert L. Kufner (eds.). 1972. *Toward a grammar of Proto-Germanic*. Tübingen: Max Niemeyer.

van Rootselaar, B., & T. F. Staal (eds.). 1968. *Logic, methodology, and philosophy of science*. Vol. 3. Amsterdam: North-Holland.

Vennemann, Theo. 1974. Theoretical word order studies: Results and problems. *Papiere zur Linguistik* 7:5–25.

Verhaar, John W. M. (ed.). 1968a. *The verb 'be' and its synonyms*. Part 2. (Foundations of Language, Supplementary Series, 6.) Dordrecht: Reidel.

————(ed.). 1968b. *The verb 'be' and its synonyms*. Part 3. (Foundations of Language, Supplementary Series, 8.) Dordrecht: Reidel.

————(ed.). 1972. *The verb 'be' and its synonyms*. Part 5. (Foundations of Language, Supplementary Series, 14.) Dordrecht: Reidel.

Viberg, Åke. 1984. The verbs of perception: A typological study. In: Butterworth, Comrie, & Dahl, *Explanations for language universals*, pp. 123–62.

Vincent, Nigel, & Martin Harris (eds.). 1982. *Studies in the Romance verb*. London: Croom Helm.

Voeltz, Erhard F. K. 1976. Inalienable possession in Sotho. *Studies in African Linguistics* (Supplement 8) (Los Angeles: University of California):255–66.

Vorbichler, Anton. 1965. *Die Phonologie und Morphologie des Balese (Ituri-Urwald, Kongo)*. (Afrikanistische Forschungen, 2.) Glückstadt: J. J. Augustin.

————. 1971. *Die Sprache der Mamvu*. (Afrikanistische Forschungen, 5.) Glückstadt: J. J. Augustin.

Watkins, Calvert. 1967. Remarks on the genitive. In: *To honor Roman Jakobson. Essays on the occasion of his 70th birthday*. Vol. 3. The Hague: Mouton, pp. 2191–2198.

Weissenborn, Jürgen, & Wolfgang Klein (eds.). 1982. *Here and there: Cross-linguistic studies on deixis and demonstration*. Amsterdam: John Benjamins.

Wells, Rulon S. 1947. De Saussure's system of linguistics. *Word* 3:1-31.

Welmers, William E. 1968. *Jukun of Wukari and Jukun of Takum*. (Occasional Publication, 16.) Ibadan: Institute of African Studies.

————. 1973. *African language structures*. Berkeley: University of California Press.

Werner, Alice. 1904. Note on the terms used for "right hand" and "left hand" in the Bantu languages. *Journal of the African Society* 13:112–16.

Westermann, Diedrich. 1907. *Grammatik der Ewe-Sprache*. Berlin: Dietrich Reimer.

————. 1924. *Die Kpelle-Sprache in Liberia: Grammatische Einführung, Texte und Wörterbuch*. (Zeitschrift für Eingeborenen-Sprachen, Beiheft 6.) Berlin: Dietrich Reimer.

Whitney, William Dwight. 1875. *The life and growth of language: An outline of linguistic science*. New York: Dover.

Whorf, Benjamin Lee. 1956. *Language, thought and reality: Selected writings of Benjamin Lee Whorf*, edited by J. B. Carroll. New York: Wiley.

Wierzbicka, Anna. 1972. *Semantic primitives*. Frankfurt: Athenäum.

————. 1980. *Lingua mentalis: The semantics of natural language*. New York: Academic Press.

————. 1988. *The semantics of grammer*. Amsterdam: John Benjamins.

————. 1992. *Semantics, culture, and cognition: Universal human concepts in culture-specific configurations*. New York: Oxford University Press.

Wilkins, David P. 1989. Mparntwe Arrernte (Aranda): Studies in the structure and semantics of grammar. Ph.D. diss., Australian National University, Canberra.

————. 1993. *From part to person: Natural tendencies of semantic change and the search for cognates*. (Cognitive Anthropology Research Group, Working Paper 23.) Nijmegen: Max Planck Institute.

————. 1996. Natural tendencies of semantic change and the search for cognates. In: Durie & Ross, *Comparative method reviewed*, pp. 264–304.

Williams, Joseph. 1976. Synaesthetic adjectives: A possible law of semantic change. *Language* 52:461–77.

Wilson, Bob. 1983. An examination of crosslinguistic constraints on the lexicalization of predications of ownership, possession, location and existence. *Working Papers in Linguistics* (University of Hawaii) 15,2:1–15.

Witkowski, Stanley R., & Cecil H. Brown. 1985. Climate, clothing, and body-part nomenclature. *Ethnology* 24:197–214.

Wolff, Ekkehard. 1993. *Referenzgrammatik des Hausa zur Begleitung des Fremdsprachenunterrichts und zur Einführung in das Selbststudium*. (Hamburger Beiträge zur Afrikanistik, 2.) Münster: Lit Verlag.

Wolff, Ekkehard, & Hilké Meyer-Bahlburg (eds.). 1983. *Studies in Chadic and Afroasiatic linguistics*. Hamburg: Buske Verlag.

Wright, S., & T. Givón. 1987. The pragmatics of indefinite reference: Quantified text-based studies. *Studies in Language* 11,1:1–33.

Wüllner, Franz. 1831. *Über Ursprung und Urbedeutung der sprachlichen Formen*. Munich: Theissingsche Buchhandlung.

Zigmond, Maurice L., Curtis G. Booth, & Pamela Munro. 1990. *Kawaiisu: A grammar and dictionary with texts*. (University of California Publications in Linguistics, 119.) Berkeley: University of California Press.

Zimzik, Helena. 1992. Komparativkonstruktionen in afrikanischen Sprachen. Unpublished manuscript, Institut für Afrikanistik, University of Cologne.

Ziv, Yael. 1976. On the reanalysis of grammatical terms in Hebrew possessive constructions. In: Cole, *Studies in modern Hebrew*, pp. 129–52.

AUTHOR INDEX

Abraham, Roy Clive, 52
Adam, Hassan, v
Allan, Keith, 153
Andersen, Elaine S., 47, 129
Andersen, Paul Kent, 109–110, 113,
116, 118, 119, 120, 130, 134, 135,
144
Anttila, Raimo, 131

Bach, Emmon, 84, 90, 106
Barr, L.I., 35, 36
Bates, Elizabeth, 4
Beckmann, Petr, 79
Beeler, M.S., 24, 25, 27
Benveniste, Emile, 90, 106
Bickerton, Derek, 84
Biermann, Anna, 99–100
Bills, Garland D., 94
Blake, Barry, 16, 61
Booth, Curtis G., 173
Bowden, John, 37, 38, 40, 43, 140
Broschart, Jürgen, v
Brown, Cecil H., 49–56, 62, 63, 64, 132,
136, 146

Brown, Penelope, 14, 38, 63
Brugman, Claudia Marlea, 9, 37, 40,
106
Buck, Carl Darling, 156
Burgess, Don, 72
Burridge, Kate, 153
Bybee, Joan, v, 6, 16, 82, 144, 147,
152

Campbell, Lyle, 6, 152
Carlin, Eithne, 92
Chafe, Wally, 66
Chappell, Hilary, 85
Chomsky, Noam, 16
Clark, Eve V., 88–90, 98, 106
Claudi, Ulrike, v, 6, 8, 30, 34, 39, 44,
47, 61, 75, 82, 88, 91, 93, 99, 106,
140, 144, 147, 152
Comrie, Bernard, v, 16
Conrad, Rudi, 67
Cooke, Joseph R., 15
Corbett, Greville G., 29, 30
Creider, Chet A., 124, 126
Creider, Jane Tapsubei, 124, 126

Creissels, D., 84
Cyffer, Norbert, 125

Dantzig, T., 21
Dimmendaal, Gerrit Jan, 94
Dixon, Robert M.W., 24, 79
Doke, Clement M., 31

Ebert, Karen, v
Emanatian, Michele, 9

Farris, Glenn J., 28
Ferguson, Charles A., 16
Fleischman, Suzanne, v
Forchheimer, Paul, 152
Fortescue, Michael, 51, 52, 55
Foulkes, H.D., 122
Frajzyngier, Zygmunt, 75, 93, 150
Freeze, Ray, 107, 150
Friedländer, Marianne, 116
Friedrich, P., 110
Fromm, Erich, 105

Gaynor, Frank, 67
Geeraerts, Dirk, 9
Gensler, Orin, v, 29, 104
Gentner, Derdre, 84
Gerhardt, Ludwig, 27
Givón, Tom, v, 73, 75, 76, 79, 150
Goldap, Christel, 37, 62. *See also* Stolz, Christel
Greenberg, Joseph H., 6, 18, 22, 23, 24, 29, 33, 129, 152

Hagège, Claude, 98, 101, 154
Hawkins, John A., 70
Heine, Bernd, 6, 8, 10, 30, 34, 37, 39, 40, 43, 44, 47, 61, 62, 67, 68, 69, 75, 76, 78, 82, 83, 91, 93, 98, 99, 101, 104, 107, 110, 112, 113, 117, 140, 144, 147–149, 152
Heine, Ingo, v
Hengeveld, Kees, 91, 106
Henry, David, 58
Henry, Kay, 58
Hetzron, Robert, 72, 77
Hill, Clifford A., 11
Hill, Deborah, 39
Hopper, Paul, v, 6, 9, 75, 90, 147, 151, 152

Hünnemeyer, Friederike, 6, 8, 30, 34, 39, 44, 47, 61, 75, 82, 99, 140, 144, 147, 152
Hurford, James R., 23, 24, 30, 31, 33, 34

Isačenko, Alexander V., 105

Jensen, Hans, 120, 122, 123, 124, 126, 130
Johnson, Mark, 16
Johnson-Laird, Philip N., 87

Kilian-Hatz, Christa, v, 43
Kirk-Greene, A.H.M., 113
Köhler, Oswin, 98
Kölver, Ulrike, 59
König, Christa, v
König, Ekkehard, 8, 60, 61, 82
Kortmann, Bernd, 60, 61
Kraft, Charles H., 113
Kuteva, Tania, v, 72

Lakoff, George, v, 9, 16, 108, 150
Langacker, Ronald W., 16, 84, 91, 108
Lehiste, Ilse, 92
Lehmann, Christian, 182
Lehmann, Thomas, 77
Lehmann, Winfred P., 110
Lessau, Donald A., 75
Levinson, Stephen C., 11, 13, 14, 38, 63, 136–43, 145
Lewis, Gilbert, 133
Lichtenberk, Frantisek, 9, 96
Locker, Ernst, 106
Lukas, Johannes, 93
Lyons, John, 9, 89–90, 92, 94

Macaulay, Monica, 37, 40
MacLaury, Robert E., 37
MacWhinney, Brian, 4
Majewicz, Alfred F., 21
Malandra, Alfred, 62
Mallinson, Graham, 16
Martin, Janice, 75
Matisoff, James A., 133, 134
Matlin, Margaret W., 91
McGregor, William, 85
Meinhof, Carl, 21
Miller, George A., 87

Moravcsik, Edith A., 67, 68, 69, 70, 80–1
Mowrey, Richard, 76
Mpaayei, ole Tompo, 63
Munro, Pamela, 115

Nichols, Johanna, 85–6
Noonan, Michael, 96
Norvig, Peter, 9

Otten, Dirk, v

Pagliuca, William, 6, 16, 76, 82, 144, 147
Paul, Hermann, 131
Pei, Mario A., 67
Perkins, Revere D., 6, 16, 82, 144, 147
Perlmutter, D.M., 80
Pott, Friedrich August, 26

Quirk, Randolph, 69

Ramat, Paolo, 6, 152
Redfield, Robert, 51, 52
Reh, Mechthild, v, 60, 62, 76, 78, 94, 152
Renzi, L., 77
Roberg, Heinz, v, 92
Romaine, Suzanne, 114
Ross, Malcolm, 49, 56
Rottland, Franz, v

Sanford, Anthony J., 91
Sapir, Edward, 16
Sasse, Hans-Jürgen, v
Saussure, Ferdinand de, 4, 31
Saxe, Geoffrey, 34
Schladt, Mathias, v, 13, 133, 134, 135, 136
Schmidt, Pater Wilhelm, 19, 26
Seiler, Hansjakob, 18, 21, 25, 26, 84, 85, 86, 89, 96, 106
Serzisko, Fritz, v
Shipley, William, 27
Stafford, R.L., 93
Stampe, David, 18, 20, 22, 23, 24, 25, 26, 33

Stassen, Leon, 101, 111, 112, 114–23, 127–130
Stern, Gustaf, 131
Stolz, Christel, 8, 109, 110, 127. *See also* Goldap, Christel
Stolz, Thomas, 8, 15, 28, 37, 62, 109, 110, 120, 127, 140, 148
Svorou, Soteria, 12, 37–45, 59, 140, 142
Sweetser, Eve, v, 8

Taylor, John R., 86, 150
Tossou, Kossi, v
Touré, Mohamed, v
Traugott, Elizabeth C., v, 6, 8, 9, 82, 144, 147
Troike, Rudolph C., 94
Tuan, Yi-Fu, 52, 57, 64
Tucker, A.N., 63
Turner, Katherine, 24

Ullmann, Stephen, 131
Ultan, Russell, 85, 88, 90, 106, 107, 109, 114, 115, 116, 117, 124–126

Vallejo, Bernardo, 94
Viberg, Åke, 145
Voeltz, Erhard, 85
Vorbichler, Anton, 20, 28

Watkins, Calvert, 87
Wells, Rulon S., 4
Welmers, William E., 90, 93
Werner, Alice, 35, 43, 48
Westermann, Diedrich, 93
Whorf, Benjamin Lee, 11, 16
Wierzbicka, Anna, 16, 108
Wilkins, David P., 132, 136, 146
Williams, Joseph, 145
Wilson, Bob, 106
Witkowski, Stanley R., 132, 136, 137, 146

Zigmond, Maurice L., 115
Zimzik, Helena, 114, 121, 128
Ziv, Yael, 100–101

LANGUAGE INDEX

Acholi, 62
African languages, 37, 40, 41, 42, 43, 46, 47, 93, 114
Afrikaans, 96
Ainu, 23
Albanian, 129
Ambrym (Lonwolwol), 54
Amharic, 124
Andamanese, 24
Angas, 121
Anutan, 56
Anywa, 94
Arabic, Classical, 101
Aramaic, 110
Aranda, 23, 95
Api, 21
Asian languages, 129
Aztec, 28, 120

Baka, 43
Balese, 28
Bantu languages, 26, 48
Berber, *see* Tamazight
Botocudo, 24

·Breton, 26
Burmese, 15

Cameroon Pidgin English, 114
Catalan, 77
Cayapo, 117
Chamus, 13
Cheremis, Eastern, 110
Cherokee, 117
Chinese, 59, 73
Coptic, 110
Cornish, 50, 101
Creole languages, 114
Czech, 51, 79, 144

Danish, 26, 126
Diyari, 95
Duala, 123
Dutch, 73, 117–8, 129

Egyptian, 57
English, Old, 74, 75
Eskimo, 51, 52, 55, 110, 116
Estonian, 92

European languages, 35, 90, 96, 102, 127, 129
Ewe, 44, 55, 59, 61, 70–71, 77, 78, 93, 110

Fijian, 49
Finnish, 116, 118–9, 129, 144, 145
French, 31, 32, 70–71, 77, 78, 90, 95, 110, 120, 126, 129

Gaelic, 129
Georgian, 116
German, 22, 59–60, 73, 92, 96, 110, 119, 121, 135, 144, 145
Germanic languages, 102, 104
Gisiga, 93
Gnau, 133
Greek, 116, 129
Gujarati, 110
Gullah, 114

Halia, 39
Hausa, 12, 27, 113, 135
Hawaiian, 50, 55
Hebrew, 73, 100–101
Hindi, 61, 127, 129
Hixkaryana, 117
Huastec, 144
Hungarian, 99–100, 110, 114, 119, 129, 132

Indo-Aryan languages, 61
Indo-European, 25
Italian, 77, 78

Jamaican Creole, 114
Japanese, 110, 127, 129
Javanese, 117–8
Jurak, 129

Kairiru, 96
Kamba, 133
Kannada, 74, 125
Kanuri, 110, 125
Kapingamarangi, 56
Kashmiri, 127, 129
Kawaiisu, 115
Khalka, 129
Kikuyu, 13
Korean, 127, 129

Koyukon, 58
Krio, 114
Krongo, 60
Kui, 110
Kxoé, 23, 32, 97–8, 104

Lamutic, 129
Lango, 96
Lapp, 116
Latin, 22, 79, 119, 120, 124, 129, 132
Latin, Late, 132
Latvian, 119, 126, 129
Longgu, 39
Lonwolwol, *see* Ambrym
Lou, 49
Lugbara, 35, 36
Luo, 93

Maasai, 26, 62, 63
Maidu, 27
Malagasy, 110, 119
Mamvu, 19–20, 22, 23, 27, 30, 32
Manchu, 101, 129
Mangareva, 56
Manus, 52
Maori, 56, 132
Marquesan, 56
Marshallese, 49
Melamela, 30
Mixtec, Chalcatongo, 40
Mopan, 127
Motu, 121
Mundari, 115
Mupun, 93

Naga, 114
Nama, 92
Nandi, 124, 126
Niger-Congo languages, 115
Nilotic languages, 48
Niuean, 56
Nomlaki, 24, 26
Nyanja, 120

Oceanic languages, 38, 41, 42, 43, 46, 47
Oksapmin, 34

Papago, 40, 45
Patwin, 26
Penutian languages, 25, 26

Pidgin languages, 114
Plateau languages, 27
Pokot, 134
Polish, 51
Polynesian languages, 56, 57
Pomo, Eastern, 28
Portuguese, 77
Proto-Oceanic, 49
Proto-Polynesian, 56
Pukapukan, 49
Punjabi, 73

Quechua, 94, 132

Rarotongan, 56
Rendille, 133
Rennellese, 56
Romance languages, 73, 96, 102, 104,
    119
Romanian, 143
Russian, 29, 72, 79, 92, 110, 116, 126,
    129

Salinan-Chumash languages, 24
Samoan, 49, 110
Senufo, 128
Sinhalese, 125
Slavic languages, 30
Slavonic, Old Church, 29
So, 28, 92
Soddo-Gogot, 72, 77
Sora, 25
Sotho, 21
Spanish, 73, 77, 81, 92, 103–4, 127
Sranan, 114
Susu, 116

Swahili, 23, 61, 72, 97, 110, 111, 113,
    123, 124, 153

Tahitian, 56
Tajik, 127, 129
Tamazight, 113
Tamil, 74, 77, 124
Tarahumara, Western, 72
Telugu, 110
Tepoztlan, 52
Thai, 59
Tigak, 49
Tikopian, 56
Tiv, 52
Toba Batak, 118
Tswana, 48, 125
Tuamotuan, 56
Turkana, 94
Turkish, 94, 115, 129
Tzeltal, 13, 136–43, 145

Uvean, 49

Walbiri, 23
Welsh, 24, 26, 132
West African Pidgin English, 95
Wintu, 24, 26
Wolof, 22
Worora, 24, 110

Yoruba, 113
Yucatec, 37, 62
Yurok, 52, 110

Zulu, 22, 30, 31, 48

SUBJECT INDEX

A-adposition, 60–1
Ablative marker, 45, 90, 95, 105
Absolute system, 63
Abstract meaning, 7
Abstract possession, 88, 105
Accidental possession, 87
Action verb, 4
Addition, 19, 20, 23, 24, 33
Addition marker, 23
Adjectival property, 30, 33
Adjunct, locative, 60
Adversative coordination, 116
Adversative predication, 121
Agreement, 100, 101
Alienable possession, 85–6
Allative marker, 45, 94, 95
Ambiguity, 107
Analytic-isolating languages, 59
Anthropomorphic model, 40, 44–6,
    140
Antithetic juxtaposition, 116
Antonymy, 117
Arbitrariness axiom, 4
Areal distribution, 130, 149

Areal forces, 126–9
Areal typology, 79
Arithmetic operation, 23
Aspect, 101
Attributive possession, 17, 85, 86, 87, 90,
    93, 94, 95, 97, 98, 103
Augmentative marker, 153
Autosemantic, 36
Auxiliary, 4, 7, 107

Bantu Model, 48–9
Base number, 25, 28, 33
Belong-construction, 87, 95, 97
Bio-cultural domain, 84–5
Bleaching, 75, 76, 78
Body-part metaphor, 139
Body-part model, 19–24, 26, 27, 28, 32,
    33, 47, 48
Borrowing, 5, 126, 149

Cardinal orientation, 12, 14, 16, 52, 53,
    54, 55, 57, 58, 62, 63
Cardinal reference point, 51
Catenative verb, 4

Chain, diachronic, 39. *See also*
    Grammaticalization chain
Clausal morphosyntax, 30
Clausal syntax, 86
Clause-initial position, 98
Cline, 152
Cliticization, 75, 76
Closed-class category, 6, 36, 81, 131, 146
Closed system of orientation, 12
Cognitive preference principle, 40
Collective noun, 29, 33
Color term, 30
Communication strategies, 150
Communicative needs, 11
Comparative notion, 17, 109, 110
Comparison, 109–30, 149
Complementary distribution, 80
Conceptualization, option for, 14
Conceptualization strategies, 150
Concrete vs. abstract meaning, 7
Connective, 24
Consecutive events, 117
Construction type of comparatives, 123
Context, 144
Context-induced reinterpretation, 140
Contextual expansion, 151
Contextual frame, 82
Contextually defined variation, 106
Contiguity, physical, 136
Continuum, 152
Control, 87
Cosmological categorization, 65
Count noun, 73, 80, 81
Counting without system, 19
Covariant, 80
Crosslinguistic regularities, 18, 68

Dative marker, 90, 94, 95, 101
Decategorialization, 104
Decimal system, 21, 24, 26, 27, 33
Definite article, 6, 17, 67, 69, 70, 77–9,
    126, 149
Deictic orientation, 11, 12, 14, 37–52, 53,
    54, 55, 56, 57, 58, 59, 64
Dependent-marked languages, 86
Description, 89, 102, 144
Diachronic evidence, 5
Diachronic linguistics, 6, 7
Diachrony, 5, 143. *See also* Synchrony
    vs. diachrony

Diminutive marker, 153
Directional marker, 45, 94
Discourse-pragmatic principle, 98
Division, 19, 23
Domain de dicto, 75
Domain de re, 75
Domain of conceptualization, 19, 132,
    138
Double subject strategy, 96
Dual locative potential, 46
Duodecimal system, 25, 27
Dynamic concept, 38, 39
Dynamic situation, 97

Elative, 109
Environment, mutually exclusive, 27
Environment-specific feature, 51, 53
Environmental landmark, *see*
    Landmark model, Landmark
    orientation
Equation, 89, 96
Equative (comparative), 109, 124
Erosion, 61–3, 76, 78
Etymology, 32
Event schema, 82, 83, 90–99, 107,
    111–23, 129, 130
Evolution, diachronic, 6
Evolutionary scenario, 122
Excessive (comparative), 109
Existential construction, 89
Explanation, 4, 6, 18, 23, 27, 32, 34, 45,
    68, 92, 101–4, 148, 149, 150, 153
Explanation, external, 3, 150

Face-to-face model, 12, 13
Family resemblance categories, 152
Folk category, 64
Form-meaning asymmetry, 151
Frequency of occurrence, 68, 69, 112
Frequency of use, 31, 125
Functionalist traditions, 150

Generalization, 78
Generalized article, 73
Generic property, 79
Genericity, 75
Genetic motivation, *see* Motivation,
    genetic
Grammar of space, 36
Grammatical concept, 66, 90, 106

Grammaticalization, 6, 10, 31, 59, 75, 76, 81, 102, 105, 106, 112, 131, 144, 146, 152, 154
Grammaticalization chain, 105, 106, 152

Have-construction, 86, 87, 90, 91, 95, 96, 97, 150
Head-marked languages, 86
Head noun, 59, 61
Head of genitival constructions, 22
Heterosemy, 9
Homonymy, 8, 10, 50
Human body, anatomic characteristics of, 34
Hybrid form, 99

Identification, 89, 105
Implication, 75
Implicational relationship, 63
Implicational scale, 47, 71, 74
Implicature, conversational, 8, 82
Inalienable possession, 85–6, 88, 95
Indefinite article, 6, 17, 66–82, 148, 151–2
Indefinite specific reference, 67, 72, 74
Inference, invited, 8, 82
Inferior comparative, 109
Inherent relation, 85
Innate mental structuring, 34
Internal geometry, 140
Intimate relation, 85
Intrafield metonymic change, 136
Intrinsic geometry, 141
Intrinsic reference frame, 12
Intrinsic system, 11

Kinship term, 85, 94, 132, 145

Landmark model, 44, 45, 48, 52, 55, 56
Landmark orientation, 12, 14, 37, 51, 56, 57, 58
Lexicon vs. grammar, 106
Lingua franca, 27
Linguistic categorization, 14
Linguistic diversity, 10
Literal-meaning fallacy, 105, 148
Locative complement, 99, 102

Main verb, 4, 7
Major schema, 115, 121, 128
Manipulation in discourse, 82

Map-model, 53
Markedness, 143
Mass noun, 68, 69, 73, 76, 77, 81
Meaning, abstract, 36
Meaning, related, 8–9
Meaning, schematic, 7–8
Medial-region, 45
Metaphor, 8, 23, 82, 139–44
Metonymy, 82, 136
Minor schema, 115
Modality, 101
Monosemy, 8
Motivation, 3, 4, 5, 31, 35
Motivation, genetic, 5, 19, 31
Motivation, psychological, 5, 31
Motivation, structural, 5, 31
Multiplication, 19, 20, 23, 28

N-adposition, 59–61
Naming, 147
Narrative discourse, 72
Nominal morphosyntax, 30
Nominal possession. *See* Attributive possession
Nominal property, 22, 30, 33, 40
Nonary system, 24, 26
Nonspecific marker, 73
Nonsubject participant, 100
Nounlike feature, 29
Numeral, 6, 18–34, 49, 70, 71, 74, 76, 77, 79, 80, 81, 82, 148, 149, 151–2
Numeral expansion, 25

Object-deictic orientation, 11, 12, 13, 37, 137
OBJECT domain, 30, 34, 44, 47
Oblique participant, 100
Onomatopoeia, 31
Opaque, 32, 48, 91, 120, 153
Open-class category, 6, 36, 81, 86, 131, 146
Open system of orientation, 12
Optimally perceptible space, 47
Overcounting, 34
Overlap Model, 74
Overlap stage, 107
Ownership, 84, 87

Pairing, 19, 26
Paradigmatic gap, 90

Part-to-whole strategy, 134, 136
Part-whole relation, 85, 145
Particle comparative, 118, 120, 127, 128, 129
Partitive, 74, 77
Partonomy, 133
Pattern transparency, 32, 91, 153
Permanent possession, 87, 88
Persistence, 151
Personal pronoun, 15
Phonetic substance, 36
Phrasal syntax, 86
Physical possession, 87, 88
Pivot, 110–1
Plural noun, 68, 69, 73, 76, 77, 81
Polysemy, 8–10, 56, 106
Polysemy, genetic, 8–10
Polysemy, psychological, 8–10
Polysemy, structural, 8–10
Positive (comparative), 109
Possession, 83–108, 129, 148, 149
Possession, definition of, 88
Possessive notion, 17, 87, 98, 105
Post-Saussurean linguistics, 4
Pragmatics of linguistic communication, 152
Predicative possession, 17, 86, 87, 88, 90, 91, 94, 98
Prediction, probabilistic, 128, 149
Presentative marker, 72–3, 74
Probability of occurrence, 43
Proper noun, 73
Psychological motivation. *See* Motivation, psychological

QUALITY domain, 30, 34
Quantification, 75
Quantifier, 148
Quaternary system, 24, 26
Quinary system, 20, 24, 28, 33

Reanalysis, 25, 26
Reference-point, absolute, 12
Referentiality, 75
Reflexive pronoun, 126
Reinterpretation, 25, 61, 98, 104
Relational concepts, 34, 39, 40, 81, 85
Relative system, 11
Relativism, 10–14

Relativist perspective, 12, 14, 146
Role relation, 15, 133

Schema blend, 120, 121
Semantic primitive, 16
Senary system, 24, 27
Separation, notion of, 116
Side-region, 45
Similarity, 133, 136
Simile, 139
Single-file model, 12, 13
Source model, 33, 38
SPACE domain, 44, 47
Spatial orientation, 35–65, 149, 152
Spatial orientation, principles of, 57–8
Specialization, 78
Specific marker, 72, 77
Status asymmetry, 15
Stereotypic description, 91
Structural linguistics, 149
Structural motivation. *See* Motivation, structural
Subject property, 100, 103
Subsequent mention, 73, 75
Subtraction, 19, 20, 23
Sun-model, 50–52, 56
Superessive link, 23
Superior comparative, 109, 124
Superlative, 109, 124–6
Synaesthetic adjectives, 145
Synchronic linguistics, 6
Synchronic profile, 78
Synchrony vs. diachrony, 4
Synsemantic, 36

Taboo strategies, 153
Temporary possession, 87, 88
Tense, 101, 107
Ternary system, 24, 26
Thematic participant, 74
Theme, 96, 99
Top-down strategy, 134–6
Topic, 96, 99
Transitional structure, 56
Transitive syntax, 104
Transitivization, 98, 99
Transparency, 32
Typological Convergence criterion, 9–10
Typological Universal Grammar, 15–16

Unidirectionality, 4, 7, 17, 53, 81, 136, 143, 144, 146
Unidirectionality principle, 6, 134
Unique reference, 126
Universal, implicational, 129
Universal of categorization, 135–6
Universal structure of possession, 107
Universalism, 10–14
Universalist perspective, 146

V-adposition, 59–61
Verb-final languages, 115, 116
Verb-initial languages, 115
Verb-medial languages, 115

Verb of existence, 94, 105
Verb of "marginal status", 89
Verbal possession. *See* Predicative possession
Vigesimal system, 20, 24, 28, 33

Western Nilotic Model, 48–9
Wind-model, 52, 56
Word order, 23, 115, 116, 129, 130
Word order alternation, 89
Word order constraints, 98

Zero anaphora, 100
Zoomorphic model, 40, 41, 42, 44–6, 140